DELIBERATE
DECEPTIONS

DELIBERATE DECEPTIONS

Facing the FACTS about the
U.S.-ISRAELI RELATIONSHIP

PAUL FINDLEY

Library of Congress Cataloging-in-Publications Data

Findley, Paul, 1921-
  Deliberate deceptions : facing the facts about the U.S.-
Israeli relationship / Paul Findley.
    p. cm.
  Includes bibliographical references and index.
  ISBN 0-937 165-09-3 (pbk.) : $14.95
    1. United States–Foreign relations–Israel. 2.
  Israel–Foreign relations–United States. I. Title.
E183.8.I7F57   1993
327.7305694--dc20

                                                          92-42294
                                                              CIP

©1993, 1995 by Paul Findley
All rights reserved
Printed in the United States of America
Second edition
American Educational Trust
P O Box 53062
Washington, D.C. 20009
1-800-368-5788

To Lucille

CONTENTS

The Dismemberment of Palestine   ix

PART ONE
STATEHOOD AND CONQUEST

One   Israel's Claims to Palestine   3

Two   The 1948 War   9

Three   The Palestinian Refugees   19

Four   The Suez Crisis of 1956   30

Five   The 1967 War   35

Six   UN Resolution 242   42

Seven   The War of Attrition: 1969–1970   48

Eight   The 1973 War   52

Nine   The 1982 Invasion of Lebanon   57

Ten   The Likud Governments   69

PART TWO
COLLUSION AND CONFLICT

Eleven   The Intifada   77

Twelve   The Palestinian Citizens of Israel   89

Thirteen   The Israeli Lobby   95

Fourteen   U.S. Aid to Israel   110

Fifteen   Loan Guarantees for Israel   116

Sixteen   Israel's Spying on America   124

Seventeen   Israel's Nuclear Weapons   130

Eighteen Israel and South Africa **136**

Nineteen Israel and the Third World **142**

PART THREE
PERILS TO PEACE

Twenty Yitzhak Rabin's Government **153**

Twenty-one The Fate of the Palestinians **164**

Twenty-two Israel's Claims to Jerusalem **170**

Twenty-three Jewish Settlements **178**

Twenty-four Israel and the United Nations **184**

Twenty-five Israel and the Peace Process **195**

Twenty-six The Other Costs of Israel **208**

Twenty-seven Israel as a Strategic Ally **218**

Twenty-eight The Illusion of Shared Values **225**

Epilogue **236**

Appendix: Major Organizations
Focused on Middle East Policy **241**

Acknowledgments **245**

Notes **247**

Bibliography and Selected Reading **295**

Index **315**

THE DISMEMBERMENT OF PALESTINE

On the morning of September 13, 1993, thirteen hundred exuberant guests met on the south lawn of the White House in Washington. Among them were long-standing critics of U.S. Middle East policy—myself included—as well as many supporters, but on this sunny day we mingled in high spirits and conversed warmly before taking seats arranged before a simple platform.

President Bill Clinton had invited us to witness the signing of peace accords between the Palestine Liberation Organization and the government of Israel. Negotiated in secret under the leadership of a Norwegian diplomat, the documents were described by many observers as an historic breakthrough in the Arab-Israeli conflict. The announcement the previous Thursday that PLO chief Yasser Arafat and Israeli prime minister Yitzhak Rabin would personally participate in the ceremony excited the nation.

The assemblage applauded enthusiastically as a smiling Arafat emerged from the White House and walked in a stately procession with Clinton and Rabin. Only days before, he had been publicly shunned as a terrorist by U.S. and Israeli officials alike.

On the platform, in the highlight of the emotion-packed ceremony, Clinton, with a sweep of his arms, brought his principal guests together in a handshake destined to rank as one of the great photographic images of the postwar era.

It was high drama.

It was also great theater, carefully scripted and rehearsed during the preceding weekend under the direction of a presidential aide. Acting with stand-ins for Arafat and Rabin, Clinton had practiced his own role. Toward the end of the proceedings, he was to stand between the two leaders, shake hands with each, then step back one pace and sweep his arms in a gesture that would elicit the desired Arafat-Rabin greeting.

The ceremony went off like clockwork, convincing, for the moment at least, Clinton's guests as well as the largest worldwide television audience in history that a watershed event had occurred that would lead inexorably to a just peace. The accords approved a timetable for establishing limited Palestinian self-rule under PLO leadership, first in the Gaza Strip and Jericho, then throughout the rest of the West Bank. Negotiations on East Jerusalem and the final status of other fundamental issues were to begin not later than April 1996.

In signing, both Rabin and Arafat provoked important constituencies. Because Arafat enthusiastically interpreted the accords as a sure step toward Palestinian statehood, Jews living in settlements in the occupied territories saw the agreement as a grave threat to their homes. Joined by leaders of the Likud Party who had lost power in the 1992 elections, they expressed sustained outrage to a degree that seemed to threaten Rabin's paper-thin control of the Israeli parliament.

The protest by Palestinians, including the well-organized Hamas movement within the occupied territories, was more fundamental and sustained. Arafat lost the support of several prominent PLO leaders who rejected the accords as an Israeli trap that legitimizes Israeli control of Palestinian land and people and will complicate the quest for statehood. One of them, Edward Said, a Palestine-born professor at Columbia University, warned in the February 14, 1994, issue of *The Nation:* "There is no such thing as partial independence or limited autonomy. Without political independence there is neither sovereignty nor real freedom." Arafat's decision, in many respects, was an act of desperation. His reaction to the coalition war against Iraq's conquest of Kuwait had destroyed his financial base and left him with no hope of substantial help from any quarter. As intermittent U.S.-

sponsored peace talks seemed to lead nowhere, his Tunis-based organization, still shunned by both Israel and the United States, seemed to verge on irrelevancy. Under these circumstances, Arafat accepted the terms offered secretly by Israel, even though they constituted high risk to his movement and an uncertain step toward his dream of Palestinian statehood.

At the White House, both Arafat and Rabin joined Clinton in heralding the accords in glowing terms, helping to create a euphoria that still survives. A year later, great expectations linger on in America, nurtured by a news media and a political establishment that frequently praise Israel for magnanimity and constancy and just as often finds fault with Palestinian conduct. Americans were reminded that, despite timetable slippage, Israel had released political prisoners, yielded police duties in the Gaza Strip and Jericho to Palestinian officers, and permitted institutions for Palestinian limited self-rule to take shape in those communities and in some other occupied territories.

Largely lost in the afterglow was Israel's continued suppression of Palestinian rights, its kidnapping of a Palestinian leader near Beirut in May 1994, its slaughter of scores of civilians during intermittent bombardment of southern Lebanon and areas near the Syrian border, and the violence provoked by Jewish settlers in the occupied territories. All this was brushed aside as the inevitable price of transition.

Rosy expectations were heightened still further at the White House on July 25, 1994, when King Hussein of Jordan and Prime Minister Rabin signed a document that won President Clinton's promise of additional U.S. aid to both Jordan and Israel. Despite high-decibel praise, the document did little beyond acknowledging formally that the state of belligerency between the two states had ended, a reality that had been universally recognized for years. Overlooked in media coverage was the profound change in the politics of the Middle East that the Hussein-Rabin handshake signified. It was proof that a long era had ended during which Arab states, with the exception of Egypt, had held off any direct agreement with Israel until Palestinian grievances had been redressed.

Actually, the era had ended nine months earlier when Arafat, the chairman of the Palestinian Liberation Organization—the institution that all Arab states years earlier had recognized as the sole, legitimate representative of the Palestinian people—secretly agreed to the accords with Israel. Arafat had accepted its terms without informing other Arab leaders, much less consulting them. Because the PLO had independently come to terms with Israel, Arab states, like Jordan, now had the same freedom.

Critics charge that Rabin lured Arafat into a deal that destroyed Arab solidarity behind Palestine. Clearly, the accords have already advanced Israel's dream of negotiating peace terms one Arab state at a time. Pan-Arab solidarity, whatever its value to the PLO cause, is a thing of the past. Palestine is on its own, more completely at the mercy of Israel and its partner, the United States, than at any time in history.

Long before Hussein met with Rabin, an emotional high in the occupied territories had already given way to harsh facts. Cynicism, resentment, and despair now abound. Many Palestinians dismiss self-rule as simply another act of deception that will give Israel time to advance a process of dismemberment. Under it, the Palestinian population is being separated into small parts that will have difficulty making common cause together. The process includes the establishment and enlargement of strategically located Jewish settlements, the construction of highways to serve them, and tightening the noose around Arabs in East Jerusalem. Israel's objective is to leave Palestinians parceled off into small pieces, forgotten by the outside world and, as a practical matter, powerless in their quest for dignity and statehood.

Clever Deceptions Are Unreported

While major U.S. media continue to extol the promise of the peace process, almost no notice is given to the harsh, restrictive steps Israel has already taken to accomplish the goal. The most extreme step is closure, begun in March 1993. Under it, all Palestinians—even those in self-rule areas like Gaza and Jericho—are kept as virtual prisoners within isolated and closely guarded cantons where external employment, trade, and travel are tightly restricted. As this is written—a full year after the Arafat-Rabin handshake—this crippling, demeaning policy remains in force throughout the occupied territories, afflicting all Palestinians like a pestilence. It is reminiscent of the suffering South African blacks experienced in isolated Bantustans before apartheid was dismantled. In the June 10, 1994, issue of *Middle East International,* Michael Jansen wrote, "Palestinians living in Gaza and Jericho are worse off than were the blacks of South Africa confined to homelands."

The Israeli government proceeds with other dismembering measures, as well. Curfew, for example, prohibits all Palestinian movement in public areas, usually on a 24-hour basis. As a control device it is even more restrictive than closure and, despite Israeli assurances to the contrary, is enforced only against Palestinians. On March 7, 1994, Israeli Foreign Minister Shimon Peres expressed a falsehood of breathtaking scope when he assured CNN's worldwide television audience that Jewish settlers and Palestinians are equally subject to curfews: ". . . if there will be a curfew for the Arabs, there will be a curfew for the Jewish settlers as well." When told by a news reporter that curfews were not enforced against Jews, Peres insisted: "There is equal treatment, and we do not discriminate in favor of anybody or against anybody." Despite Peres's declaration, Jewish settlers are exempt from these restrictions and can move about as they wish. Furthermore, they enjoy the greater liberties permitted by Israel's civilian laws, while Palestinians are kept under harsh military rules.

Whether Rabin's Labor Party stays in power, or is replaced by Likud, the process of dismemberment seems assured. While Likud leaders prefer open defiance of world opinion, under Labor—by Rabin's own admission—repression is carried out quietly and deceptively.

In the fall of 1990, preparing for the political campaign that would restore him two years later to the position of prime minister, Rabin acknowledged publicly a deception that had already put major obstacles on the road to peace.

At the time, on the assumption that the spread of Jewish settlements in the occupied territories was broadly popular among Israelis and certain to win votes on election day, Prime Minister Yitzhak Shamir's Likud Party was boasting about its leadership in expanding the settlements. Indeed, Shamir, never known for subtlety, had been brazen about settlement construction. On several occasions he participated in groundbreaking ceremonies for new ones, celebrations that were deliberately scheduled to coincide with days a strong critic of settlements, U.S. Secretary of State James A. Baker, arrived for official visits.

In the 1990 campaign arena, Rabin, too, discarded subtlety. He informed the electorate that the Labor Party had led the way in building settlements years before the Shamir administration came to power but added that Labor had carried out the construction "cleverly" so as to avoid criticism by the U.S. government.

The October 18, 1990, issue of the Israeli periodical, *Davar,* quoted Rabin's response to the Likud boasting: "For all its faults, Labor has done more and remains capable of doing more in the future [in expanding Jewish settlements] than Likud with all of its doing. We have never talked about Jerusalem. We just made a 'fait accompli.' It was we who built the suburbs in [the annexed part of] Jerusalem. The Americans didn't say a word, because we built these suburbs cleverly." The suburbs he cited are Jewish settlements built on expropriated Palestinian land bordering East Jerusalem. In his amazing but little-noted burst of candor,

Rabin could accurately have broadened Labor claims beyond the East Jerusalem area. All of the early and many of the later settlements in the West Bank and Gaza were built when the Labor Party was in power.

Rabin's admission is a convincing rejoinder to those who claim that the settlements are the unfortunate legacy of the Likud Party alone and would never have come into being had Labor stayed in power.

The main difference on settlement policy is that Labor is more deceptive than Likud. When he became prime minister, Rabin pledged publicly a "settlement freeze" but proceeded privately with expansion. He began to carry out the Sheves Plan, named after Shimon Sheves, the director-general of the prime minister's office. It cleverly obscures in "development" terminology plans for the expansion of settlements and highways that serve them. According to the Palestine Human Rights Information Center in Jerusalem: "[Under Rabin] there has not been an abrupt break, or settlement 'freeze,' as publicly claimed [by Rabin]. Instead, there has been a shift from Ariel Sharon's stark vision of the transfer of Palestinians and outright Israeli annexation of the territories to a more sophisticated concept of quantitative control, selective annexation of the territories to a more sophisticated concept of quantitative control, selective annexation, separation [through closure], and containment of Palestinian population centers within contiguous Jewish settlements."

Deception surfaced again when Rabin's office announced that Israel was terminating government financial benefits to Jewish settlers. The announcement worked wonders in America; it gave U.S. President George Bush the excuse to go forward in the last months of his administration with $10 billion in Israeli loan guarantees that, among other goals, facilitated settlement expansion. In reality, the announcement was a fraud. Financial benefits to Jewish settlers did not end. The Rabin government continued generous grants and subsidies to Jews in seventy-six separate settlements— nearly half the total—in amounts ranging as high as $18,000 per settler. Far from being frozen, subsidies rose. For example, living space that costs $145,000 in West Jerusalem could be purchased by settlers for $60,000.

Rabin specifically excluded East Jerusalem and its suburbs from the so-called freeze. New settlers there are exempt from municipal taxes for five years and then benefit from a reduced rate. Because of this bias, Palestinians in East Jerusalem pay taxes five times higher than many settlers.

Palestinian living conditions in East Jerusalem—long known as Arab Jerusalem—are even more desperate than in other parts of the occupied territories. After the 1967 war, the 17,625 acres of Arab land that comprise East Jerusalem were expropriated and annexed to West Jerusalem. According to the Jerusalem Information Center, only 13.5 percent of this land was designated for Arab neighborhoods, and this small allocation consisted mainly of small, scattered parcels that were already fully developed and crowded at the time of annexation.

By contrast, 42 percent of East Jerusalem was set aside exclusively for Jewish settlements. On this land, more than 50,000 government-sponsored Jewish housing units have been constructed and 22,000 more are planned. Israel designates the remaining annexed land, about 42 percent of the total, as unzoned or protected for environmental preservation. It is expected to be made available, as needed, for additional settlement construction.

Israel is steadily tightening rules that reduce the number of Palestinians entitled to live in East Jerusalem. Over 50,000 have been denied permanent residency rights because they were away from home in 1967 or moved, even temporarily, to a different location. Young people often find their residency rights blocked when they attempt to return from attending universities overseas. Unification of divided families is more difficult in East Jerusalem than elsewhere in the occupied territories. Only Palestinians bearing proof that they, or their parents, have resided in East Jerusalem since 1967 can move freely to and from the city. Others may enter only if they receive special permits from Israeli authorities. This policy sharply restricts religious practice, as a practical matter blocking most Palestinians in the West Bank and Gaza from visiting holy places in East Jerusalem. It stands as a cynical reversal of Israel's long-proclaimed guarantee that all people will have free access to religious shrines.

Ninety-one percent of owner-built housing units in East Jerusalem are substandard or overcrowded, but because of Israeli controls, improvement is almost impossible. Israeli authorities approve only about 150 Palestinian licenses for housing construction a year, notwithstanding the hardship this means for 21,000 families that are virtually homeless, some subsisting in caves, tents, or temporary lean-tos. By contrast, Jewish settlers secure construction permits and government subsidies without delay.

Broadly, throughout the occupied territories, Rabin is making steady progress in the creation of a series of isolated cantons whose residents Israeli authorities can efficiently control through closures, curfews, and other restrictions.

Israel's Apartheid Well Advanced

Working "cleverly" and without complaint from his chief financier, the U.S. government, Rabin's administration is building new settlements and a $600 million highway project in the occupied territories, in each instance ordering the confiscation of Palestinian land and the destruction of Palestinian property, including many homes and farms. In December 1993 alone, three months after the Arafat-Rabin handshake, Israel confiscated 9,000 acres.

The new highways serve Israeli interests in two ways:

First, they enable settlers to bypass Palestinian cities and villages in moving to and from Jerusalem and from one settlement to another. This process helps to strengthen their status as an integral part of Israel's body politic.

Second, they form barriers that make travel more difficult for Palestinians, a challenge that is intensified by Israel's edict forbidding the establishment of non-Jewish enterprises adjacent to the highways.

The creation of the network of Jewish settlements and highways facilitates the division of the Palestinian population among six substantially isolated parts:

▪ A northern canton in which Nablus and Jenin are the largest communities.

▪ A canton just north of Jerusalem consisting of Ramallah and surrounding villages.

▪ East Jerusalem, where 155,000 Palestinians are crowded onto small bits of land scattered amid settlements where 160,000 Jews now reside. They are further isolated from other Palestinians by the ring of suburban settlements Rabin credits the Labor Party with cleverly building years ago.

▪ A southern canton that includes the city of Hebron.

▪ The northern part of the Gaza Strip, in which Gaza City is the population center.

▪ The southern part of the Gaza Strip in which Khan Yunis and Rafah are the main communities.

The Gaza Strip may be viewed as a single canton, but Israeli forces stationed in the settlement of Netzarim, consisting of 1,000 acres, can easily and swiftly divide the north part from the south.

Future prospects for Palestinians are grim. Even if Israel lives up to all terms of the accords, these sobering realities will remain:

▪ Israel's government will continue to be in full, unfettered command of all important aspects of Palestinian political life. The powers reserved to Israel are so sweeping and intimate that the accords have become an instrument of oppression, legitimizing Israel's program of dismemberment. The PLO is a negotiating partner in name only, as the disparity in strength between Israel and the Palestinians is absurdly wide. Israeli Foreign Minister Peres observed candidly in March 1994: "The PLO can give us very little. They have no land. They have no authority. They have no means."

■ The entirety of the occupied territories will remain smothered by Israel's military might, no matter what self-rule steps may be taken.

Israel reserves the right to protect all 253,500 Jewish inhabitants of the 160 settlements that are widely scattered throughout the occupied territories, including East Jerusalem. As a practical matter, this stipulation enables Israeli military forces to blanket the occupied territories, even in self-rule areas like the Gaza Strip. (See map.)

The deadly, racist character of this stipulation became apparent five months after the Arafat-Rabin handshake when a settler, Baruch Goldstein, used an automatic assault gun to massacre twenty-nine Palestinians at prayer in a Hebron mosque. The Israeli official responsible for security at the mosque disclosed at an official inquiry that government orders forbade Israeli soldiers to fire at Jewish settlers, even one like Goldstein who was shooting down Palestinians without cause. Hebron Police Superintendent Meir Tayar testified that in such a circumstance Israeli soldiers are instructed to "take cover and wait for the clip to finish, then stop [the settler] in some other way, not by shooting."

■ Even the modest advances toward a decent existence that self-rule may achieve hang by slender threads that can snap at any time. The accords are substantially in the personal custody of two men, Arafat and Rabin, each of whom must still contend with fierce opposition within his own constituency. If either should depart from leadership, the future of the accords would be seriously threatened.

The peace accords leave untouched the most fundamental Palestinian demands: the removal of the Jewish settlements from the occupied territories, the establishment of an independent Palestinian state with East Jerusalem as its capital, and the right of all refugees to return home. Although the resolution of these issues is essential to a just and lasting peace, they are put off—even for discussion—until April 1997. The United States, the only nation with enough leverage to force Israel to put these demands on the current agenda, instead continues to shower Israel with unconditional economic and military aid, as well as uncritical political support.

The most depressing reality is that the peace accords, even in their most optimistic interpretation, fail to lift Palestinians from their status as vassals of a foreign state. They offer no assurance that these beleaguered people, even in the distant future, will attain the rights to which they are entitled as human beings. How these rights have been denied for nearly a half century is the focus of this book.

By supporting the severe limits of the accords and continuing to reject self-determination and statehood, the U.S. government opposes real freedom for the Palestinians, a posture that violates America's traditions and principles. It is complicity in discrimination on a massive and shameful scale. The consequences are more harsh and demeaning to Palestinians, with whom we have never been at war, than those we imposed on Germans and Japanese following World War II.

Our posture projects a glaring double standard that mocks our government's professed support for the rules of international conduct proclaimed in the United Nations Charter, and it seriously undercuts the ability of our government to exert moral leadership as it deals with other foreign policy challenges. For example, during the spring of 1994 our pro-Israel bias forced our government to a new level of hypocrisy that must have both amused and depressed world leaders. Pressured by pro-Israel interests who were worried that Iran and Iraq might buy nuclear weapons from Pyongyang, the United States threatened military action in demanding international inspection of North Korea's nuclear facilities. At the same time, Washington did nothing to force Israel, at long last, to accept the same inspections and halt its own well-known nuclear weapons buildup.

To all people concerned about violations of human rights, it is a bitter irony that Israel, with massive U.S. help, is building an ugly new apartheid while South Africa, responding to substantial U.S. pressure, is dismantling the old.

Our citizens must, at long last, make amends for our government's misconduct. First and foremost, we owe it to the Palestinians, as Israel could not maintain its occupation of Arab land, its subjugation of the Palestinian people and its denial of their nationhood, or its refusal to deal under the peace accords with these violations without the powerful, unconditional support of the U.S. government.

But we also owe it to ourselves. Our government's moral integrity must be restored so it can provide effective leadership, not only for justice in the Middle East but to advance America's other worthy interests worldwide.

Israel must be pressed into accepting fundamental change in its agenda with the Palestinians. Because the accords permit a long delay in addressing the final status questions and, meanwhile, facilitate the dismemberment of the Palestine nation, they are becoming an instrument of oppression, not justice.

The final status of East Jerusalem, the settlements, the refugees, and statehood must be moved from the bottom of the agenda to the top. And only the American people, acting through their government and utilizing government aid as an instrument of influence, can force Israel to accept this urgent, essential change in priority.

We must demand, as an absolute condition of further aid, that this change occur. Given the consistently pro-Israel bias that the Clinton administration projects and the domination of Congress by Israel's lobby, the difficulty of this mission is formidable. A powerful, sustained outcry from the American people is required.

Our duty is clear, because our own responsibility for Palestine's plight is inescapable. Prime Minister Rabin's handshakes with Chairman Arafat and King Hussein intensify rather than lessen our obligation to undertake this urgent task.

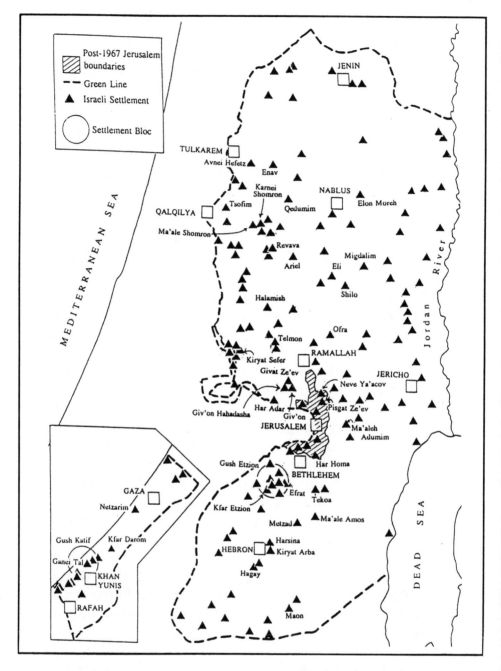

Jewish Settlements, built by Israel on confiscated Palestinian land, blanket the occupied territories and surround major Palestinian cities. The broken line (Green Line) shows the pre–June 1967 border between Israel and the West Bank. The insert at lower left shows the Gaza Strip. The small black triangles locate the 160 settlements inhabited by 1992 by over 253,500 Jewish Israelis. Map reproduced from *Clever Concealment,* by permission of the publisher, Palestine Human Rights Information Center, Jerusalem.

PROLOGUE

The Arab-Israeli conflict is fraught with disastrous consequences for the United States, and much of the trouble is of our own making. The damage goes far beyond the financial and economic burdens that are created as our government continues to donate billions of dollars each year to Israel and to lavish tax and trade favors on that state. The worst of the consequences arise from U.S. collusion in the dreadful, long-standing violation of human rights that Israel has perpetrated on a vast scale.

The United States maintains a pivotal role in Israel's control and exploitation of the occupied territories—the West Bank, East Jerusalem, the Gaza Strip, southern Lebanon, and the Golan Heights—all of it Arab land. Our government provides unwavering financial, diplomatic, and military support while Israel persists in the violation of international law, maintains a tight and often brutal military rule over nearly two million Arabs, and masks all of this behind a shield of deliberate deceptions.

Beyond the suffering Arabs, the principal casualty of this collusion is America's reservoir of goodwill in the Middle East. Respect for the United States—once deeply rooted and widespread among Arabs and Israelis alike—is being squandered in the unseemly, perpetual quest by politicians in this country for the approval of pro-Israel interest groups.

The collusion is transparent in the appalling double standard that the U.S. government applies in the enforcement of Middle East–related UN Security Council resolutions.

When Iraq invaded and annexed Kuwait in 1990, the United States organized and led a massive multinational military assault that, under UN sanction, reversed the conquest. In contrast, the U.S. government does nothing beyond expressing a few words of rebuke when Israel commits gross violations of international law.

For example, the UN Security Council has called on Israel to withdraw from the Arab land it seized years ago by force of arms, condemned Israel's annexation of East Jerusalem and the Golan Heights and the construction of Israeli housing in the occupied territories, and, most recently, on December 18, 1992, demanded that Israel reverse its expulsion of 413 Palestinians (UN Security Council Resolution 799).

Instead of leading the international community in forceful action—political, economic, or military—to secure compliance with the council's demand that Israel reverse the expulsions, the United States did just the opposite. It continued without interruption its steady flow of unrestricted financial and military aid to the offending state. Almost concurrently, just before the inauguration of President Bill Clinton in January 1993, the Bush administration, responding to far less egregious violations, began a new military campaign against Iraq for its violation of postwar no-fly zones. Saudi Arabia's King Fahd deplored this double standard: UN Security Council resolutions, he asserted, "must be respected and implemented, whether they pertain to the situation in the Gulf or the Palestinian case. . . . "[1]

U.S. goodwill is threatened even in Israel, where a rising number of citizens view the U.S.-applied double standard as a roadblock to peace. They believe that, in the absence of the uninterrupted flow of unconditional financial and military support from the United States, their government long ago would have withdrawn its forces from the occupied territories and established a normal, peaceful relationship with the Arab states.

The difficulty for the United States will become more burdensome and more menacing when the Arab-Israeli conflict escalates, as it surely must in the absence of peace. The site of the conflict is the crossroads of highly competitive religious, economic, political, and military influences, all of which involve vital U.S. interests. Those interests straddle both sides and cannot be protected by favoring either Arab nations or Israel.

We alone have the resources needed to secure the cooperation of all major parties to the conflict. But to act effectively the United States must first overcome two formidable obstacles, both of them domestic. One is the excessive influence that pro-Israel interests exercise in the formulation of U.S. policy in the Middle East. The other is the false facade that most Americans innocently accept as the real Israel. Supporters of Israel exploit that misleading image with great skill in their program to maintain U.S.-Israeli collusion.

The path to a just peace in the region cannot come into clear focus until the fiction about Israel is recognized and cleared away. Wise judgments about future U.S. policy must be based on reality, not fallacies. They must take into account the most complete and accurate information that is available, including an unbiased profile of Israel, and proceed from a genuine acceptance of the responsibility the United States bears for Israel's past and present actions.

This volume, I believe, fills that critical need. In reading it, you will share an unsettling experience: a long quest for a report that encompasses Israel's expansionist behavior and discriminatory social structure. The journey is arduous, because truth is often elusive. In this case, it must be sorted from voluminous published information about the U.S. relationship with Israel and the Palestinians, much of which is fallacious and must be debunked. In addition, the popular media—newspapers, books, articles, television dramas and documentaries, and movies—deal for the most part only with the heroic side of Israeli history and current behavior, ignoring or glossing over its persistent violations of human rights, its expansionist policies, and its violations of international law. (For instance, Leon Uris's vastly popular 1950s novel *Exodus* was actually commissioned by the New York public relations firm of Edward Gottlieb to "create a more sympathetic attitude toward Israel." As public relations expert Art Stevens concluded: "The novel did more to popularize Israel with the

American public than any other single presentation through the media."[2]

I bring to this task a unique experience in Middle East politics. I served for twenty-two years as a member of the U.S. House of Representatives, twelve of them on the House Foreign Affairs Subcommittee on Europe and the Middle East. During those years I often decried Israel's violations of human rights and its military aggression, but I never once voted against the legislation that provided Israel with the means to carry out those misdeeds. On several occasions I urged the Carter administration to suspend all aid, but when the roll was called in committee and in the House of Representatives chamber on basic legislation for aid, my vote was always affirmative. When I now lament the hypocrisy of continuing U.S. aid to Israel while criticizing its violations of human rights, I reflect with sadness on my own record.

The congressional years gave me for the first time an awareness of Middle East politics. Through foreign travel and scores of official hearings and private meetings, I dealt personally with all of the principal leaders who shape policy in the region. In my acquaintance, as well, were the officials of lobbying groups, many of them organized by U.S. citizens with ethnic ties to the Middle East, including the American Israel Public Affairs Committee (AIPAC), the powerful organization that serves the interests of the state of Israel on Capitol Hill. My experience also included candidacy in twelve federal election cycles. In the last two, I found myself the primary target of the nation's major pro-Israel lobbying groups. Those campaigns provided new insight into the domestic factors that influence foreign policy. When I departed Congress in January 1983, I innocently considered myself something of an expert on Israel and the Arab states.

My education began in earnest when, after leaving Congress, I began research for my book *They Dare to Speak Out: People and Institutions Confront Israel's Lobby.*[3] I soon realized that my congressional experience had provided only a glimpse of the network that Israel's supporters utilize in influencing both Middle East policymaking and the public perception of Israel.

This influence is pervasive throughout government and in almost every aspect of life, private and public, across the United States. On Capitol Hill it is so powerful that no debate worthy of the name ever occurs on the Arab-Israeli conflict. Except for Senators Robert C. Byrd of West Virginia and Bob Dole of Kansas and Representatives James A. Traficant, Jr., of Ohio and Nick Joe Rahall of West Virginia, no members of either chamber question Israel's behavior in a sustained way. As former Under Secretary of State George W. Ball observes: "On Middle East policy, Congress behaves like a bunch of trained poodles, jumping through the hoop held by Israel's lobby."[4]

Each year the U.S. Congress donates to Israel the equivalent of $1,000 for every Israeli man, woman, and child. No matter how sharply Congress cuts other items in the federal budget, gifts to Israel sweep through without restrictive amendment or murmur of opposition. My years on Capitol Hill led me to conclude that aid to Israel is more sacrosanct there than even Social Security and Medicare.

Israel's influence is nearly as great in the executive branch. Donald McHenry, a respected career diplomat and former ambassador to the United Nations, makes this somber appraisal: "Because of the [Israeli] lobby's influence, our government is unable to pursue its own national interests in the Middle East."[5]

They Dare to Speak Out explains how the lobby's power is established and maintained—and why. The response to the book's publication—sales have exceeded 210,000—is almost as astounding as the facts the book reveals. At this writing, more than one thousand readers have sent messages by mail and telephone. Some traveled across the country to my midwestern home. All are troubled and want to help loosen the lobby's grip on Middle East policymaking. Many of these readers became the founding members of the Council for the National Interest, a Washington-based nonprofit, nonpartisan organization established in 1989. Its exclusive purpose is to organize support at the community level for policies that advance the American national interest in the Middle East (see Appendix).

The letters and calls have raised important questions. Is Israel a democracy? Why did the United Nations equate Zionism with racism? Is Israel open to all refugees? Is Israel important to U.S. security? Does Israel pay its debts to the United States? Are Arab citizens of Israel treated the same as Jewish citizens? Is Israel's military occupation of the West Bank and Gaza a violation of international law? How does Israel justify its control over the Palestinians who live there? Which side started the Arab-Israel wars? Does the United States have a moral duty to help Israel with its problems, especially the settlement of Jewish immigrants from the former Soviet republics?

Most Americans, influenced by the false image Israel's supporters have created, would probably answer this way: "Israel is a democracy that shuns racism, treats all its citizens equally, promptly pays its debts to the U.S. government, has shared values with America, and is vital to U.S. security. Because the United States helped to bring Israel into being and encouraged immigration it has a moral obligation to help Israel with its problems. Israel has fought against Arabs only when attacked. It must maintain strict control in the West Bank and Gaza because the Palestinians who reside there want to destroy Israel." My answers challenged these views. But while I believed my opinions to be well founded I did not have readily at hand the basic sources. Nor could I find them in a single volume.

As I continued my research following publication of the revised edition of *They Dare to Speak Out* in 1989, I discovered a shocking number of broadly accepted assertions about the nature of Israel and its relationship with the United States that are proved false by authoritative documents. It is obvious that the acceptance of fallacies about Israel is not a happenstance. It is the handiwork of many people applying their energy to the task with perseverance and commitment.

The drive to sustain these fallacies arises, in part at least, from the reverence with which many Jews and Christians view Israel. Its creation in 1948 is the major achievement of Judaism in recent history, culminating years in which "next year in Jerusalem" had served as the rallying cry and dream of many Jews worldwide. The cry intensified in the wake of the dreadful oppression and extermination of Jews in Nazi Germany during World War II. This awful example of the crime of genocide against Jews will receive lasting public attention with the opening of the new Holocaust Museum near the Washington Monument in Washington, D.C. It is ironic, however, that Nazi Germany's systematic attempt to destroy European Jewry, for which the U.S. government had no direct responsibility, is the subject of a national memorial, while examples for which our government must accept full responsibility—slavery, the slaughter of American Indians, and now Israel's violation of Arab human rights—are overlooked.

Although the creation of Israel was strongly resisted by many prominent Jews in the United States and its subsequent misbehavior remains a topic of broad concern in the Jewish community here, Israel shines in the consciousness of other Jews. The Jewish state is seen as a haven where Jews can be safe from any future wave of anti-Semitism. A 1983 survey of American Jews reports: "Caring for Israel still ranks with attending a Passover Seder and lighting Hanukkah candles as among the most popular and widespread contemporary expressions of American Jewish commitment."[6] Rabbi Arthur Hertzberg comes to a similar conclusion: "The sense of belonging to a worldwide Jewish people, of which Israel is the center, is a religious sentiment, but it seems to persist even among Jews who regard themselves as secularists or atheists."[7]

Intellectual Irving Kristol confesses his concern for Israel in the pages of *The Wall Street Journal*: "Why am I so deeply affected? I am not an Orthodox Jew, and only a barely observant one. I am not a Zionist and I did not find my two visits to Israel to have been particularly exhilarating." Yet he adds that he cares desperately about Israel because he senses "deep down that what happens to Israel will be decisive for

Jewish history, and for the kinds of lives my grandchildren and great-grandchildren will be leading."[8]

In recent years Israel has become viewed as more than a place of refuge. Ralph Nurnberger, another scholar and keen observer of Judaism, notes the sharp decline in Jewish participation in religious services and concludes: "For many American Jews, Israel has replaced Judaism as their religion."[9] The result is that Israel is the focus of unwavering and uncritical devotion by leaders of America's traditional Jewish organizations.

There are exceptions, however. In academia, business, and journalism a number of prominent Jewish professionals speak and write about Israel with candor, balance, and sensitivity, among them Anthony Lewis, Mike Wallace, Roberta Feuerlicht, Rita Hauser, Milton Viorst, Seymour M. Hersh, Michael Lerner, Noam Chomsky, and Philip Klutznick. They make valuable contributions to public discourse on Middle East policy. But at times their voices can scarcely be heard over the incantations of those Americans whose judgment is clouded by emotional fervor.

Israel also derives enormous political support from millions of fundamentalist Christians who are driven by religious conviction to embrace fallacies about Israel. They believe that the Israelis of today inherit God-given privilege from the Israelites of biblical times. They contend that Israel must be kept strong as part of God's plan for the "end of times" prophesied in the Bible. They ignore the sectarian anti-Semitic and anti-Catholic underpinnings of this apocalyptic belief system, which foretells the destruction of all people, Jews included, who are not "born again" to Christianity.[10]

These fundamentalist Christians and the Jews who accept Israel as their religion seem constrained to defend it from all criticism. In their zeal they often wrongfully castigate Israel's critics as anti-Semites or as "self-hating Jews." The effect is intimidation. Free speech is stifled and thoughtful study and appraisal inhibited. In contrast, frank discussion of Israel's shortcomings is commonplace among its citizens. The Hebrew press, a major forum for Israeli debate, is filled with candid reports of misconduct by the Israeli government, but these are rarely quoted in the United States.

Also to be found among Israel's strong defenders are people who have no religious motivation but believe that the state of Israel protects vital American military, economic, or political interests in the region. For years, they viewed Israel as a bulwark against Soviet intervention. Today they see it, mistakenly in my view, as an effective counter to the menace of religious radicalism centered in Iran and the military threat already given substance by Iraq's Saddam Hussein.

Most of the fallacies about Israel are the work of religious partisans, both Jewish and Christian, who repeat these fallacies so frequently year after year that they are accepted almost universally as fact. For most Americans, this skein of myths defines Israel and constitutes the case for still more U.S. economic, political, and military aid.

In this book, I attribute each fallacy to a well-known authority and then examine and refute it with facts meticulously reported and footnoted from the public record, often from Israeli sources. The resulting picture of Israel, supported by facts rather than myths, will be a revelation to many readers.

If the history of the Arab-Israeli conflict were written today, it would record that the overwhelming majority of U.S. citizens, both Christians and Jews, have been either silent about the inhumane policies being carried out by Israel or directly complicit in their implementation. The intent of this book is to provide the information that will inspire thoughtful citizens to demand change.

PART ONE

STATEHOOD
AND
CONQUEST

ONE

ISRAEL'S CLAIMS TO PALESTINE

Israel bases its claims to establishment of a state in Palestine on three major sources: the legacy of the Old Testament of the Bible,[1] the Balfour Declaration issued by Great Britain in 1917, and the partition of Palestine into Arab and Jewish states recommended by the UN General Assembly in 1947.

FALLACY

"By virtue of our natural and historic right . . . [we] do hereby proclaim the establishment of a Jewish State in the Land of Israel—the State of Israel."
—Israel's Declaration of Independence, 1948[2]

FACT

Historically, Jews were not the first inhabitants of Palestine, nor did they rule there for as long as a number of other peoples did. Modern archaeologists now generally agree that Egyptians and Canaanites inhabited Palestine from the earliest recorded days of around 3000 B.C. to around 1700 B.C.[3] There followed other occupiers such as Hyksos, Hittites, and Philistines. The Hebrew period of rule started only in 1020 B.C. and lasted until 587 B.C. The Israelites were then overrun by Assyrians, Babylonians, Greeks, Egyptians, and Syrians until the Hebrew Maccabeans regained partial rule in 164 B.C. However, in 63 B.C. the Roman Empire conquered Jerusalem and in 70 A.D. destroyed the Second Temple and scattered the Jews into other lands. In sum, ancient Jews controlled Palestine or some major parts of it for less than six hundred years in the five-thousand-year period of Palestine's recorded history—less than Canaanites, Egyptians, Muslims, or Romans.[4] The U.S. King-Crane Commission concluded in 1919 that a claim "based on an occupation of two thousand years ago can hardly be seriously considered."[5]

On May 14, 1948, a total of thirty-seven men attended the Tel Aviv meeting at which Israel's independence was declared as a "natural and historic right." But critics charge that their action had no binding legal force in international law because they did not represent the majority population at the time. In fact, only one of them had been born in Palestine; thirty-five were from European countries and one was from Yemen. Asserts Palestinian scholar Issa Nakhleh: "The Jewish minority had no right to declare an independent state on a territory belonging to the Palestinian Arab nation."[6]

FALLACY

"Israel's international 'birth certificate' was validated by the promise of the Bible."

—AIPAC, * *1992*[7]

FACT

Claims of divine support for tribal or national ambitions were common in the ancient world. Sumerians, Egyptians, Greeks,

---

*AIPAC is the American Israel Public Affairs Committee, the major lobby supporting Israel in the United States.

and Romans all cited divine inspiration for their conquests. As historian Frank Epp notes: "Every phenomenon and process of life was attributed to the agency of a god or gods . . . of good land being promised to better people by superior gods."[8] No court of law or world body today would honor as legal a title of ownership based on a claim that purported to come from God.[9] Even for those who take the biblical grant literally as God's grant, biblical scholars such as Dr. Dewey Beegle of Wesley Theological Seminary point out that the ancient Jews failed to be obedient to God's commandments and therefore forfeited the promise.[10]

FALLACY

"The right [of Jews to national restoration in Palestine] was acknowledged by the Balfour Declaration."
                    —*Israel's Declaration of Independence, 1948*[11]

FACT

The Balfour Declaration deliberately did not endorse establishment of a Jewish nation. The declaration was contained in a letter sent by British Foreign Secretary Arthur James Balfour to Lord Rothschild, president of the British Zionist Federation, on November 2, 1917. The declaration had been approved by the British cabinet and said: "His Majesty's Government view with favor the establishment in Palestine of a national home for the Jewish people, and will use their best endeavors to facilitate the achievement of this object, it being clearly understood that nothing shall be done which may prejudice the civil and religious rights of existing non-Jewish communities in Palestine, or the rights and political status enjoyed by Jews in any other country."[12] In 1939 a British White Paper specifically stated that Great Britain "could not have intended Palestine should be converted into a Jewish State against the will of the Arab population of the country."[13]

"[Palestine is] the land without people—for the people [Jews] without a land."

—*Israel Zangwill, early Zionist, c. 1897*[14]

At the time of the 1917 Balfour Declaration there were about 600,000 Arabs in Palestine and about 60,000 Jews.[15] Over the next thirty years the ratio narrowed as Jewish immigration increased, especially as a result of the anti-Semitic policies of Adolf Hitler. However, on the eve of the 1947 UN plan to partition Palestine, Arabs still were a large majority, with Jews amounting to only one-third of the population—608,225 Jews to 1,237,332 Arabs.[16] When Max Nordau, an early Zionist and friend of Zangwill, learned in 1897 there was an indigenous Arab population in Palestine, he exclaimed: "I didn't know that! We are committing an injustice!"[17]

Not only were a people already in Palestine, but they had a well-established society that was recognized by other Arabs as uniquely "Palestinian." It consisted of respected intellectual and professional classes, political organizations, and a thriving agrarian economy that was expanding into the crude beginnings of modern industry.[18] Observes scholar John Quigley: "The Arab population had been stable for hundreds of years. There was no substantial in-migration in the nineteenth century."[19]

"By virtue of . . . the resolution of the General Assembly of the United Nations [we] do hereby proclaim the establishment of a Jewish State in the Land of Israel—the State of Israel."

—*Israel's Declaration of Independence, 1948*[20]

It was only strong pressure exerted by the Truman administration that secured passage of the UN Partition Plan by the General Assembly on November 29, 1947, by a vote of 33 to 13 with 10 abstentions and 1 absent. Among those nations that succumbed to U.S. pressure were France, Ethiopia, Haiti, Liberia, Luxembourg, Paraguay, and the Philippines.[21] Former Under Secretary of State Sumner Welles wrote: "By direct order of the White House every form of pressure, direct and indirect, was brought to bear by American officials upon those countries outside of the Muslim world that were known to be either uncertain or opposed to partition. Representatives or intermediaries were employed by the White House to make sure that the necessary majority would at length be secured."[22]

The partition plan, adopted as Resolution 181, divided Palestine between "independent Arab and Jewish states and the Special International Regime for the City of Jerusalem."[23] Future Israeli Foreign Minister Moshe Sharett argued that the resolution had "binding force," and Israel's Declaration of Independence cited it three times as legal justification for the establishment of the state.[24] But the General Assembly, in contrast to the Security Council, has no powers beyond making recommendations. It cannot enforce its recommendations nor are they legally binding except on internal UN matters.[25]

The Palestinians, as was their right, rejected the plan because it granted the Jews more than half of Palestine despite the fact that they made up only one-third of the population and owned only 6.59 percent of the land.[26] In addition, the Palestinians maintained that the United Nations had no legal right to recommend partition when the majority inhabitants of Palestine opposed it. Nonetheless, by rejecting partition Palestinians did not reject their own claim to an independent nation. Their opposition was to a Jewish state established on Palestinian land, not to the Jews' rights as a people.

Jewish leader David Ben-Gurion advised his colleagues to accept partition because, he told them, "there is no such thing in history as a final arrangement—not with regard to the regime, not with regard to borders, and not with regard to international agreements."[27]

One of Zionism's great pioneers, Nahum Goldmann, expressed pragmatism in a different vein: "There is no hope for a Jewish state which has to face another 50 years of struggle against Arab enemies."[28]

FALLACY

"Originally Palestine had included Jordan."
        —*Ariel Sharon, Israeli trade minister, 1989*[29]

FACT

At no time in the long history of the Islamic/Ottoman Empire did Palestine exist as a separate geopolitical or administrative unit. When the area of the eastern Mediterranean between Lebanon and Egypt was taken over by Great Britain from Turkey at the end of World War I, certain parts of what was called Palestine were under the administrative region of Beirut while Jerusalem was a sanjak, an autonomous district.[30] The area east of the river Jordan—Transjordan—was, in the words of Tel Aviv University scholar Aaron Klieman, "virtually *terra nullius* under the Turks and was left undefined in the partition of the Ottoman Empire."[31]

In assuming the League of Nations Palestine mandate in 1922, Britain was granted Palestine and Transjordan eastward to Mesopotamia, which became Iraq. In today's terms, this included Israel, Jordan, the West Bank, the Gaza Strip, and Jerusalem. In December 1922, Britain declared its recognition of "the existence of an independent constitutional Government in Transjordan." And in 1928 it specifically defined Palestine as the area west of the Jordan River.[32] It was only in Palestine that Britain recognized as applicable its promise in the Balfour Declaration to aid in establishing a Jewish homeland.

TWO

THE
1948 WAR

The 1947 UN Partition Plan for Palestine recommended the establishment of Jewish and Palestinian states. Jewish forces took to the field almost immediately, quickly securing areas designated Jewish and then expanding into parts of Palestine reserved for Palestinians. The war lasted a year, until January 6, 1949. The first part was marked by regular Jewish troops fighting Arab irregular forces and the second half by battles between Jewish units and five Arab armies that entered Palestine the day after Israel's founding on May 14, 1948.[1]

FALLACY

"We were, of course, totally unprepared for war."
—*Golda Meir, Israeli prime minister, 1975*[2]

FACT

Israeli plans for war began in earnest the day after passage of the UN Partition Plan on November 29, 1947. All Jews age seventeen to twenty-five were ordered to register for military service.[3] On December 5, Zionist leader David Ben-Gurion ordered "immediate action" to expand Jewish settlements in three areas assigned by the UN to the Arab state of Palestine.[4] By mid-December they began organized military action against the Arabs in Palestine under a strategy spelled out in military Plan Gimmel. Aims of Plan Gimmel were to buy time for the mobilization of Jewish forces by seizing strategic points vacated by the British and to terrorize the Arab population into submission.[5] The first major Jewish assault came on December 18 when Palmach troops ("assault companies"), the shock force of the Jewish underground Haganah army, attacked the Palestinian village of Khissas in northern Galilee in a nighttime raid, killing five adults and five children and wounding five others.[6]

Christopher Sykes, a contemporary British observer, notes that the Khissas attack represented a new phase in the struggle, with its character changing from "indiscriminate raiding and counter-raiding to more calculated attack and atrocity."[7] On December 19, Ben-Gurion ordered that Jewish forces strike aggressively: "In each attack, a decisive blow should be struck, resulting in the destruction of homes and the expulsion of the population."[8] Thus by the time the five Arab armies entered Palestine on May 15, 1948, the Zionists were already well advanced in carrying out their war plans.

FALLACY

"Total war was forced on the Jews."
—*Jacob Tzur*, Zionism, *1977*[9]

FACT

Israel's army was on the march within weeks after the 1947 UN Partition Plan. Organized military action by the Zionists began in mid-December under Plan Gimmel.[10] By early March 1948, the Jews were pursuing Plan Dalet, aimed at capturing areas in the Galilee and between Jerusalem and Tel Aviv that had been assigned by the United Nations Partition Plan to the envisioned Palestinian state.[11] Thus, by May 15 when five Arab armies entered Palestine, Israel had already conquered substantial portions of Palestine outside its own UN-defined state.[12]

By contrast, it was not until April 30, 1948, that the Arab chiefs of staff met for the first time to work out a plan for military intervention. Even at this late date, adds Israeli historian Simha Flapan, "the Arab leaders were still desperately searching for a face-saving formula that would extricate them from a commitment to military action."[13] On May 13, the U.S. ambassador to Egypt reported on the low morale of the Arabs, adding: "Informed circles inclined to agree that Arabs would now welcome almost any face-saving device if it would prevent open war."[14]

Jordanian war aims were not against the Jewish state or partition—which it conditionally accepted—but were against Israel's efforts to annex parts of Palestine not included as Jewish in the UN Partition Plan. As a result, as Israeli historian Abraham Sela recorded, "all of the battles with [Jordan's] Arab Legion were fought in the areas outside the territory of the Jewish state . . . including those fought in Jerusalem."[15]

On June 1, Israel's UN delegation issued a statement reporting that in the two weeks of fighting since Israel's independence the new country had gained control of 400 square miles beyond the borders assigned to it by the partition plan and that no fighting was taking place within Israel's UN borders. The communiqué said: "The territory of the State of Israel is entirely free of invaders."[16]

FALLACY

"[The Arabs had] an absolute superiority of arms, and an overwhelming superiority of manpower conscripted, volunteer, or potential."
—*Yigal Allon, Israeli deputy prime minister, 1970*[17]

The Jews of Palestine consistently had better and more weapons than the Palestinians or the other Arabs in neighboring states. While both Arabs and Jews were officially embargoed from buying weapons in the United States and most Western countries, the Jews clandestinely received major supplies of arms from Czechoslovakia starting in early 1948. These included in one contract alone 24,500 rifles, 5,000 light machine guns, 200 medium machine guns, 54 million rounds of ammunition, and 25 Messerschmitt warplanes.[18] By the time the war of organized units began on May 15, 1948, the Israelis were capable of fielding 800 armored vehicles against the combined Arab total of 113, and 787 mortars and 4 field guns to the Arabs' 40 mortars and 102 guns.[19]

At the same time, another major supply of arms to the Jews came from American Zionists in the United States in violation of the U.S. arms embargo. Such suppliers included the Sonneborn Institute, a group composed of wealthy Jewish Americans headed by Rudolf G. Sonneborn, a millionaire New York industrialist.[20] Two others were the Joint Distribution Committee and Service Airways, which was headed by Jewish American Adolph ("Al") William Schwimmer, a former TWA flight engineer.[21] Another major player was Austrian-born Teddy Kollek, who headed Israel's underground arms purchases in New York and later became the mayor of Jewish West Jerusalem.[22]

Schwimmer and his airline were one of the few underground Jewish groups actually prosecuted for their illegal trade; he was convicted in federal court in Los Angeles in 1950 and fined $10,000 for exporting planes and spare parts to Israel and other countries. Schwimmer went on to become head of Israel's aircraft company, Israel Aircraft Industries, and reappeared in 1985 as a major player in the Reagan administration's worst scandal, the Iran-Contra affair.[23]

"Our enemies have failed in their efforts to beat us by brute force although they outnumbered us twenty to one."
—*Chaim Weizmann, provisional president of Israel, 1948*[24]

FACT

Trained Jewish forces outnumbered the total forces committed to battle by five Arab countries on May 15, 1948, and continued to do so throughout the war. Frontline, armed Israeli troops totaled 27,400 compared with 13,876 from the Arab states: Egypt 2,800; Iraq 4,000; Lebanon 700; Syria 1,876; and Transjordan 4,500.[25] At the time, on May 18, U.S. army intelligence estimated forces as 40,000 Jewish troops and 50,000 militia against 20,000 Arab troops and 13,000 guerrillas.[26] Israeli historian Simha Flapan observed: *"The Israelis were not outnumbered.* In spite of differences in their estimates, particularly over Jewish figures, various observers agree on this fact."[27]

FALLACY

"[The Arabs were so strong in 1948 that] many military experts expected that Israel would soon be overrun."
—*Terrence Prittie and B. Dineen,*
The Double Exodus, *1976*[28]

FACT

Israel had such an advantage in both troops and weapons that there was never any serious doubt among observers that Israel would win the war. U.S. Secretary of State George Marshall notified U.S. embassies the day before the war began that the Arab armies were weak and would be no match for Israel. His major worry was that "if Jews follow counsel of their extremists who favor contemptuous policy toward Arabs, any Jewish State to be set up will be able to survive only with continuous assistance from Abroad."[29] On May 13, two days before the war, the U.S. ambassador in Egypt reported that the Arabs had not been successful in obtaining weapons abroad and that their morale was low, adding: "[It is] feared that Arab armies will probably be soundly defeated by Jews."[30]

Jordan's King Abdullah had repeatedly warned: "The Jews are too strong—it is a mistake to make war."[31] Great Britain's legendary Glubb Pasha, head of Jordan's Arab Legion, later recalled: "I missed no opportunity to inform [Jordan's government] that Transjordan had not sufficient resources to wage war on the Jewish state."[32] Reports Israeli historian Simha Flapan: "A Jewish Agency assessment of Arab intentions and capacities . . . reported that the Arab chiefs of staff had warned their governments against the invasion of Palestine and any lengthy war."[33] Concludes Pakistani military historian Syed Ali el-Edroos of the Arab effort: "In professional military terms, there was, in fact, no plan at all."[34]

Nearly forty years later, Israeli historian Benny Morris concludes: "The Yishuv [Jewish community in Palestine] was militarily and administratively vastly superior to the Palestinian Arabs."[35]

FALLACY

"We too had our terrorist groups during the War of Independence: the Stern, the Irgun. . . . But neither of them ever covered itself with such infamy as the Arabs have done with us."

—*Golda Meir, Israeli prime minister, 1972*[36]

FACT

In the 1947–1948 period that resulted in the birth of Israel, terrorism raged in Palestine, conducted mainly by Zionists.

Jewish leader David Ben-Gurion recorded in his personal history of Israel: "From 1946 to 1947 there were scarcely any Arab attacks on the Yishuv [the Jewish community in Palestine]."[37] As war approached in 1948, terrorist actions were launched by both sides, but the Arabs were no match for the organized and systematic campaign waged by Zionist terrorists.[38] As British Major R. D. Wilson reported in 1948, they made "bestial attacks on Arab villages, in which they showed not the slightest discrimination for women and children, whom they killed as opportunity offered."[39]

Zionist acts of terror, carried out mainly by members of two major groups, the Irgun and Lehi, or Stern Gang, included the 1946 bombing of the King David Hotel in Jerusalem, which killed ninety-one people—forty-one Arabs, twenty-eight British, and seventeen Jews;[40] the 1947 hanging of two British soldiers and booby trapping of their bodies;[41] the 1948 bombing of the Arab-owned Semiramis Hotel in Jerusalem, which killed twenty-two Arabs, including women and children;[42] the 1948 massacre of 254 Arab men, women, and children villagers of Deir Yassin;[43] the massacre of scores of civilians at the village of Dawayima in 1948;[44] and the 1948 assassination of UN Special Representative Count Folke Bernadotte of Sweden.[45]

Menachem Begin led the Irgun, and Yitzhak Shamir was one of the leaders of the Stern Gang. Both men later became prime ministers of Israel.

FALLACY

"We do not intend to push the Arabs aside, to take their land, or to disinherit them."
—*David Ben-Gurion, as an early Zionist, circa 1915*[46]

FACT

After the conquest of Arab land in the 1948 war, looting occurred, followed by confiscation of Palestinian property by

Jews. "Plundering and looting were very common," writes Israeli historian Tom Segev. He quotes Israeli writer Moshe Smilansky, an eyewitness: "The urge to grab has seized everyone. Individuals, groups and communities, men, women and children, all fell on the spoils." Cabinet minister Aharon Cizling complained: "When they enter a town and forcibly remove rings from the fingers and jewelry from someone's neck, that's a very grave matter. . . . Many are guilty of it."[47]

Nearly two-thirds of the original 1.2 million Palestinian population had been displaced, turned into refugees.[48] This massive loss was the reason that the war became known to Arabs as the *Nakba*, the Catastrophe.[49]

New York Times correspondent Anne O'Hare McCormick reported that Israelis were going at "top speed" to repopulate the land, adding: "If the influx continues at the contemplated 200,000 a year it will not be long before the newcomers outnumber the displaced."[50]

When Israeli scholar Israel Shahak conducted a study in 1973, he discovered that of the original 475 Palestinian villages caught inside Israel's self-proclaimed frontiers in 1949 only 90 remained; 385 had been destroyed.[51] Later studies showed that the total was more than 400.[52]

The villages, Shahak reported, were "destroyed completely, with their houses, garden-walls, and even cemeteries and tomb-stones, so that literally a stone does not remain standing, and visitors are . . . being told that 'it was all desert.'"[53]

FALLACY

"The best evidence against this myth [of Israeli expansionism] is the history of Israeli withdrawal from territory captured in 1948, 1956, 1973 and 1982."

—*AIPAC, 1992*[54]

In the midst of the 1948 war, British diplomat Sir Hugh Dow reported: "The Jews are frankly expansionist."[55] Israel never gave up any major portions of the land it captured in 1948 outside the borders set down in the UN Partition Plan. The plan confined the Jewish state to 5,893 square miles, equal to 56.47 percent of Palestine, but by the end of the 1948 war Israel controlled an area of 8,000 square miles, 77.4 percent of the land.[56] Significantly, Israel's Declaration of Independence did not mention any borders, and the Jewish state has never publicly declared the extent of its limits.[57]

Israel held an area of Palestine that included 475 Palestinian towns and villages, the vast majority of them empty or soon to be made so. (This compares with a total of 279 Jewish settlements throughout Palestine that were in existence as of November 29, 1947, the day of adoption of the UN Partition Plan.[58])

As Defense Minister Moshe Dayan told a class of Israeli students in 1969: "There is not one single place built in this country that did not have a former Arab population."[59] Indeed, the Israelis confiscated 158,332 out of a total of 179,316 housing units, including homes and apartments.[60] At a minimum the property taken over by Jews also included 10,000 shops and 1,000 warehouses.[61] About 90 percent of Israel's olive groves were taken from the Arabs and 50 percent of the citrus orchards,[62] a confiscation so massive that income from the groves and orchards was "instrumental in alleviating the serious balance-of-payments problem which Israel suffered from 1948 to 1953," according to scholar Ian Lustick.[63]

After the 1967 war, Israeli military forces controlled all of Palestine, the West Bank and Gaza Strip, plus Syria's Golan Heights and Egypt's Sinai Peninsula, a spread of territory totaling 20,870 square miles.[64]

After Israel's Operation Litani invasion of Lebanon in March 1978, Israel's frontiers again expanded to include a self-proclaimed "security belt" in southern Lebanon, a strip along the frontier extending an average of three to six miles inside Lebanon.[65] The "security belt" was extended as deep as twelve miles after Israel's 1982 invasion of Lebanon.[66] The "security belt" continues to exist today, making southern Lebanon what some Israelis call Israel's occupied "North Bank."

Although Israel later did return the Sinai Peninsula in exchange for peace with Egypt, it has continued to occupy all the other Arab territory it has seized by force over the years except for Syria's town of Quneitra, which it destroyed before withdrawing in 1974 as a result of its disengagement agreement with Syria.[67]

THREE

THE PALESTINIAN REFUGEES

Two major waves of Palestinian refugees have been created by the Arab-Israeli conflict. The first wave resulted from the 1948 war and numbered 726,000, two-thirds of the total Palestinian population of 1.2 million. The second wave came in the 1967 war when 323,000 Palestinians became homeless, 113,000 of whom were already refugees from 1948.[1]

FALLACY

"There are no refugees—there are fighters who sought to destroy us, root and branch."
—*David Ben-Gurion, Israeli prime minister, 1949*[2]

FACT

Reports from a variety of independent and reliable sources show that the vast majority of the Palestinian refugees were children, women, and old men.

After Israeli troops—under the command of future prime minister Yitzhak Rabin—captured the Arab city of Lydda in mid-1948 and drove out the population, the British military commander of Jordanian forces, Glubb Pasha, reported: "Perhaps thirty thousand people or more, almost entirely women and children, snatched up what they could and fled from their homes across the open fields."[3] On September 16, UN mediator Count Folke Bernadotte noted that "almost the whole of the Arab population fled or was expelled from the area under Jewish occupation. Large numbers of these are infants, children, pregnant women and nursing mothers. Their condition is one of destitution."[4]

On October 17, 1948, the U.S. representative in Israel, James G. McDonald, reported urgently and directly to President Truman that the Palestinian refugees' "tragedy is rapidly reaching catastrophic proportions and should be treated as a disaster. Present and prospective relief and resettlement resources are utterly inadequate. . . . Of approximately 400,000 refugees approaching winter with cold heavy rains will, it is estimated, kill more than 100,000 old men, women and children who are shelterless and have little or no food."[5]

By February 1949 the death rate of Palestinian refugees in the Gaza Strip alone was reported at 230 a day.[6] William L. Gower, the delegate for the American Red Cross, reported: "Eighty to 85 percent of the displaced persons consist of children, old women, pregnant women and nursing mothers."[7]

By mid-March 1949, a secret State Department report said: "The International Children's Emergency Fund considers 425,000 or 58 percent of the refugees eligible for assistance under its program: this group consists of infants, young children, pregnant women, and nursing mothers. Approximately 15 percent of the refugees are aged, sick, and infirm. It would appear that the able-bodied men and women amount to a maximum of 25 percent of the total, or 180,000."[8]

Reaction in the United States was largely indifference. The American news media generally ignored the plight of the Palestinian refugees. The secret March 1949 State Department report observed that the public in the United States "generally is unaware of the Palestine refugee problem, since it has not been hammered away at by the press or radio."[9]

FALLACY

"The total number of bona fide Arab refugees who left Israel was about 590,000."

—*AIPAC, 1989*[10]

FACT

The AIPAC figure is too low by at least 150,000 . After many attempts by various countries and international agencies to estimate the total number of Palestinian refugees, the United Nations concluded in late 1949 that 726,000 of the 1.2 million Palestinians had been uprooted from their homes and turned into refugees by the 1948 war. Another 25,000 were listed as borderline-case refugees but were not included in the total.[11] These have remained the official UN figures, generally accepted outside the Middle East.

Arabs maintain that the true number is closer to 1 million while Israel officially claims the figure was between 520,000 and 530,000.[12] But internal documents show that Israeli officials early on realized the number was much higher than they claimed in public. Israeli historian Benny Morris has documented Israel's early awareness of the actual number from records in Israel's archives. One document shows the director general of the Foreign Ministry, Rafael Eytan, reporting that "the real number was close to 800,000." But officially Israel kept to the low figure because, in the words of another Foreign Ministry official, "It would . . . seem desirable to minimize the numbers."[13]

The refugee number swelled in the 1967 war when 323,000 additional Palestinians were driven from their homes. Of these, 113,000 were second-time refugees from among the 726,000 who had been made homeless in the 1948 war.[14] In addition to those uprooted by war, Israel also deliberately drove out thousands of others from their homes—4,000 Palestinians from the Old City of Jerusalem's Jewish and Mughrabi quarters; 10,000 residents of the villages of Imwas, Yalu, and Beit Nalu in the Latrun Salient, not allowing them even to take their possessions; and 6,000 to 20,000 Bedouin from their homes in the Gaza Strip's Rafah area near the Sinai Peninsula.[15]

FALLACY

"In numerous instances, Jewish leaders urged the Arabs to remain in Palestine and become citizens of Israel."

—*AIPAC, 1992*[16]

FACT

The focus of Israel's leaders was to get rid of the Palestinians, not to encourage them to remain in the Jewish state.[17]

Israeli historian Benny Morris reports: "Ben-Gurion clearly wanted as few Arabs as possible to remain in the Jewish State. He hoped to see them flee. He said as much to his colleagues and aides in meetings in August, September and October [1948]."[18]

A 1949 State Department study noted that despite its past promises, Israeli officials had "very clearly indicated" they would not now allow "more than a small number of refugees" to return to their homes.[19]

In their internal discussions, a number of Israeli officials proclaimed they wanted no non-Jews in their new state. Knesset member Eliahu Carmeli said: "I am not willing to take back even one Arab, not even one *goy* [non-Jew]. I want the Jewish state to be wholly Jewish." Moshe Dayan's father, Shmuel, also a Knesset member, said he opposed any return "even in exchange for peace. What will this formal peace give us?"[20]

By early March 1948, the Israeli military command had produced Plan Dalet, which was aimed at capturing areas in the Galilee and between Jerusalem and Tel Aviv that had been assigned by the UN Partition Plan to the envisioned Palestinian state. In the words of historian Morris: "Plan Dalet provided for the conquest and permanent occupation, or leveling, of Arab villages and towns. It instructed that . . . in the event of resistance, the [Arab] armed forces in the villages should be destroyed and the inhabitants should be expelled from the State."[21]

Israeli historian Simha Flapan notes that "the plan dealt in detail with the 'expulsion over the borders of the local Arab population.' . . . In retrospect, it can be seen that the aim of the plan was annexation—the destruction of Arab villages was to be followed by the establishment of Jewish villages in their place."[22] Flapan concluded: "Hundreds of thousands of [Palestinians], intimidated and terrorized, fled in panic, and still others were driven out by the Jewish army, which, under the leadership of [David] Ben-Gurion, planned and executed the expulsion in the wake of the UN Partition Plan."[23]

One operation against Galilee was called Matateh (Broom), and Jewish commander Yigal Allon spoke openly of the need to "cleanse the Upper Galilee."[24] Ben-Gurion assured his colleagues that the assault on Galilee would result in the region being "clean" of Arabs.[25] As he observed: "Land with Arabs on it and land without Arabs on it are two very different types of land."[26]

Flapan writes: "That Ben-Gurion's ultimate aim was to evacuate as much of the Arab population as possible from the Jewish state can hardly be doubted."[27]

Obviously, the flight of the Palestinians was not, as Israel's first president, Chaim Weizmann, claimed, "a miraculous simplification" of Israel's demographic problem.[28] It was, instead, a chilling fulfillment of the prophecy of Zionism's founder, Theodor Herzl, although he had a less violent scheme in mind: "We shall try to spirit the penniless population [the Palestinians] across the border by procuring employment for it in the transit countries, while denying it any employment in our own country."[29]

"The demographic problem will disappear."
—*Ezer Weizman, Israeli minister of defense, 1981*[30]

The imbalance beween Palestinian and Jewish populations—the "demographic problem"—has long plagued Zionism's leaders. Zionists were early aware that Jews were on a population collision course with Palestinians who not only were Palestine's majority but also had a higher birthrate than Jews. Although it is a subject that receives little note in the United States, in Israel this question of which ethnic group is the majority is of acute concern and is acknowledged as the "demographic time bomb."[31]

As early as 1938, Jewish leader David Ben-Gurion told his colleagues that "the starting point for the solution of the Arab problem" was to work out an agreement with the neighboring Arab states for the peaceful transfer of the Palestinians from a Jewish state.[32] In 1943, noting the higher birthrate of Arabs over Jews, he stressed that 2.2 children per family was insufficient and urged Jewish parents to fulfill their "demographic duty."[33]

The next year, revisionist leader Zeev Jabotinsky wrote: "We should instruct American Jewry to mobilize half a billion dollars in order that Iraq and Saudi Arabia will absorb the Palestinian Arabs. There is no choice: The Arabs must make room for the Jews in Eretz Israel. If it was possible to transfer the Baltic peoples, it is also possible to move the Palestinian Arabs."[34]

At the time of UN partition in 1947 the demographic problem was of the greatest concern for the Zionists because Palestinians outnumbered Jews by two to one in Palestine. The partition plan called for a Jewish state that would have had barely a Jewish majority: 498,000 Jews and 435,000 Palestinians.[35] (The proposed Palestinian state would have had 725,000 Arabs and 10,000 Jews).[36]

With such a thread-thin majority, Jews could not be sure they would continue for long to be the majority of their own state. Thus chasing Palestinians from their land and turning them into refugees was a practical imperative in the eyes of many Zionists. As an official memorandum to Ben-Gurion in mid-1948 observed: "The uprooting of the Arabs should be seen as a solution to the Arab question in the state of Israel."[37] Ben-Gurion was well aware of that fact and decreed: "We cannot allow the Arabs to return to those places that they left."[38]

Israeli policy quickly hardened into an official stance that the Palestinian refugees should not be allowed to return—and almost none succeeded in reclaiming their homes. By the end of May 1948 an unofficial "transfer committee" came into being with the specific aim of preventing the return of the Arab refugees by settling Jews in the abandoned homes and destroying Palestinian villages.[39] By June 1 direct orders were issued to Israel's military units to forcibly prevent the return of refugees.[40]

As a result of the uprooting of the Palestinians, there were only 170,000 of them left within the land controlled by Israel at the end of fighting in 1949. These men, women, and children became citizens of Israel and made up about 15 percent of the population, a far more tolerable minority than the 40 or more percent they would have represented if no refugees had been created.[41]

Ben-Gurion remained concerned enough about the demographic problem that in 1949 he initiated an award for mothers bearing their tenth child. The program was halted a decade later because of the number of Palestinian mothers of Israeli citizenship claiming the award. In 1967, an Israeli demographic center was established because "an increase in natality in Israel is crucial for the future of the whole Jewish people."[42]

Today the demographic problem remains of central concern in Israel. From the 1967 war to the start of the intifada in 1987, the Palestinian population doubled, almost wholly because of natural increase. The proportion of Palestinians inside Israel rose to 18 percent. During the same period, the Jewish population grew by 50 percent, much of this due to immigration. Without the newcomers, the Jewish increase would have been only 29 percent. By 2005, Palestinian citizens of Israel are projected to number 1.35 million. Added to these figures must be the Palestinians living under occupation in the West Bank and Gaza. The total was approaching 2 million in the early 1990s and is projected to reach 2.5 million by 2002.[43]

FALLACY

"[The Palestinian refugees] left partly in obedience to direct orders by local military commanders and partly as a result of the panic campaign spread among Palestinian Arabs by the leaders of the invading Arab states."

—*Moshe Sharett,*
Israeli provisional foreign minister, 1948[44]

FACT

As early as 1961 Irish journalist Erskine Childers examined the British record of all the radio broadcasts by Arab leaders during 1948 and concluded: "There was not a single order, or appeal, or suggestion about evacuation from Palestine from any Arab radio station, inside or outside Palestine, in 1948. There *is* repeated monitored record of Arab appeals, even flat orders, to the civilians of Palestine *to stay put.*"[45]

Even before Childers, Glubb Pasha, the British commander of the Jordanian army, had written: "The story which Jewish publicity at first persuaded the world to accept, that the Arab refugees left voluntarily, is not true. Voluntary emigrants do not leave their homes with only the clothes they stand up in. People who have decided to move house do not do so in such a hurry that they lose other members of their family—husband losing sight of his wife, or parents of their children. The fact is that the majority left in panic flight, to escape massacre (at least, so they thought). They were in fact helped on their way by the occasional massacre. Others were encouraged to move by blows or by indecent acts."[46]

Since then, abundant documentation has emerged showing that Israeli troops used psychological warfare, threats, violence, and murder to force many Palestinians to leave their homes. This new documentation comes mainly from Israeli sources.[47]

Concludes Israeli historian Simha Flapan: "The recent publication of thousands of documents in the state and Zionist archives, as well as Ben-Gurion's war diaries, shows that there is no evidence to support Israeli claims [that Arab leaders ordered the Palestinians to flee]. In fact, the declassified material contradicts the 'order' theory, for among these new sources are documents testifying to the considerable efforts of the AHC [Arab Higher Committee] and the Arab states to constrain the flight."[48]

Similarly, Israeli historian Benny Morris reports: "I have found no evidence to show that the AHC issued blanket instructions, by radio or otherwise, to Palestine's Arabs to flee."[49]

Yet the fallacy persists that it was Arab leaders who ordered the flight. Journalist Christopher Hitchens noticed a pro-Israeli ad in the *New Republic* in the late 1980s saying: "In 1948, on the day of the proclamation of the State of Israel, five Arab armies invaded the new country from all sides. In frightful radio broadcasts, they urged the Arabs living there to leave, so that the invading armies could operate without interference." Hitchens asked the sponsor for evidence of the "frightful" broadcasts but never received an answer.[50]

As late as May 27, 1991, the *Near East Report*, the newsletter of AIPAC, asserted that "in 1948 Arab leaders had repeatedly urged the Palestinians to leave so that Arab armies would have an easier time crushing the nascent Jewish state."[51] By then, Benny Morris's well-documented *The Birth of the Palestinian Refugee Problem* had already been out for three years, reporting that there was no evidence of Palestinians being ordered to flee.[52]

"Can anyone doubt that the Arab governments have been determined that the refugees shall remain refugees?"

—*Abba Eban,*
Israeli ambassador to the United Nations, 1955[53]

FACT

Although the UN General Assembly called on Israel as early as December 1948 to allow the Palestinian refugees to return to their homes, Israel refused.[54] Israel maintained that the refugees were the responsibility of the Arab states, whom it accused of indifference to the refugees' fate.[55]

However, a secret State Department study in early 1949 noted that the Arab nations were overwhelmed by the refugee problem: The Cairo embassy reported that if the refugees were driven into Egypt the "result would be almost catastrophic for Egypt financially." The embassy in Jordan reported that the refugees were a serious drain on "almost nonexistent resources" and that "money, jobs and other opportunities [were] scarce." The embassy in Lebanon reported that the refugees were an "unbearable burden" on that government while Syria had "practically abandoned its relief expenditures as unsupportable budgetary drain."

The study concluded by noting that assistance to the refugees by the Arab governments had been $11 million in cash or kind over the last nine months of 1948, a "relatively enormous" sum in "light of the very slender budgets of most of these governments." Israel's "total direct relief . . . to date consists of 500 cases of oranges."[56]

A major reason why Israel would not contemplate the return of the refugees to their homes was that most of those homes had already been taken over by Jews or had been destroyed to make way for new Jewish housing.[57]

A major 1949 State Department report noted that "the great bulk of the refugees wish to return to their homes."

However, their return was unrealistic because "Israeli author-ities have followed a systematic program of destroying Arab houses in such cities as Haifa and in village communities in order to rebuild modern habitations for the influx of Jewish immigrants from DP [displaced persons] camps in Europe [estimated at 25,000 per month]. There are, thus, in many instances, literally no houses for the refugees to return to. In other cases incoming Jewish immigrants have occupied Arab dwellings and will most certainly not relinquish them in favor of the refugees. Accordingly, it seems certain that the majority of these unfortunate people will soon be confronted with the fact that they will not be able to return home."[58]

New York Times correspondent Anne O'Hare McCormick reported on January 17, 1949, that Israelis were going at "top speed to repopulate the land left empty by the Arab exodus. . . . This means, obviously, that very few of the 750,000 refugees stranded in Arab Palestine and neighboring countries will ever return to their former abodes in Israeli territory. Their place is being taken by Jewish settlers now coming in for the first time in unrestricted numbers as fast as transport is available to carry them."[59]

Nonetheless, Israel has waged a relentless propaganda cam-paign to shift the blame onto the Arab states. How successful it has been is indicated by the 1960 Democratic platform, which asserted: "We will encourage direct Arab-Israel peace negotiations, the resettlement of Arab refugees in lands where there is room and opportunity for them, an end to boycotts and blockades, and unrestricted use of the Suez Canal by all nations." AIPAC has continued up to the present day to blame the Arabs for not accepting the refugees. Its 1992 issue of Myths and Facts compares the plight of Palestinians to Turk-ish refugees in Bulgaria in 1950, noting that despite difficulties the Turkish government repatriated 150,000 refugees. The book adds: "Had the Arab states wanted to alleviate the refugees' suffering they could easily have adopted an attitude similar to Turkey's."[60]

FOUR

THE SUEZ CRISIS OF 1956

In the Suez crisis of 1956, Israel, Great Britain, and France colluded secretly in violation of international law to attack Egypt with the aim of toppling its young leader, Gamal Abdel Nasser.[1] Although all three countries were friendly with the United States, they hid their plan from Washington. When President Dwight D. Eisenhower finally realized their intentions, he exerted such strong diplomatic pressures that they halted their invasion and surrendered the Egyptian territory they had captured. The military action began on October 29 and ended on November 7, 1956.

FALLACY

"It is not Israel which has sought to encompass Egypt with a ring of steel."

—*Israeli Foreign Ministry statement, 1956*[2]

Israeli troops moved into the Sinai Peninsula on October 29, 1956, to begin the invasion of Egypt jointly planned in secret with Britain and France. To hide its intentions from the United States, Israel instructed its Washington ambassador, Abba Eban, to assure U.S. officials that the deployment of Israeli troops "arose from 'security matters' and to stress that there was no connection between what we were doing and the conflict of other powers [Great Britain and France] with Egypt."[3]

At that very moment Israeli troops were on the attack across Sinai. When President Eisenhower heard the truth of Israel's sneak attack, he told his secretary of state, John Foster Dulles: "Foster, you tell 'em . . . we're going to apply sanctions, we're going to the United Nations, we're going to do everything that there is so we can stop this thing." Later Eisenhower recalled: "We just told the Israelis it was absolutely indefensible that if they expect our support in the Middle East and in maintaining their position, they had to behave. . . . We went to town right away and began to give them hell."[4]

The Suez crisis erupted just as Eisenhower's campaign for reelection was concluding. On the night of the Israeli attack, a group of prominent Republicans called on him, worried that Eisenhower might be tempted to use U.S. troops to drive out the Israelis because they had "committed aggression that could not be condoned."[5] The politicians feared that reaction to Eisenhower's opposition among Israeli partisans in the United States would be so great that he would lose the election. Commented Eisenhower: "I thought and said that emotion was beclouding their good judgment."[6] The next day Eisenhower had a resolution introduced in the UN Security Council calling for a ceasefire and withdrawal of Israeli troops. Within the next week, he successfully pressured Great Britain, France, and Israel to stop their attacks against Egypt, and handily won the election.

FALLACY

"[T]he armistice lines between Israel and Egypt have no more validity."

—*David Ben-Gurion, Israeli prime minister, 1956*[7]

FACT

Israeli troops had swept almost unhindered across the Sinai Peninsula to the Suez Canal and south to Sharm el-Sheikh, completing their conquest of Egyptian territory in less than a week while Egypt fought off simultaneous attacks from Great Britain and France. On November 7 Israeli leader David Ben-Gurion declared: "The armistice agreement with Egypt is dead and buried and cannot be restored to life."[8] Ben-Gurion's declaration that the 1949 armistice with Egypt was null and void signaled to President Eisenhower that Israel sought to retain the territory it had captured by force from Egypt.

Eisenhower immediately wrote a personal message to Ben-Gurion to express his "deep concern" and warning: "Any such decision [to occupy Sinai] could not but bring about the condemnation of Israel as a violator of the principles as well as the directives of the United Nations."[9] To give substance to Eisenhower's message, Under Secretary of State Herbert Hoover, Jr., called in Israel's Washington representative and warned that the United States was ready to take serious action against Israel, including "termination of all United States government and private aid, United Nations sanctions and eventual expulsion from the United Nations. I speak with the utmost seriousness and gravity."[10]

That same day, November 7, the UN General Assembly, in a 65-to-1 vote, demanded that all foreign troops leave the Sinai.[11] Israel cast the lone no vote. But still Israel refused to remove its troops, even after the General Assembly passed another resolution in February 1957 "deploring" Israel's refusal to withdraw.[12]

Eisenhower's patience began running out on February 11. He sent another message to Ben-Gurion, demanding the "prompt and unconditional" withdrawal of Israeli troops from Gaza. Ben-Gurion again refused.[13]

By February 20, Eisenhower had had enough. He sent a stiff note to Ben-Gurion warning that the United States might support UN sanctions against Israel and that such sanctions might include not only bans against government aid but private donations by individuals as well. That same night he also went on national television to plead his case against Israel: "I believe that in the interests of peace the United Nations has no choice but to exert pressure upon Israel to comply with the withdrawal resolutions."[14]

Ben-Gurion called Eisenhower's demands "perverted justice."[15] But under the impact of such threats Israeli troops were shortly withdrawn and the Suez crisis finally ended. Israel had been forced by the United States to surrender its acquisition of territory.

FALLACY

"The United States performance in the Suez crisis of 1956 [was] deplorable."
—*Henry Kissinger, secretary of state, 1979*[16]

FACT

Despite criticism from Israel and its supporters, Eisenhower and the United States emerged from the Suez crisis with great moral authority and prestige around the world. Eisenhower's authoritative biographer, Stephen E. Ambrose, notes: "Eisenhower's insistence on the primacy of the UN, of treaty obligations, and of the rights of all nations gave the United States a standing in world opinion it had never before achieved. . . . The introduction of the American [ceasefire] resolution to the U.N. was, indeed, one of the great moments in U.N. history."[17]

The enormous boost to America's prestige became immediately clear at the United Nations. The U.S. ambassador to the UN, Henry Cabot Lodge, telephoned the president and reported: "Never had there been such a tremendous acclaim for the president's policy. Absolutely spectacular." From Cairo, Ambassador Raymond Hare cabled: "The U.S. has suddenly emerged as a real champion of right."[18] Nearly four decades later, historians view Eisenhower's handling of the crisis as a high point of his presidency. It upheld the authority and moral stance of the United Nations and the ideals of the United States.

FIVE

THE 1967 WAR

The 1967 war was the third in the Arab-Israeli conflict, and the most successful for Israel. Israel achieved all its war aims, chief among them the occupation of all of Palestine, including Arab East Jerusalem, as well as Egypt's Sinai Peninsula and Syria's Golan Heights. Unlike the 1956 Suez crisis, when Washington's opposition forced Israel to withdraw from the territory it had captured, Israeli officials this time had been careful to cultivate the understanding of U.S. officials for their position.[1] As a result Israel did not suffer any U.S. pressure to surrender its gains. The fighting began June 5 and ended June 10.

FALLACY

"It is beyond all honest doubt that . . . Arab governments . . . methodically prepared and mounted an aggressive assault designed to bring about Israel's immediate and total destruction."

—*Abba Eban,*
Israeli ambassador to the United Nations, 1967[2]

FACT

As in the 1956 war, Israel started the fighting in 1967 by a surprise attack against Egypt. Once again, as in 1956, the Israelis deceived the United States. Foreign Minister Abba Eban personally assured U.S. Ambassador to Israel Walworth Barbour that Egypt had attacked first.[3] Since the war, however, Israel's leaders—unlike many of its supporters in the United States[4]—have openly admitted that Israel was the attacker and, moreover, that Israel faced no immediate threat to its existence.

Menachem Begin, while prime minister in 1982, said the 1967 war was one of "choice," that "we decided to attack him [Egyptian President Gamal Abdel Nasser]." Ezer Weizman, father of the Israeli air force and later defense minister, said in 1972 that there was "no threat of destruction" from the Arabs. General Mattityahu Peled, a former member of the general staff who later became a dove, said in 1972: "To claim that the Egyptian forces concentrated on our borders were capable of threatening Israel's existence not only insults the intelligence of anyone capable of analyzing this kind of situation, but is an insult to Zahal [the Israeli army]." And Chief of Staff Yitzhak Rabin said in 1968: "I do not believe that Nasser wanted war. The two divisions he sent into Sinai on May 14 would not have been enough to unleash an offensive against Israel. He knew it and we knew it."[5]

David Ben-Gurion said he "doubt[ed] very much whether Nasser wanted to go to war."[6] Moreover, the combined intelligence services of the United States had concluded just before the war that Israel faced no imminent threat and that if attacked Israel could quickly defeat any Arab state or combination of Arab states.[7]

Israeli cabinet member Mordecai Bentov revealed in 1972 that Israel's "entire story" about "the danger of extermination" was "invented of whole cloth and exaggerated after the fact to justify the annexation of new Arab territories."[8]

"The GOI [Government of Israel] has no, repeat no, intention of taking advantage of the situation to enlarge its territory."
—*Walworth Barbour, U.S. ambassador to Israel, 1967*[9]

FACT

Within two days of the start of the war, Israeli troops captured the Old City of Jerusalem from Jordan. Israeli leaders immediately declared that they would never give up the city. Shlomo Goren, the chief Ashkenazi rabbi of the Israel Defense Forces, arrived at the Wailing Wall within a half hour and declared: "I, General Shlomo Goren, chief rabbi of the Israel Defense Forces, have come to this place never to leave again."[10] Defense Minister Moshe Dayan also arrived, saying: "We have united Jerusalem, the divided capital of Israel. We have returned to the holiest of our holy places, never to part from it again."[11] By the time fighting ended after six days, Israeli troops had overrun all of Egypt's Sinai Peninsula, the West Bank and Gaza Strip, and Syria's Golan Heights. The captured territory increased Israel's control of land from the original 5,900 square miles awarded it in the 1947 UN Partition Plan to 20,870 square miles.[12] Despite Israel's initial promise that it sought no territory, it immediately moved to expel Palestinians and establish Jewish settlements in the occupied territories, including Arab East Jerusalem.[13]

FALLACY

"Do not forget that we are neutral in word, thought and deed."
—*Eugene Rostow, under secretary of state, 1967*[14]

Eugene Rostow's tongue-in-cheek declaration was greeted with knowing smiles by other U.S. officials since the United States was never, at any point, neutral in the 1967 war. The Johnson administration was thoroughly pro-Israel. Thus when State Department spokesperson Robert McCloskey repeated to the media Rostow's words about neutrality on the first day of the war, the reporters were incredulous. Such an astonishing assertion, if taken seriously, was big news and the Associated Press immediately sent a special bulletin across the wires.[15]

Reaction to Rostow's statement among American supporters of Israel was outrage. Presidential speech writer John Roche was so incensed that he sent a memo directly to the president protesting, "I was appalled to realize that there is a real underground sentiment for kissing some Arab backsides. . . . The net consequence of trying to 'sweet talk' the Arabs is that they have contempt for us—and we alienate Jewish support in the United States."[16]

The strong partisanship of Israel's supporters in the Johnson administration became blatant from the first days of the war.[17] In the State Department's summary of the first day of combat, national security adviser Walt Rostow, the brother of Eugene, flippantly wrote in a cover letter: "Herewith the account, with a map, of the first day's turkey shoot."[18]

In reality, the relationship between the United States under President Johnson and Israel was so close that policy was frequently coordinated with Israel at the expense of the Arabs. McGeorge Bundy, who served as a special presidential adviser, touched on the closeness of the two countries in a memorandum to Johnson in the midst of the war when he suggested that the president make a speech to "emphasize that this task to secure a strong Israel and a stable Middle East is in the first instance a task for the nations in the area. This is good LBJ doctrine and good Israeli doctrine, and therefore a good doctrine to get out in public."[19]

The intimacy of the two countries has raised suspicions that Johnson and his officials gave a "green light" to Israel's launching of the war. The presumed rationale was a U.S. desire, shared with Israel, to depose Egypt's Gamal Abdel Nasser. But Nasser, while an annoyance, was not at the time a major concern in Washington, where the growing war in Vietnam held the capital in a trance. Moreover, no smoking gun showing collusion has emerged.

Yet there is no doubt that Johnson at least signaled his acceptance of Israel's decision to go to war, even if he did not actively encourage it in some sort of collusive scheme. Middle East expert William Quandt, a former member of the National Security Council under President Jimmy Carter, examined all the evidence that has emerged over the quarter century since the war and concluded in a 1992 study: "With all of this information at hand, it should now be possible to resolve the red-light versus green-light debate. Both views are inaccurate in important ways." Quandt concluded that President Johnson sought to deter Israel from going to war during May—the "red light"—but then realized that short of force the United States was powerless to prevent a determined Israel from following its own policy. At that point the administration gave Israel a "yellow light," meaning, in Quandt's words, "the president acquiesced in Israel's decision to launch a preemptive war." Added Quandt: "In brief, in the crucial days before Israel undertook the decision to go to war, the light from Washington shifted from red to yellow. It never turned green, but yellow was enough for the Israelis to know that they could take action without worrying about Washington's reaction."[20]

A notable example of how Israeli and U.S. officials worked together during the war occurred in the United Nations. Israel's UN ambassador, Gideon Rafael, recalled that U.S. Ambassador Arthur Goldberg "was frightfully worried about Israel and the military equation." Goldberg called Rafael and asked: "Gideon, what do you want me to do?"[21] Rafael said that what Israel needed was time to avoid having the Security Council pass a ceasefire resolution while Israeli troops were scoring dramatic victories in the first days of the war. To accomplish this, he wanted Goldberg to avoid meeting with his Soviet counterpart, Nikolai Federenko. Rafael said to Goldberg: "You are not so available for the next few days." And Goldberg wasn't.[22]

FALLACY

"It is concluded clearly and unimpeachably from the evidence and from comparison of war diaries that the attack on USS *Liberty* was not in malice; there was no criminal negligence and the attack was made by innocent mistake."
—Government of Israel statement, 1967[23]

FACT

In bright daylight on June 8, with no other combat taking place nearby, Israeli warplanes and torpedo boats repeatedly attacked the U.S. intelligence ship *Liberty* off the Sinai coast, killing 34 of its crew and wounding 171. The attack involved the use of napalm, rockets, machine guns, and torpedoes. It had been preceded by reconnaissance by Israeli planes for at least five and a half hours, during a time when the ship was flying a new flag that flew freely in a light breeze.[24]

Though Israel through the years has insisted it was a case of mistaken identity and an accident, abundant evidence emerged to strongly support the charge that Israel deliberately attacked the intelligence ship, apparently because it feared the *Liberty* would monitor Israeli preparations for invading the Golan Heights the next day. The Johnson administration accepted Israel's claim that the assault resulted from misidentification. Even years later, Johnson was evasive about the incident, claiming in his memoirs that only ten men died in the attack.[25] It was a clear indication of how Johnson colluded with Israel.

As late as 1991, survivors of the attack charged the U.S. government with continuing to cover up Israel's role. Wrote

James Ennes, a lieutenant on the bridge on the day of the attack: "[T]he official lid on this story remains almost as tight as the day it was first applied." This was despite the fact that such former officials as Secretary of State Dean Rusk and Chairman of the Joint Chiefs of Staff Admiral Thomas Moorer had gone on record blaming Israel for deliberately assaulting the *Liberty*.

Rusk's words in his memoirs: "I was never satisfied with the Israeli explanation. . . . I didn't believe them then, and I don't believe them to this day. The attack was outrageous." Concluded Ennes: "Yet despite such strong opinions of key leaders, not a single person while still in government has ever made any apparent effort to set the record straight."[26]

It was not until June 8, 1991, that the survivors were finally awarded a presidential unit citation signed by Johnson in 1967 but not presented at that time.[27] Then on November 6, 1991, columnists Rowland Evans and Robert Novak finally discovered that the U.S. embassy in Beirut had intercepted Israeli radio traffic in which an Israeli pilot reported: "It's an American ship." The Israeli command ignored the report and ordered the pilot to press his attack. Evans and Novak concluded that Israel attacked "because [the *Liberty*] would have picked up every word of communication between IDF headquarters and Israeli units preparing to invade Syria." The Israeli invasion of the Golan Heights came the day after Israel had silenced the *Liberty*. The report was confirmed by Dwight Porter, who was the American ambassador to Lebanon at the time.[28] Thus, after twenty-four years, the truth has finally emerged.

SIX

UN RESOLUTION 242

The passage of Resolution 242 by the UN Security Council on November 22, 1967, was a major diplomatic achievement in the Arab-Israeli conflict.[1] It emphasized "the inadmissibility of the acquisition of territory by war" and contained the formula that has since underlain all peace initiatives—land for peace. In exchange for withdrawing from Egyptian, Jordanian, and Syrian territory captured in the 1967 war, Israel was promised peace by the Arab states. The resolution provides the basis on which the peace talks between Israel and the Arabs begun in Madrid, Spain, in 1991 are being conducted.

FALLACY

"[N]either this international document [Israel's 1949 armistice with Jordan] nor Resolution 242 forms an obstacle to the Jewish People's basic claim that the Land of Israel belongs by right to the Jewish People."
        —Menachem Begin, Israeli prime minister, 1977[2]

FACT

A major confrontation on the interpretation of UN Security Council Resolution 242 erupted between the United States and Israel after Menachem Begin came to power in 1977. Although previous Israeli governments accepted the applicability of the resolution to all territories—the Sinai, the West Bank, including Arab East Jerusalem, Gaza, and the Golan Heights—Begin argued that the resolution did not apply to Jordan's West Bank, or Judea and Samaria, as he insisted on calling it. When Begin first declared publicly that Resolution 242 did not negate Israel's claim to the West Bank, the U.S. Department of State immediately responded by declaring publicly: "We consider that this resolution means withdrawal on all three fronts in the Middle East dispute. . . . This means no territories—including the West Bank—are automatically excluded from the items to be negotiated."[3]

A 1978 State Department study of the issue, made after Begin continued to put forward his unique interpretation, concluded: "We have researched the records of the public and private negotiations leading up to adoption of Resolution 242, and the explanations of vote at its adoption, and we conclude that there is no room for doubt that members of the Council, and Israel . . . shared a common core of understanding that the principle of withdrawal was applicable to all three fronts."[4]

This stand was later authoritatively endorsed by the resolution's author, Lord Caradon of Great Britain, who wrote: "It was from the occupied territories that the Resolution called for withdrawal. The test was which territories were occupied. That was a test not possibly subject to doubt. As a matter of plain fact East Jerusalem, the West Bank, Gaza, the Golan, and Sinai were occupied in the 1967 conflict; it was on withdrawal from occupied territories that the Resolution insisted."[5]

U.S. officials have reiterated this position in public many times. In June 1977, the Carter administration released a paper on its views of the elements of a comprehensive peace. The paper pointedly said that Israel, "within the terms of Resolution 242, in return for this . . . peace, clearly should withdraw from occupied territories. We consider that this resolution means withdrawal on all three fronts—that is, Sinai, Golan, West Bank–Gaza. . . . [N]o territories, including the West Bank, are automatically excluded from the items to be negotiated."[6] More than a decade later, Secretary of State George Shultz said: "The provisions of Resolution 242 apply to all fronts."[7]

FALLACY

"[UN Resolution 242] speaks of withdrawal from occupied territories without defining the extent of withdrawal."
—*Arthur Goldberg,*
U.S. ambassador to the United Nations, 1973[8]

FACT

There was deliberate ambiguity in Resolution 242. It occurs in the withdrawal phrase, which says "from territories" instead of "the" or "all" territories. The point of the phrase was to allow for minor border adjustments that would rectify the zigzag lines left by the end of fighting in 1948. Arab East Jerusalem was not specifically mentioned in the resolution but was considered by all countries except Israel as included in the preambulatory paragraph that emphasized "the inadmissibility of the acquisition of territory by war."[9]

Despite the ambiguity, King Hussein of Jordan was repeatedly assured by high-ranking U.S. officials in the days before passage of the resolution that only small alterations in territory were envisioned and that any change would be reciprocal. As Secretary of State Dean Rusk explained to Hussein on November 6, sixteen days before passage of the resolution: "[T]he United States was prepared to support return of a substantial part of the West Bank to Jordan with boundary adjustments, and would use its influence to obtain compensation to Jordan for any territory it was required to give up." By way of illustration, Rusk told Hussein that if Jordan gave up an awkward bulge of territory between Jerusalem and Tel Aviv known as the Latrun Salient, "the United States would then use its diplomatic and political influence to obtain in compensation access for Jordan to a Mediterranean port in Israel." Hussein received similar assurances from President Johnson and U.S. Ambassador Arthur Goldberg.[10]

All administrations since Johnson's have repeated similar assurances to King Hussein. For instance, in January 1983 Reagan's secretary of state, George Shultz, wrote in a letter to Hussein that "the President believes, consistent with Resolution 242, that territory should not be acquired by war. He believes, as well, however, that Resolution 242 does permit changes in the boundaries which existed prior to June 1967 but only where such changes are agreed between the parties." Shultz added that the "United States considers [Arab] East Jerusalem part of the occupied territories."[11]

It was only under the Bush administration that the United States began backing its words supporting the resolution with actions. In early 1992, Bush refused to grant Israel $10 billion in loan guarantees unless it promised to impose a total freeze on all settlement activity in the occupied territories and negotiate on the basis of Resolution 242.[12] However, in the midst of the 1992 presidential campaign and the coming to power of Yitzhak Rabin, Bush relented and granted the guarantees, dropping nearly all conditions.

FALLACY

"[UN Resolution 242] required negotiations between the parties."
—*Yitzhak Rabin, Israeli prime minister, 1979*[13]

There was no mention of direct negotiations in the resolution or of the need for negotiations preceding Israel's withdrawal.

In the resolution's words, it merely "requests the Secretary-General to designate a Special Representative to proceed to the Middle East to establish and maintain contacts with the States concerned in order to promote agreement and assist efforts to achieve a peaceful and accepted settlement in accordance with the provisions and principles in this resolution."

U.S. officials privately agreed with Israel that negotiations would have to precede Israel's withdrawal from the territories captured in the war. But what they thought was meant by negotiations was far different from Israel's later contention.

The U.S. officials naively thought that once the UN resolution was adopted only technical and brief negotiations would be needed between Israel and its Arab neighbors to work out the details of Israeli withdrawal. They assured the Arabs that this would be the case, and the Arabs henceforth maintained that Israel had to withdraw without conditions. But Israel contended that negotiations would have to cover all the aspects of both withdrawal and peace, including disposition not only of Palestinian refugees but of Jewish refugees from Arab countries as well.[14]

It was on the specific issue of prior negotiations that Israel stalled enactment of the resolution for the next six years. The United States repeatedly urged Israel to withdraw without detailed negotiations but Israel refused, insisting on direct negotiations. On June 9, 1970, Secretary of State William Rogers criticized Israel's stand by saying: "Israel should make clear that it accepts the principle of withdrawal as laid down in the November 1967 Security Council resolution and that it will no longer insist on the formula of 'direct negotiations without preconditions.'"[15] But Israel refused.

War broke out in 1973 as Egypt and Syria sought to break the diplomatic logjam by military assault on Arab territory held by Israel. The question of prior negotiations was finally settled at the end of the 1973 war with passage of UN

Resolution 338, which said that "negotiations will start between the parties concerned under appropriate auspices aimed at establishing a just and durable peace in the Middle East."[16] However, having won that point, Israel then began insisting that withdrawal did not mean on all fronts. It maintains that unique interpretation of Resolution 242 to this day.

SEVEN

THE WAR OF ATTRITION: 1969–1970

The War of Attrition was fought between Israel and Egypt by artillery and commandos along the Suez Canal in the Sinai Peninsula and by missiles and jet warplanes over Egyptian skies. At no time did combat take place within Israel itself. The underlying dispute centered on Israel's determination to remain on Egyptian territory captured in 1967 and Egypt's efforts to regain it.[1]

FALLACY

"We observe the ceasefire agreement—and the other side violates it."

—*Levi Eshkol, Israeli prime minister, 1968*[2]

FACT

Continuation of the ceasefire that ended the 1967 war suited Israel's expansionist policy. This was because the fighting ended with Israeli troops stationed on land belonging to all of

Israel's surrounding Arab neighbors except Lebanon. Observance of a ceasefire thus meant that Israel could continue its occupation without serious cost and at the same time colonize the captured land.

Immediately after the 1967 war Israel made clear that "the position that existed up till now shall never again return," in Prime Minister Levi Eshkol's words. To Arabs, this sent a message that Israel planned to retain the captured lands and that the only way to make Israel surrender its conquests in accordance with UN Resolution 242 was by military pressure.[3]

The War of Attrition developed slowly. One major step came a year after the 1967 war when Israeli gunners lobbed some 450 artillery shells into Suez City at the southern terminus of the canal, killing forty-three Egyptian civilians and wounding sixty-seven others. At least one hundred buildings—homes, shops, a mosque, a chapel, a cinema—were damaged or destroyed in the bombardment.

Israel said that Egypt had started the incident by firing on its troops stationed on the Suez Canal and that Israeli troops had fired into Suez City to silence the Egyptian guns. It had been a city of 260,000, but after heavy Israeli bombardments the previous October some 200,000 had evacuated. Since then about 40,000 had returned, leaving the city's current population at about 100,000. Many of those fled after the mid-1968 Israeli shelling.[4]

Another major stepping-stone to the outbreak of the war was Israel's decision in September 1968 to construct the Bar-Lev Line along the canal. This was an extremely heavily fortified system of military positions along its entire 101-mile length aimed at blunting Egyptian artillery attacks across the canal. But in Egyptian eyes it marked Israel's determination to retain the Sinai by permanently stationing Israeli troops at the Suez Canal.[5]

Egyptian President Gamal Abdel Nasser repeatedly warned in public that if Israel continued its occupation of Egyptian land he would use force to get it back: "The first priority, the absolute priority in this battle is the military front, for we must realize that the enemy will not withdraw unless we force him to withdraw through fighting."[6] Nasser put his words to action in early 1969 by unleashing unrelenting artillery and commando attacks against the Israeli forces in the Sinai.

Before the fighting ended, Israel employed its new U.S.-made F-4 warplanes to stage deep raids inside Egypt, wreaking heavy damage on civilians and attacking areas near Cairo. The Soviet Union responded by taking the extraordinary measure of sending Soviet pilots and planes to protect Egypt's skies. Once again, the Middle East threatened to engulf the superpowers in a direct confrontation.[7] The entry of the Soviets spurred the United States actively to seek a ceasefire, which it achieved in August 1970.[8]

FALLACY

"Since March this year Nasser has transformed the Canal into a focus of large scale aggression."
—*Golda Meir, Israeli prime minister, 1969*[9]

FACT

The War of Attrition started in earnest on March 8, 1969, with daily Egyptian artillery attacks against Israel's heavily fortified Bar-Lev Line on the east bank of the Suez Canal.[10] The attacks were aimed specifically against Israeli troops occupying Egyptian land. No Israeli civilians or their property were endangered. As historian Lawrence Whetten observed: "The Arab aim in resuming the fighting was to restore national honor through regaining lost territory."[11] The exchange of artillery fire grew so fierce that by July 7, 1969, UN Secretary-General U Thant warned that the level of violence along the Suez Canal had become worse than at any time since the 1967 war.[12]

The war included numerous Israeli air strikes against Egyptian civilians, although there were no Egyptian attacks against Israeli civilians. Israel employed its U.S.-made F-4 warplanes for deep penetration raids inside Egypt, killing many civilians. Sixty-eight Egyptian workers were killed in an Israeli air raid in February 1970, when Israeli warplanes bombed a scrap metal factory at Abu Za'abal, fifteen miles northeast of Cairo;[13] and forty-six children were killed on April 8 in an attack on an elementary school at Bahr el-Bakr.[14]

FALLACY

"Israel has never been stronger, or more dominant."
—Jon Kimche, Zionist writer, 1970[15]

FACT

At the end of the War of Attrition in August 1970, Israel officially declared it had been victorious since its troops still stood on Egyptian territory on the east bank of the Suez Canal. But more thoughtful Israeli military leaders such as Ezer Weizman and Mattiyahu Peled considered the war the first in which Israeli forces had been defeated. Peled argued that one of leadership's basic failures was in not understanding that Egypt could not acquiesce in the continued Israeli occupation of its land. Israeli military historian Yaacov Bar-Siman-Tov agreed there were major Israeli failures: "Israel's political and military blunders in the Yom Kippur War [of 1973] were rooted in mistaken evaluation of the results of the War of Attrition."[16]

Whatever the lesson, the price for Israel's refusal to give up its military conquests was steep. Egyptian losses were at least five thousand killed during the war. Israeli casualties were more than eleven hundred, including more than four hundred deaths.[17]

EIGHT

THE
1973 WAR

The 1973 attacks launched by Egypt and Syria against Israeli forces are variously known as the October or Ramadan or Yom Kippur War. As in the War of Attrition three years earlier, the aim of the Arabs was to regain territory occupied by Israel since the 1967 war. The Arabs failed, but the political earthquake caused by the war led to a frenzy of diplomatic activity by the United States that ended in 1979 with the signing of the peace treaty between Israel and Egypt. The war lasted from October 6 to October 25, 1973.

FALLACY

"Since the [1967] War there has been no substantial change in the refusal of the Arab Governments, headed by Egypt, to reach an agreed peace with us."
—*Golda Meir, Israeli prime minister, 1972*[1]

FACT

Within three months after he became Egypt's president in the fall of 1970 on the death of Gamal Abdel Nasser, Anwar el-Sadat sent President Nixon an urgent secret message: "I want peace; move fast."[2] The White House ignored the message, largely because national security adviser Henry Kissinger agreed with the Israeli assessment that Sadat was not a serious leader and would not long survive in power.[3]

Throughout 1971 Sadat publicly and repeatedly called for Israeli withdrawal, warning that it was a "year of decision"— Israel would either withdraw peacefully or be forced to do so. Israel was openly scornful of Sadat's threats and flatly declared: "Israel will not withdraw to the pre–June 5, 1967, lines."[4] In 1972 Sadat took the dramatic step of expelling Soviet advisers from Egypt. Although the Soviet Union was Egypt's major supporter, Sadat hoped to enlist Washington's help in achieving peace with Israel. But Kissinger failed to understand Sadat's seriousness and dismissed his gesture as impetuous.[5] In early 1973 Sadat encouraged secret talks between Kissinger and a high-ranking Egyptian official to find a peaceful solution. But Kissinger still doubted Sadat's capabilities and declined to make any move until after Israel's election, scheduled for October 30.[6]

The result of this long stalemate became known as the period of no-war/no-peace, which was what Israel desired. As Kissinger observed, one of Prime Minister Golda Meir's chief aims was "to gain time, for the longer there was no change in the status quo, the more Israel would be confirmed in the possession of the occupied territories."[7] Kissinger was content to support Israel in this aim since he believed that a stalemate would build up pressure on the Arabs to make concessions.[8] Analyst William Quandt, who served as the Carter administration's Middle East expert on the National Security Council, concludes: "During 1972, United States Middle East policy consisted of little more than open support for Israel. . . . It required the October [1973] war to change United States policy."[9]

"Egypt has no military option at all."
—*Yigal Allon, Israeli deputy prime minister, 1973*[10]

FACT

The arrogance of Israelis toward the Arabs resulted in misleading not only the world but also themselves. As it turned out, Israel suffered one of the greatest failures of military intelligence when it did not anticipate the combined Egyptian-Syrian attack against Israel's occupation troops on October 6, 1973. The months preceding the outbreak of war were filled with Israeli boasts about Israel's power and the Arabs' weakness.

Defense Minister Moshe Dayan, less than two months before war, told the general staff: "The balance of forces is so much in our favor that it neutralizes the Arab considerations and motives for the immediate renewal of hostilities."[11] And General Ariel Sharon declared that "there is no target between Baghdad and Khartoum, including Libya, that our army is unable to capture." He assured Israelis that "with our present boundaries we have no security problem."[12] So great was Israel's confidence that on July 15 it decided to cut its three-year compulsory military service by three months, starting the next year.[13]

Israel's intelligence failure arose from a combination of excessive self-confidence about its own strength and disdain for the Arabs' cause. Since the end of the 1967 war, Israeli troops had been sitting on Arab territory, refusing to withdraw under the provisions of UN Resolution 242. During a White House visit with President Nixon in March 1973, Israeli Prime Minister Golda Meir said: "We never had it so good." Meir said she would be willing to enter peace talks but left the strong impression that she was in no hurry to see a new diplomatic initiative. When Meir returned home, she said there was "no basis or reason for changing our policy."[14]

Defense Minister Moshe Dayan urged Israelis to settle in the occupied territories since there was no chance of Arab-Israeli negotiations for "ten to fifteen years."[15] At about the same time, a poll showed that a vast majority of Israelis opposed returning most of the occupied territories.[16]

In April 1973, Sadat openly warned in an interview: "Everything was very discouraging. Complete failure and despair sum it up. . . . Every door I've opened has been slammed in my face by Israel—with American blessings. . . . The time has come for a shock. . . . Everything in the country is now being mobilized for the resumption of the battle—which is now inevitable."[17]

But no high-ranking official in Israel or America paid any attention.

FALLACY

"We won the Yom Kippur war."
—Golda Meir, Israeli prime minister, 1975[18]

FACT

Israel "won" the 1973 war much like Lyndon Johnson "won" the disastrous Tet Offensive of 1968 in Vietnam. The Arabs regained a large measure of self-respect from their early battlefield achievements. This was particularly true of Egypt's spectacular crossing of the Suez Canal, which most military men around the world believed could not be accomplished against Israel's powerful fortifications along the canal's east bank.[19]

Certainly Israeli troops finally prevailed, though not nearly as easily as they later claimed. But the magnitude of the war and its ending with a tense direct confrontation between the United States and the Soviet Union forced world attention on the basic questions underlying the Arab-Israeli conflict. Almost unanimously the world community concluded that Egypt and Syria had a right to try to reclaim their lost land

and that Israel had been wrong to ignore UN Resolution 242 and refuse to surrender its 1967 conquests. Condemnations came from countries around the world, including European nations, African nations, Asian nations—almost every nation except the United States.[20]

Although Israel and its supporters asserted that the world community was motivated by fear of the Arab oil boycott—or, alternatively, by "old-fashioned" anti-Semitism—the reality is that most objective observers saw Israel as more interested in retaining Arab land than in peace.[21]

It is now clear that the Arabs went to war out of desperation to regain their land, not, as Israel claimed, to destroy the Jewish state. Often forgotten is the fact that the 1973 war was fought, as had been the War of Attrition before it, solely on occupied Arab land. No combat took place inside Israel.

Even Israeli Prime Minister Yitzhak Rabin has admitted: "The Yom Kippur War was not fought by Egypt and Syria to threaten the existence of Israel. It was an all-out use of their military force to achieve a limited political goal. What Sadat wanted by crossing the canal was to change the political reality and, thereby, to start a political process from a point more favorable to him than the one that existed. In this respect, he succeeded."[22]

Or, in Sadat's words: "We simply could not allow the situation to continue as it was before October—no peace, no war. The two superpowers froze the Middle East dispute and put it in a refrigerator. The Americans have viewed us as a motionless corpse since the six-day war in 1967. This was worse than war."[23]

NINE

THE 1982
INVASION
OF LEBANON

The entry of Israeli troops into Lebanon in 1982 was a full-scale invasion involving armor, planes, and ships, most of them U.S.-made. The name of the operation was Peace for Galilee, implying that Israel's aim was to push Palestinian guerrillas back from the frontier to prevent attacks inside Israel. In reality Israeli troops marched on Beirut and for the first time besieged an Arab capital. Israeli aims, it turned out, were to rid all of Lebanon of Palestinian fighters and Syrian troops and to intimidate Lebanon into signing a peace treaty. The major combat took place between June 6 and September 26, 1982, when Israeli troops withdrew from West Beirut.

FALLACY

"A series of provocative incidents and retaliations throughout the first months of 1982 reached a climax in June when [Israeli Ambassador] Shlomo Argov was shot down in London. . . . Israeli troops pushed into Lebanon on June 6, 1982."
    —*Hyman Bookbinder, former representative of
    the American Jewish Committee, 1987*[1]

FACT

Up to Israel's invasion of Lebanon on June 6, 1982, Palestinian guerrillas had scrupulously observed a ceasefire that had been in effect since July 24, 1981. Israel's northern frontier with Lebanon had been quiet. There had been no attacks.[2]

Yet when Israeli Ambassador to London Shlomo Argov was shot on June 3, Prime Minister Menachem Begin quickly seized on the incident to justify the invasion of Lebanon. This despite the fact that Israel's intelligence analysts immediately determined that the assassination gang was part of the terrorist group Fatah Revolutionary Council, a group totally outside the PLO. It is headed by Abu Nidal, born Sabri Khalil Banna, one of the worst enemies of the PLO's Yasser Arafat.[3] Nonetheless, Begin declared, "They're all PLO," and ordered heavy air attacks to begin the next day against PLO offices in crowded West Beirut and in southern Lebanon, killing at least 45 and wounding 150. Israel's massive invasion occurred three days after Argov's wounding.[4]

As an Israeli critic of Israeli Defense Minister Ariel ("Arik") Sharon has written: "Arik Sharon took a relatively peaceful country, whose northern border had been quiet for a full year, and plunged it into a maelstrom of death and destruction whose calamitous effects spread to every corner."[5]

FALLACY

"We don't covet even one inch of Lebanese territory."
—*Menachem Begin, Israeli prime minister, 1982*[6]

FACT

More than a decade after its 1982 invasion Israel continues to control southern Lebanon. By late 1992, there were still about a thousand Israeli troops occupying the "security belt" that Israel seized in 1978 and expanded up to twelve miles deep inside Lebanon in 1982.[7] This "security belt" (some

Israelis called it the "North Bank") amounted to 9 percent of Lebanon's territory and added several hundred square miles more to the list of Arab land Israel had expanded on since 1948.[8]

Since Israel's earliest days its leaders had ambitions to take over the southern part of Lebanon. For instance, in 1955, Moshe Dayan, then chief of staff, discussed the subject with Prime Minister David Ben-Gurion, saying that "the only thing that's necessary is to find an officer, even just a major [in Lebanon]. We should either win his heart or buy him with money, to make him agree to declare himself the savior of the Maronite [Christian] population. Then the Israeli army will enter Lebanon, will occupy the necessary territory, and will create a Christian regime which will ally itself with Israel. The territory from the Litani southward will be totally annexed to Israel and everything will be all right."[9]

FALLACY

"[The invasion of Lebanon] is an operation that will take about twelve hours. I don't know how matters will develop, so I suggest we view it in terms of twenty-four hours."
—*Ariel Sharon, Israeli defense minister, 1982*[10]

FACT

Defense Minister Ariel Sharon's reassuring words on the eve of Israel's invasion of Lebanon to the Israeli cabinet and Israel's subsequent assurances to Washington were deliberately misleading, a deceitful effort to mask Sharon's grandiose plans for forcing a peace treaty on Lebanon, smashing the PLO, and, incidentally, defeating the Syrian army.[11]

In reality, Israel's invasion force of tens of thousands of troops could not have moved into Lebanon within Sharon's stated schedule, much less accomplished his goals, in that short a period. As it turned out, the Israeli invasion force remained in Lebanon for three years. (At its peak in the initial weeks of the invasion, Israel fielded 90,000 troops, 12,000 troop and supply trucks, 1,300 tanks, 1,300 armored personnel carriers, 634 warplanes, and a number of warships. What all this power finally achieved was the evacuation of an estimated 8,300 PLO fighters from Beirut.[12]) Although Israel announced that its withdrawal was completed on June 6, 1985, it in fact left behind about 1,000 troops to man its "security belt" in southern Lebanon, where troops remain to this day.[13]

FALLACY

"Operation Peace for Galilee is designed not to capture Beirut but to drive the PLO's rockets and artillery out of the range of our settlements. We're talking about a range of forty kilometers [twenty-four miles]."
—Ariel Sharon, Israeli defense minister, 1982[14]

FACT

Within a week of the invasion Israeli forces were in Beirut, nearly sixty miles from Israel. By that time the landscape of southern Lebanon was shattered and 200,000 of its people uprooted, and at least 20,000 injured or killed.[15]

Israeli Prime Minister Menachem Begin rejected international pleas for a halt to the slaughter, claiming that the invasion would usher in an era of "forty years of peace."[16] Instead he ordered the siege of West Beirut and its more than 500,000 civilians.[17] West Beirut was repeatedly bombed from the air and subjected to ceaseless bombardment by artillery and naval gunfire. Cluster bombs, napalm, phosphorus, and even advanced fuel-air weapons were used against residential sections.[18]

FALLACY

"It never occurred to anyone dealing with the Lebanese military units which subsequently entered the Shatila and Sabra camps that they would perpetrate a massacre."
—*Menachem Begin, Israeli prime minister, 1982*[19]

FACT

It was obvious by September 16 that a massacre was in the making in some of the Palestinian refugee camps of Lebanon.[20]

U.S. Special Envoy Morris Draper was concerned enough to bring up the question of the safety of the refugees with Israeli Defense Minister Ariel Sharon and Chief of Staff Rafael Eitan. Draper proposed that the Lebanese army be sent into the Palestinian refugee camps south of Beirut to search for "terrorists" Sharon insisted were hiding there. However, Eitan said the regular army was not up to the task, adding: "Lebanon is at a point of exploding into a frenzy of revenge. . . . I'm telling you that some of their commanders visited me, and I could see in their eyes that it's going to be a relentless slaughter."[21]

At the time, Israeli troops had surrounded the refugee camps of Sabra and Shatila and completely controlled the area. Yet despite his words to the American envoy Eitan allowed the Lebanese Christian Phalange militia to enter the two refugee camps on September 16 to use "their own methods." Eitan explained to the Israeli cabinet that the camps were surrounded "by us, that the Phalangists would begin to operate that night in the camps, that we could give them orders whereas it was impossible to give orders to the Lebanese Army."[22]

The slaughter of women, children, and old men—but apparently not of the "terrorists" the Israelis insisted were hiding in the camps, since none could be found—began that same night, September 16, and lasted until September 18. When word of the massacre spread and international criticism was raised against Israel, Israeli Prime Minister Menachem Begin indignantly declared: "*Goyim* kill *Goyim* and they blame the Jew."[23]

A prepared statement by the Israeli cabinet said: "A blood libel has been perpetrated against the Jewish people."[24] In a letter to California Democratic Senator Alan Cranston, one of Israel's strongest supporters, Begin wrote: "The whole campaign . . . of accusing Israel, of blaming Israel, of placing moral responsibility on Israel—all of it seems to me, an old man who has seen so much in his lifetime, to be almost unbelievable, fantastic and, of course, totally despicable."[25]

However, within a few months the official Israeli Commission of Inquiry, better known as the Kahan Commission, concluded that Israeli officials shared major blame for the massacre. The report found the Phalange militia guilty of "direct responsibility" and eight Israelis of "indirect responsibility": Prime Minister Begin, Foreign Minister Yitzhak Shamir, Defense Minister Sharon, Chief of Staff Lieutenant General Eitan, Director of Military Intelligence Major General Yehoshua Saguy, Major General Amir Drori, Brigadier General Amos Yaron, and the unidentified head of Mossad. Yaron was later posted as Israel's military attaché in Washington after having been rejected by Canada because of his involvement in the massacre.[26]

The commission said: "In our view, everyone who had anything to do with events in Lebanon should have felt apprehension about a massacre in the camps, if armed Phalangist forces were to be moved into them without the IDF [Israel Defense Forces] exercising concrete and effective supervision and scrutiny of them."[27]

Not only did Israel aid in the Phalange's entry into the camps, but once it became clear that massacres were occurring Israeli officials did nothing to stop them. The commission said: "It is clear . . . no energetic and immediate actions were taken to restrain the Phalangists and put a stop to their actions."[28] *New York Times* correspondent Thomas L. Friedman later noted: "The Israelis knew just what they were doing when they let the Phalangists into those camps."[29]

Israel said 700 to 800 persons were killed in the Sabra and Shatila massacre.[30] Other estimates were considerably higher. The Palestine Red Crescent put the number at over 2,000 while Lebanese authorities reported 762 bodies recovered and 1,200 death certificates issued.[31]

FALLACY

"I want to promise you . . . that the IDF—following the government's orders—did not even once deliberately harm the civilian population."
—*Menachem Begin, Israeli prime minister, 1982*[32]

FACT

In addition to the Sabra and Shatila massacre, many Lebanese civilians were killed in Israel's invasion. Israelis, reporters, diplomats, international observers, and others all have testified about the horrendous loss of civilian life.[33] Estimates vary greatly, but all estimates have placed the toll in the thousands. The Israeli military reported 12,276 killed as of October 6, 1982.[34] Lebanese police put the toll at 19,085 killed and 30,302 wounded, including 6,775 in Beirut, where 84 percent of them were civilians and a third of them children.[35]

The American Friends Service Committee's Advisory Committee on Human Rights estimated that nearly 200,000 Palestinians were made homeless as a result of the systematic destruction of refugee camps by Israeli forces in the first four months of the invasion.[36]

Additionally, Israeli troops indulged themselves in widespread looting of civilian property, as they had in previous wars.[37] Truckloads of the plundered booty were seen heading back toward Israel in convoys as Israel retreated in late September 1982. Dr. Sabri Jiryis, director of the Palestine Liberation Organization's Research Center in Beirut, complained that Israeli soldiers carted away the center's entire 25,000-volume research library of books in Arabic, English, and Hebrew. Dr. Jiryis said Israeli soldiers spent a week in the center taking files, manuscripts, documents, microfilms, a printing press, telephones, and electric appliances. They also smashed desks, filing cabinets, and other equipment.[38]

Left behind by the Israelis were graffiti such as "Palestinian? What's That?" and "Palestinians, fuck you."[39] Under pressure from the United Nations, Israel returned the archives on November 24, 1983.[40]

Israel also used U.S.-made cluster bombs against civilians in violation of an agreement with the United States to employ them only in self-defense. As a result, the Reagan administration reported to Congress on June 24 that Israel "may have" violated the Arms Export Control Act by using U.S. weapons for purposes other than its own defense in the invasion of Lebanon. Three days later the shipment of cluster bomb units to Israel was halted, but only briefly.[41]

The London *Sunday Times* reported that in the first two months of the invasion up to August 6 Israeli gunners had hit in Beirut 5 UN buildings, 134 embassies or diplomatic residences, 6 hospitals and clinics, 1 mental institution, the Central Bank, 5 hotels, the Red Cross office, and innumerable homes.[42] All traffic into the western part of the city was stopped. Water, power, food, gasoline, and other essential civilian supplies were cut off by Israeli troops.[43] When President Reagan urged Prime Minister Begin to make Israeli troops stop violating UN-supported ceasefires, Begin responded: "Nobody, nobody is going to bring Israel to her knees. You must have forgotten that the Jews kneel but to God."[44]

Begin added powerful action to his defiant words a week later when Israel unleashed its most devastating attack against Beirut. The massive assault on August 12 by planes, artillery and naval guns became known as Black Thursday. The day of destruction began with a massive artillery attack at dawn that was followed by eleven straight hours of saturation air bombardment.[45] As many as five hundred persons were killed in the assault.[46]

President Reagan was so outraged that he personally telephoned Begin twice that day, charging that Israel was causing "needless destruction and bloodshed."[47] The bombings were "unfathomable and senseless," Reagan complained.[48] The White House publicly announced that "the President was shocked this morning when he learned of the new, heavy Israeli bombardment of West Beirut."[49]

By the end of August the Lebanese newspaper *an-Nahar* estimated that 5,515 persons had been killed and 11,139 wounded in Beirut. Although Israel maintained that "only 3,000" were killed and that most of them were "terrorists," others estimated that for every Palestinian guerrilla killed or wounded, four civilians had been killed or wounded.[50]

FALLACY

"The Lebanese war, like all of Israel's wars, had been a defensive struggle."
          —*Ariel Sharon, Israeli defense minister, 1989*[51]

FACT

Not even Israeli Prime Minister Begin maintained that the threat from Lebanon was so grave that Israel was forced to launch war. In a speech before the Israeli National Defense College, Begin noted that Israel had fought three wars in which it had no alternative but to fight and three wars in which it had a "choice"—including the 1982 invasion of Lebanon.[52] Begin listed as the wars of no choice the 1948 War of Independence, the 1969–1970 War of Attrition and the 1973 Yom Kippur/Ramadan War. He added: "Our other wars were not without an alternative."

The wars of choice that Begin listed were those in 1956, 1967, and 1982. "In November 1956 we had a choice. The reason for going to war then was the need to destroy the fedayeen, who did not represent a danger to the existence of the state. . . . In June 1967, we again had a choice. The

Egyptian army concentrations in the Sinai approaches do not prove that Nasser was really about to attack us. We must be honest with ourselves. We decided to attack him.

"As for the [1982] Operation Peace for Galilee, it does not really belong to the category of wars of no alternative. We could have gone on seeing our civilians injured in Metulla or Qiryat Shimona or Nahariya. . . . True, such actions were not a threat to the existence of the state."

FALLACY

"Much of what you have read in the newspapers and news-magazines about the war in Lebanon—and even more of what you have seen and heard on television—is simply not true."
—*Martin Peretz, publisher of the* New Republic, *1982*[53]

FACT

Israel's 1982 invasion of Lebanon was the first of the Middle East wars that was televised in all its horrors. The daily picture reports of Israeli troops bombarding civilians brought international protests. In the United States Israel's supporters rallied to Israel's side, professing to see a silver lining in all the suffering.

Former Secretary of State Henry Kissinger declared that the invasion "opens up extraordinary opportunities for a dynamic American diplomacy throughout the Middle East."[54] Arthur Goldberg, former U.S. ambassador to the United Nations, concluded that now "it should be possible to conclude an autonomy agreement with all deliberate speed."[55] Historian Barbara Tuchman contended that Israel had no choice because the actions of the Arabs were beyond Israel's control. She added that what concerned her most was "the survival and future of Israel and of Jews in the diaspora—myself among them."[56]

As worldwide protests against Israel mounted, Israelis and their supporters launched a fierce campaign against the media.

Thomas L. Friedman of *The New York Times* was called a "self-hating Jew" by Israeli army radio; the *New Republic* attacked the press as anti-Israel, and an article in *Penthouse* asked readers why "American journalists enthusiastically joined the lynch mob against Israel." The respected Hebrew daily *Ha'aretz* printed a long article headlined "The Media Sold Their Conscience to the PLO." A book written by an American-born Israeli claimed that Western journalists in Beirut had been "terrorized" by Muslim thugs and "by accident or design . . . engaged in a conspiracy to defame Israel." And former U.S. Ambassador to the United Nations Jeane Kirkpatrick declared that the reporting was "unfair" to Israel.[57]

Aside from demonizing the press, supporters of Israel sought other avenues for condoning or excusing Israel's behavior. Morris B. Abrams, a former U.S. representative on the UN Commission on Human Rights, attempted to justify Israel's actions by comparing them to atrocities committed by the West: "The moral culpability for the loss of innocent lives in Lebanon, as in Dresden, Germany, and Normandy, in France, during World War II, rests primarily on those who initiated the terror rather than those who ended it." He concluded that the war "would never have occurred" if the Arab states had resettled the Palestinian refugees.[58]

Zionist author Norman Podhoretz and others, including anti–Vietnam War activist Jane Fonda, saw anti-Semitism at the root of criticism of Israel's invasion. Critics of the invasion, Podhoretz argued, were denying Jews "the right of self-defense. . . . What we have here is the old anti-Semitism modified to suit the patterns of international life."[59]

After the war, a group called Americans for a Safe Israel applied heavy pressure on NBC, protesting its coverage. The group produced a documentary called *NBC in Lebanon: A Study of Media Misrepresentation* and a monograph, *NBC's War in Lebanon: The Distorting Mirror*, seeking to discredit the network's coverage. Later, ABC also came under attack. Another pro-Israeli organization that grew out of the war was the Committee for Accuracy in Middle East Reporting (CAMERA). It successfully prevented all fifteen radio stations in Baltimore, Maryland, from running advertisements opposing aid to Israel paid for by the National Association of Arab Americans.[60]

Why such exaggerated reactions to the media coverage?

Robert Fisk, a veteran reporter for *The Times* of London, who lived through Israel's invasion while stationed in Beirut, concluded that the reason for the hysteria was that the 1982 invasion showed the world that Israeli troops acted much like other troops in time of war. The difference was that in 1982, "for the very first time, reporters had open access to the Arab side of a Middle East war and found that Israel's supposedly invincible army, with its moral high ground and clearly stated military objective against 'terrorists,' did not perform in the way that legend would have suggested. The Israelis acted brutally, they mistreated prisoners, killed thousands of civilians, lied about their activities, and then watched their militia allies slaughter the occupants of a refugee camp. In fact, they behaved very much like the 'uncivilized' Arab armies whom they had so consistently denigrated over the preceding 30 years."[61]

TEN

THE LIKUD GOVERNMENTS

The emergence of a Likud (Unity) government under Menachem Begin in 1977 was an earthquake in Israeli politics and policies. Begin's victory swept aside David Ben-Gurion's socialist Labor party, which had ruled Israel since its birth in 1948 and replaced it with Revisionist Zionism. It was the triumph of messianic nationalism over Zionism's pragmatic and secular mainstream. Likud dominated from 1977 to 1992, except for the period 1984–1988, when it shared power with the Labor party.

FALLACY

"The right of the Jewish people to Eretz Yisrael is eternal and indisputable."

—*Manifesto of the Likud party, 1973*[1]

FACT

A bitter split had raged for decades between the two factions of secular and messianic Zionism and their two proponents David Ben-Gurion and Menachem Begin. Ben-Gurion used to call the Revisionists Nazis and compare Begin to Hitler. Begin and his followers called Ben-Gurion a traitor to the Jewish cause.[2] Labor party officials professed a humane and compromising form of Zionism—even if they did not always practice it—and accepted the idea of the partition of Palestine in 1947 as well as the formula of trading land for peace as embodied in UN Resolution 242, but Likud officials made no such pretense. The core and guiding principle of their belief was the Jewish claim to Eretz Yisrael.

In Hebrew, Eretz Yisrael means "Land of Israel," a phrase invested with strong nationalist and messianic feelings and implying Jewish rule over all of Palestine as well as Jordan. To Revisionists, the Jewish claim encompassed all the land between the Nile and the Euphrates rivers.

The concept of Eretz Yisrael, a Greater Israel, was the most cherished belief of Likud's two first prime ministers, Menachem Begin and Yitzhak Shamir, and the essence of Likud philosophy. Both men were natives of Poland who became leaders of the two major Jewish terrorist groups in pre-1948 Palestine. Both were disciples of Vladimir Jabotinsky's blood-and-honor Revisionist Zionism, and both devoted their lives to establishing Jewish control over all of Palestine. Both rejected the 1947 UN Partition Plan because it did not give Jews the whole of Palestine.

As Begin said in 1947: "Our fatherland is indivisible. Any attempt to cut it up is not just criminal but invalid. He who does not recognize our right to the entire homeland does not recognize our right to any of its parts."[3] He added: "We shall never acquiesce in the partitioning of our homeland."[4] Begin's terrorist organization, Irgun, had as its insignia and slogan "Both sides of the Jordan," referring to Jewish claims to all of Palestine and Jordan.[5] Begin never renounced that ambition.

"Some Israeli commentators predicted that the creation of the new [Likud] bloc would mark the beginning of the end of Begin's career."

—*Eric Silver*, Begin, *1984*[6]

There was considerably more support for Begin and his expansionist policy in Israel than generally realized. Formation of the Likud bloc in 1973 out of an amalgam of rightist parties led by Begin's Herut party set the stage for his rise to power four years later. The new Likud coalition, like Begin himself, was openly dedicated to retaining the conquests of 1967. Likud's 1973 manifesto declared: "The State of Israel has a right and a claim to sovereignty over Judea, Samaria, and the Gaza Strip. In time, Israel will invoke this claim and strive to realize it. Any plan involving the handover of parts of western Eretz Yisrael to foreign rule, as proposed by the Labor Alignment, denies our right to this country."[7] Use of the phrase "western Eretz Yisrael" to describe the West Bank was shorthand to signal Likud's claim to Jordan as well.

Begin ruled for six years and three months between 1977 and 1983, longer than any other prime minister except his old nemesis David Ben-Gurion. During his term of office Begin exerted all of his formidable energies to secure for Israel the whole of the ancient homeland of the Jews.

There were about 50,000 Jews living in occupied Arab East Jerusalem and about 7,000 in forty-five settlements in the rest of the occupied territories when Begin assumed power.[8] (Those numbers, by the way, represent strong evidence that the Labor party was not opposed to settlements. Its officials were just less truthful about their goals.) When Begin resigned six years later, there were 112 Jewish settlements in the West Bank and five in the Gaza Strip; and the Golan Heights and Arab East Jerusalem had been officially annexed as integral parts of Israel. The number of Jewish settlers was more than 40,000, not counting a rough estimate of about 100,000 Jews living in Arab East Jerusalem.[9]

When asked how he wanted to be remembered in history, Begin replied: "As the man who set the borders of Eretz Yisrael for all eternity."[10] Concluded Begin's most insightful biographer, Eric Silver: "His overriding priority was to secure the whole of the ancient homeland west of the Jordan for the Jewish people. By the time he retired even his opponents acknowledged that it would take a leader no less dedicated and no less commanding to restore the partition lines. . . . The Israel Menachem Begin created in his own image was more narrowly Jewish, more aggressive, and more isolated."[11]

FALLACY

"Those who doubt the sincerity and the willingness of Israel to make sacrifices . . . to achieve peace should put Israel to the test."

—*Moshe Arad,*
Israeli ambassador to the United States, 1988[12]

FACT

When Yitzhak Shamir succeeded Menachem Begin in 1983 he vowed in his inaugural speech to continue the "holy work" of establishing settlements in the West Bank.[13] Shamir was as good as his word. He enormously accelerated the pace of establishing Jewish settlements in the occupied territories, promoting the greatest settlement activity in Israel's history.

When Shamir was defeated in 1992, there were, according to a State Department report, nearly double the number of settlers as when he took power: 129,000 Jews in Arab East Jerusalem (compared with 155,000 Palestinians); 97,000 Jews in 180 settlements in the West Bank with half of the land under exclusive Jewish control; 3,600 in 20 settlements in the Gaza Strip; and 14,000 in 30 settlements in the Golan Heights.[14]

Shamir's defeat came just as he was involved in the greatest campaign of construction in the occupied territories. A study by Israel's Peace Now group showed that Israel had started 13,650 housing units in the occupied territories in 1991, an increase in one year equal to 65 percent of all the units established over the previous twenty-three years in the territories.[15] The figure did not include more than 10,000 units under construction in Arab East Jerusalem.[16] In the words of *The Washington Post*: "In the last 18 months, [Prime Minister Yitzhak] Shamir's government has launched the biggest housing construction campaign in the 24-year history of its rule of the territories."[17]

Typical of the attitude of Israel's Likud leaders toward exchanging land for peace was the statement by Shamir after his defeat for reelection in 1992: "I would have conducted the autonomy negotiations for ten years, and in the meantime we would have reached half a million souls in Judea and Samaria [the West Bank]."[18] Shamir had begun his reelection campaign by declaring that he planned to "tell the Gentiles of the world" that nothing could stop establishment of settlements in the occupied territories.[19]

As a result of the accelerated pace of moving Jewish settlers into the occupied territories during the rule of the Likud prime ministers, the struggle between Israel and the Palestinians has become more complex than ever. If peace is to be achieved, Israel will have to return to the Palestinians the land it has taken for settlements. With tens of thousands of Jews now living on Palestinian land that essential action will be more difficult.

PART TWO

COLLUSION AND CONFLICT

ELEVEN

THE
INTIFADA

The intifada—Arabic for "shaking off"—erupted on December 9, 1987, in the crowded Gaza Strip and quickly spread to the West Bank, involving all 1.7 million Palestinians living under Israeli occupation since 1967. The immediate stimulus for the uprising occurred on December 8, when an Israeli army truck ran into a group of Palestinians near the Jabalya refugee camp in the Gaza Strip, killing four and injuring seven. A Jewish salesman had been stabbed to death in Gaza on December 6, and Palestinians suspected that the traffic collision had been deliberate.[1] Observers speculated that the Palestinians also were motivated by two dramatic events of the previous month: by the daring exploit of a Palestinian guerrilla who single-handedly killed six Israeli soldiers in a hang-glider attack and by despair at the apparent lack of support for the Palestinians' plight among the Arab states at the Arab League summit in Amman.

Significantly, the intifada has involved confrontations between heavily armed Israeli soldiers and thousands of young children and women armed only with stones. Israel's violent methods in trying to suppress the uprising have claimed well over one thousand lives and have been widely condemned throughout the world. As of March 1993 the intifada continues.

FALLACY

"In our view, Israel clearly has not only the right, but the obligation, to preserve or restore order in the occupied territories and to use appropriate levels of force to accomplish that end."

—*Richard Schifter,*
assistant secretary of state for human rights, 1988[2]

FACT

Israel has killed, wounded, maimed, tortured, imprisoned, or expelled tens of thousands of Palestinians in trying to suppress the Palestinian uprising. As the uprising began its fifth year toward the end of 1991, the Palestine Human Rights Information Center of Jerusalem and Chicago reported the following cumulative statistics: 994 Palestinians killed by Israeli troops; 119,300 estimated injuries; 66 deportations; 16,000 administrative detentions; 94,830 acres of land confiscations; 2,074 home demolitions or sealings; 10,000 round-the-clock curfews of areas over 10,000 population; and 120,000 tree uprootings.[3]

Statistics have been among the controversial subjects of the uprising. But even by the conservative count of the State Department, at least 930 Palestinians were killed by Israeli troops in the first four years of the intifada.[4]

The brutality of Israel's efforts to suppress the intifada was spelled out early by Defense Minister Yitzhak Rabin. On January 19, 1988, he announced a policy of "broken bones," saying Israel would use "force, power and blows" to suppress the uprising.[5] Prime Minister Yitzhak Shamir said: "Our task now is to re-create the barrier of fear between Palestinians and the Israeli military, and once again put the fear of death into the Arabs of the areas so as to deter them from attacking us anymore."[6]

The Israeli government seemed to take to heart advice offered by former Secretary of State Henry Kissinger to a private group of Jewish American leaders in New York in February 1988. *The New York Times* reported that Kissinger had suggested Israel should put down the intifada "as quickly as possible—overwhelmingly, brutally and rapidly. The insurrection must be quelled immediately, and the first step should be to throw out television, a la South Africa. To be sure, there will be international criticism of the step, but it will dissipate in short order." He added: "There are no awards for losing with moderation."[7]

In suppressing the uprising, Israeli troops appear to especially seek out for beatings old men, women, and children. An official of the UN Relief and Works Agency in the Gaza Strip, acting director Angela Williams, early on said: "We are deeply shocked by the evidence of the brutality with which people are evidently being beaten. We are especially shocked by the beatings of old men and women."[8] The Swedish Save the Children Fund, in research financed by the Ford Foundation, reported by mid-1990 that Israeli troops used "severe, indiscriminate and recurrent" violence against Palestinian children. It said 159 children with an average age of ten had been killed in the first two years, 6,500 wounded by gunfire, and 35,000 to 48,000 others (40 percent of them ten years old or younger) treated for injuries during the first two years of the intifada.[9]

The claim by Israel and its supporters that the intifada was not the result of outrage against the occupation but of meddling by outside forces is untrue. The *New York Times* correspondent in Israel at the time was Thomas L. Friedman, winner of Pulitzer Prizes for his coverage of the 1982 Israeli invasion of Lebanon and his 1987 coverage of Israel. He wrote at the beginning of the uprising:

"The Israeli-Palestinian clashes of the last two weeks only underscore that there is already a civil war going on here. . . . Just because Palestinians or Israelis are not dying in such numbers each week does not mean that their war is not constantly present; barely a week has gone by in the last three years without a Palestinian or Israeli killed or wounded."[10]

As UN Undersecretary-General for Special Political Affairs Marrack Goulding reported after visiting the territories in early 1988: "The unrest of the past six weeks has been an expression of the despair and hopelessness felt by the population of the occupied territories, more than half of whom had known nothing but an occupation that denies what they consider to be their legitimate rights."[11]

FALLACY

"Israel's administration of the West Bank (Judea and Samaria) and the Gaza Strip was recognized as comparatively benign."
—AIPAC, 1989[12]

FACT

There has been nothing benign about Israel's occupation of the territories captured in 1967.

Palestinian rights have been systematically violated by the Shabak, Israel's secret police previously known as Shin Bet. Shabak has absolute power over the occupied territories. One of its more effective forms of harassment comes with the power of its operatives to decide whether Palestinians in the occupied territories will be granted permits for the most routine aspects of daily life.[13] At first glance, the practice seems fairly benign. But the Israeli occupation authorities have perfected the issuance of such permits into an art form of bureaucratic harassment.

The Washington Post reports that Israel deliberately employs the system to make daily life difficult and frustrating for Palestinians under occupation. According to Jonathan Kuttab, a prominent Palestinian lawyer: "The whole point of the process is to grind people down, to break their resistance and to force them to realize that whatever they do, the system has power over them and can deny them their rights."[14]

The all-inclusive permit system was put in place in early 1988 and since then it has made life miserable for Palestinians. The heart of the system is a one-page application form generally titled "Judea and Samaria Area Civil Administration Application for Permission." Since 1988, Palestinians have had to fill out the form to carry out any of twenty-three categories of activities ranging from registering a car to building a new factory. It is needed for applicants of all ages and covers such daily activities as registering babies, enrolling in school, getting a telephone, receiving a pension, traveling abroad, and buying a burial plot.

For approval, the form must be stamped by seven different widely scattered Israeli offices where lines are usually hours long. The applicants must prove there are no outstanding obligations against them, including traffic tickets and unpaid taxes. Reported *Washington Post* correspondent Jackson Diehl: "For Palestinians, the war of daily life means that activities as simple as registering for a driver's license, or obtaining a birth certificate, can require weeks of formalities at more than a half-dozen government offices, including regional and local tax audits."[15]

It was the Palestinians' total sense of despair and anger at the military occupation that sparked the uprising. Israel's tactics, especially since the uprising, have been roundly condemned by nearly every human rights organization in the world, by individual witnesses, and repeatedly by members of the United Nations, including the United States.[16] A few of many critical reports:

▌ *UN Goulding Report, January 21, 1988.* UN Undersecretary-General for Special Political Affairs Marrack Goulding conducted an investigation in early 1988 and concluded that Israel violated a broad range of human rights guaranteed by the Fourth Geneva Convention Relative to the Protection of Civilian Persons in Time of War of August 12, 1949. Specifically, Israel violated Article 33, collective punishment; Article 47, attempts to alter the status of Jerusalem; Article 49, deportation of Palestinians and establishment of settlements in the occupied territories; and Article 53, destruction of property. In addition, there was also evidence of violations of Article 32, brutality against civilians.[17]

■ *European Community Report, February 8, 1988.* The twelve nations of the EC condemned Israel's harsh actions, saying the member states "deeply deplore the repressive measures taken by Israel, which are violations of international law and human rights." They said Israel's "repressive measures must stop" and expressed the EC's "profound concern at the deteriorating situation."[18]

■ *Physicians for Human Rights Report, February 11, 1988.* A group of four American doctors, three from Harvard and one from City University of New York, representing Physicians for Human Rights, an independent monitoring group in Boston, reported after a week-long visit to the territories that Israel had unleashed "an unrestrained epidemic of violence by the army and police." The physicians said their research on injured Palestinians indicated that many of the injuries had been inflicted in a systematic fashion by Israeli troops. The doctors also said it appeared that many beatings had been deliberately aimed at breaking hands, arms, and legs.[19]

■ *Medical and Human Rights Groups Report, May 30, 1988.* Palestinian doctors, UN officials, and representatives of Amnesty International reported that indiscriminate and widespread use of tear gas by Israeli troops had injured 1,200 Palestinians and caused dozens of miscarriages and eleven deaths since the uprising's beginning. The groups charged that there were well-documented cases of troops firing gas into homes, into closed rooms, and into hospitals.[20]

■ *Amnesty International Report, June 17, 1988.* AI issued a special report critical of the widespread use by Israeli troops of live ammunition that resulted in killing women, children under fourteen years of age, and the elderly. Some of the dead were not in violent demonstrations when they were killed. The report said there was "evidence to suggest that the Israeli authorities at a high level have actively condoned if not encouraged the use of live ammunition and unreasonable force."[21]

■ *UN General Assembly Condemnation, November 3, 1988.* The UN General Assembly voted 130 to 2 to condemn Israel for "killing and wounding defenseless Palestinians" and said it "strongly deplores" Israel's disregard for earlier UN resolutions condemning such actions. The United States and Israel cast the only two negative votes.[22]

■ *UN General Assembly Condemnation, April 20, 1989.* The General Assembly condemned Israel's human rights abuses and demanded that it halt excessive gunfire and restrictions on worship in the occupied West Bank and Gaza Strip. The vote was 129 to 2, with only the United States and Israel voting against.[23]

■ *Private Witness Report, March 2, 1990.* Dr. Martin Rubenberg, a practicing physician in Florida, worked as an unaffiliated volunteer physician in the Gaza Strip in 1989 and found that Israel was preventing proper health care to the Palestinians. He reported: "Bureaucratic obstruction is used to limit medical care. . . . Radio facilities, including physicians' beepers, have been banned. . . . Medical care is also limited by the Israeli authorities when they prevent the return of Palestinian physicians who have been trained abroad. The absence of adequate services, continuous nightly curfews, frequent 24-hour curfews for days or weeks at a time, military closures and regulations prohibiting Gazans from remaining in Israel overnight, all combine to increase the pain, suffering, debilitation and mortality of Palestinian patients."[24]

■ *Jimmy Carter Report, March 19, 1990.* Former President Carter toured Israel in early 1990 and said: "What we are talking about is an authoritarian government, that is in charge, that is depriving the people [Palestinians] under its control of their basic human rights."[25] He added: "There is hardly a family that lives in the West Bank and Gaza that has not had one of its male members actually incarcerated by the military authorities. . . . There have been about 650 Palestinians killed by excessive use of firearms by the military that are not under life-threatening situations, and they are still demolishing homes and still putting people in prison without charges."[26]

■ *Middle East Watch, July 25, 1990.* The U.S. human rights organization found that Israel's rules governing the use of firearms were "unduly permissive" and urged immediate modification "in order to reduce the number of Palestinians killed unjustifiably at the hands of Israeli troops." The report criticized Israel for failing to prosecute soldiers for illegal killings.[27]

■ *Secretary-General of the United Nations Report, November 1, 1990.* UN Secretary-General Javier Perez de Cuellar proposed that the Security Council involve itself directly in finding a way to protect Palestinians living under Israeli occupation.[28] One of Perez de Cuellar's proposals was that the 164 signatories to the 1949 Fourth Geneva Convention Relative to the Protection of Civilian Persons in Time of War be convened to discuss Israel's human rights violations in the territories captured by Israel in 1967. He noted that "the determination of the Palestinians to persevere with the intifada is evidence of their rejection of the occupation and their commitment to exercise their legitimate political rights, including self-determination. . . . The issue before us today is what practical steps can, in fact, be taken by the international community to ensure the safety and protection of the Palestinian civilians living under Israeli occupation. Clearly, the numerous appeals—whether by the Security Council, by myself as Secretary-General, by individual Member States or by ICRC [International Committee of the Red Cross] . . . to the Israeli authorities to abide by their obligations under the Fourth Geneva convention have been ineffective."[29] Israel dismissed the report as "one-sided" and the United States showed no interest in pursuing the matter.[30]

United Nations Condemnation, January 6, 1992. The UN Security Council unanimously passed a resolution that "strongly condemns the decision of Israel, the occupying power, to resume deportations of Palestinian civilians" in violation of the Fourth Geneva Convention. The resolution referred to the lands occupied by Israel as "Palestinian territories . . . including Jerusalem."[31] It was the seventh time since the start of the intifada that the Security Council had passed a resolution urging Israel not to deport Palestinians or deploring such deportations; the United States had abstained in three of the previous resolutions.[32] It was the sixty-eighth time the council had passed a resolution critical of Israel.

FALLACY

"There is no doubt in my mind that Israel is being held to a higher standard than others."

—Richard Schifter,
assistant secretary of state for human rights, 1990[33]

FACT

Schifter made his statement in testimony before the first House committee hearing on the intifada held on May 9, 1990—two and a half years after the uprising began. His testimony was rebutted by other witnesses such as Michael Posner, executive director of the Lawyers Committee for Human Rights; Kenneth Roth, deputy director of Human Rights Watch; and Sarah Roy, an academic expert on the Gaza Strip. They all testified that Israel's use of force was excessive and had caused many unnecessary deaths, including those of 102 children under sixteen years of age. They also criticized Israel's torture of prisoners, its administrative detentions under which Palestinians were arrested without charge or trial, its deportation of Palestinians, and its demolition of Arab homes.[34]

The American-Arab Anti-Discrimination Committee (ADC) called for Schifter's firing, charging he had deliberately muted criticism of Israel. The Bush administration refused. ADC noted that Schifter was the founding president of the Jewish Institute for National Security Affairs (JINSA), a group organized to "inform the defense and national security community of the value of strategic cooperation between the U.S. and Israel." ADC President Abdeen Jabara charged that "Ambassador Schifter is more concerned about Israel's image than he is about protecting human rights and effectuating the mandate of American law." A request by Jabara to meet with Schifter was refused.[35]

In spite of his testimony to the contrary, Richard Schifter's own State Department office issued reports on the intifada that left no doubt about the nature and extent of Israel's abuses. Following are some excerpts from the U.S. State Department's *Country Reports on Human Rights Practices* from 1988 to 1991:

■ *1988:* The State Department reported that 366 Palestinians were killed by Israelis in 1988; another twenty-three were killed between the start of the uprising on December 9, 1987, and the end of that year. Thus the total deaths were 389 in less than thirteen months of uprising—more than one a day. The report cited "five cases in 1988 in which unarmed Palestinians in detention died under questionable circumstances or were clearly killed by the detaining officials." More than 20,000 Palestinians had been wounded or injured—an average of fifty-five per day during the year. The report said that 36 Palestinians were deported during 1988, well over 2,600 were held in "administrative detention," at least 108 houses were demolished, and 46 were sealed. The report added that "many avoidable deaths and injuries" were caused because Israeli "soldiers frequently used gunfire in situations that did not present mortal danger to troops. . . . [R]egulations [governing the use of gunfire] were not rigorously enforced; punishments were usually lenient; and there were many cases of unjustified killing which did not result in disciplinary actions or prosecution." The report noted "widespread beating" of Palestinians. "I.D.F. troops used clubs to break limbs and beat Palestinians who were not directly involved in disturbances or resisting arrest. Soldiers turned many people out of their homes at night, making them stand for hours, and rounded up men and boys and beat them in reprisal for stone-throwings. At least thirteen Palestinians have been reported to have died from beatings. By mid-April [1988] reports of deliberate breaking of bones had ended, but reports of unjustifiably harsh beatings continued."[36]

■ *1989:* The State Department reported that 304 Palestinians were killed by Israelis in 1989, including eleven by Israeli settlers and ten by beatings during interrogation. Reports of Palestinians wounded by Israeli forces ranged from 5,000 to 20,000. The report said that 26 Palestinians were deported during the year, well over 1,271 were held in "administrative detention," 88 houses were demolished, and 82 were sealed. It added that "reports continue of harsh and demeaning treatment of prisoners under investigation or interrogation, as well as beatings of suspects."[37]

■ *1990:* The State Department reported that 140 Palestinians were killed by Israelis in 1990. Ten were killed by Jewish settlers and the rest by Israeli security forces, including at least 5 by personnel not in uniform. Human rights groups charged that the plainclothes security personnel acted as death squads who killed Palestinian activists without warning, after they had surrendered, or after they had been subdued.[38] Reports of Palestinians wounded by Israeli forces ranged from 4,000 to over 10,000. The report said that no Palestinians were deported during the year, but well over 1,263 were held in "administrative detention," 93 houses were demolished, and 83 were sealed. It added that "reports continue of harsh and demeaning treatment of prisoners under investigation or interrogation, as well as beatings of suspects."[39]

■ *1991:* The State Department reported that 97 Palestinians were killed by Israeli occupation forces during 1991, including at least 27 by personnel not in uniform. It said human rights groups, as in 1990, charged that Israeli plainclothes agents acted as death squads who killed Palestinian activists without warning, after they had surrendered, or after they had been subdued.[40] Reports of Palestinians wounded by Israeli forces ranged from 841 to over 5,000. The report said 8 Palestinians were deported during the year, well over 1,400 held in "administrative detention," 55 houses were demolished, and 62 were sealed. It added that human rights groups had published "detailed credible reports of torture, abuse and mistreatment of Palestinian detainees in prisons and detention centers."[41]

TWELVE

THE PALESTINIAN CITIZENS OF ISRAEL

Palestinian citizens form a sizable minority within Israel, numbering in 1992 about 800,000, equal to 18 percent of Israel's population.[1] Officially, the Palestinians are citizens of Israel. But in practice they enjoy few of the advantages of citizenship and have been discriminated against in a number of laws that reserve rights to Jews.[2] No Israeli government, whether led by the Likud or the Labor party, has ever proposed genuine equality for Palestinian citizens.

FALLACY

"The state [Israel] will not be Jewish in the sense that its Jewish citizens will have more rights than their non-Jewish fellows."
—*Jewish Agency statement, 1947*[3]

FACT

A highly praised history of Palestinians and Israel published in 1989 concluded: "In practice . . . the Palestinian citizens of

Israel have always been subject to systematic and widespread discrimination. To argue, as some dovish Israelis do, that this discrimination is a social and economic issue, ignores the fact that it is fundamentally political. It is about power. . . . Palestinians have never shared political power and have no prospect in the foreseeable future of doing so. Although some have played a role as co-opted members of Zionist political parties, they have never been given full ministerial authority or party power. Their role has been token, to give credibility to the claim on Arab votes and to the impression of a fully fledged democracy. For Palestinians it has been a democracy bereft of substance."[4]

Discrimination began as soon as Israel came into being. The 1948 war left 160,000 Arabs inside Israel, a minority equal to 12.5 percent of the new country's population at the end of 1949—aliens in their own land.[5] But they were not safe from expulsion. Thousands of Palestinians were selectively driven from the country. As late as 1950 Israel drove out 14,000 Palestinian inhabitants of Majdal to create the new Jewish city of Ashkelon.[6]

The Palestinians remaining inside Israel's expanded frontiers automatically became Israeli citizens, though with a distinctly second-class status. Palestinian citizens were subject to Israel's Defense (Emergency) Regulations under which they were prosecuted before military rather than civilian courts, severely restricted in their movements, vulnerable to exile and town arrest without appeal, prohibited from organized political action, forced to submit to censorship of their newspapers and school textbooks, and severely circumscribed in obtaining building permits.[7]

Israeli Arabs remained under military rule until 1966, when the Knesset finally abolished the special laws against them.[8] However, many of the restrictive rules of the Defense (Emergency) Regulations were retained in other forms and continue to be used against Israeli Arabs to this day.[9]

"The sole legal distinction between Jewish and Arab citizens of Israel is that the latter are not required to serve in the Israeli army."

—AIPAC, 1992[10]

FACT

When Israelis say that Palestinian citizens of Israel are not required to serve in the armed forces, they are trying to disguise the fact that they are not allowed to serve. By not being allowed to serve in Israel's armed forces, Palestinians lose out on a whole range of social benefits provided to veterans such as housing, social services, and other subsidies.[11]

Discrimination against Palestinians living in Israel is deep and endemic, and it is embodied in Israel's laws and government regulations.[12] The most obvious example of this discrimination is the fact that no Palestinian has the basic right to return to his or her homeland while any Jew anywhere in the world can receive automatic citizenship in Israel under the 1950 Law of Return.[13] Another example is that Palestinians have to carry identification cards noting that the bearer is not Jewish. Under the 1952 Nationality Law, "Jewish nationality" confers automatic Israeli citizenship on Jews anywhere. But it sets citizenship rules so stringently for non-Jews that many Palestinians are denied citizenship even though their families have lived in Palestine for generations.[14]

Another law passed in 1952, the World Zionist Organization–Jewish Agency (Status) Law, legalized special economic, political, and social benefits for Jews only. It gave exclusive rights to Israelis of "Jewish nationality," including the right to purchase land. Jewish institutions such as the Jewish National Fund are prohibited by law from selling land in Israel to non-Jews and are enjoined to hold all land "for the whole Jewish people."[15] The law also affirmed that the state of Israel regarded itself as the creation of the entire Jewish people and that therefore its gates were open to all Jews.[16]

Other laws discriminating against Arabs include a skein of rules for expropriating Arab property: the Law for Requisitioning of Property in Time of Emergency (1949), the Absentee's Property Law (1950), and the Land Acquisition Law (1953). Under the 1953 law alone about a million acres of land owned by 18,000 Palestinians was confiscated.[17] Israeli reporter Moshe Keren of Tel Aviv's Hebrew-language daily, *Ha'aretz*, characterized the land laws and land confiscation as "wholesale robbery in legal guise. Hundreds of thousands of dunams were taken away from the Arab minority."[18]

Once land is acquired by the state or the Jewish National Fund, a subordinate body of the World Zionist Organization–Jewish Agency, it cannot be sold or alienated in any way, meaning it is "forever" held in trust for the Jewish people. A 1961 "covenant" between the fund and the government describes the fund's function as being "beneficial to persons of Jewish religion, race or origin." Between them, the fund and the state owned 93 percent of the land inside Israel by the early 1990s, most of it confiscated from Palestinians. When it was discovered that some Jews were subletting land to Palestinians, another law was passed in 1967, the Agricultural Settlement Law, which prohibited the subleasing of land without the authority of the minister of agriculture. Palestinians thus were further restricted in where they could live or operate a business—and continue to be so.[19]

As Dani Rubinstein, the Israeli reporter on Arab affairs for the Hebrew daily *Davar*, reported in 1975: "The official policy towards the Israeli Arabs was and is not to allow them any activity within a political, social, or economic framework which is independent and Arab."[20]

FALLACY

"The State of Israel . . . will ensure complete equality of social and political rights for all its citizens, without distinction of creed, race, or sex."

—*Israeli Declaration of Independence, 1948*[21]

Though Israel's Declaration of Independence promised equality to all citizens, the same document specified that Israel was "a Jewish state . . . open to Jewish immigration" and called on all Jews throughout the world "to join forces with us." Over the years, Israel's laws have increasingly emphasized the exclusively Jewish character of the state. For instance, a 1985 law declared that no one could run for public office who rejects "the existence of the State of Israel as the state of the Jewish people."[22] The 1949 Flag and Emblem Law mandated the Star of David as Israel's state flag to reflect the "identification between the new state and the Jewish people" and the menorah, a Jewish candelabra, as the state emblem.[23]

As a result of exclusivist laws, *New York Times* reporter David Shipler reported in 1983 that Palestinians were "aliens in their own land" who were not "wholly part of a nation conceived as a Jewish state."[24] As former foreign minister Yigal Allon once stated: "It is necessary to declare it openly: Israel is a single-nationality Jewish state. The fact that an Arab minority lives within the country does not make it a multinational state."[25]

The most dramatic public evidence of Israel's official discrimination against Palestinians emerged in 1976 in a document called the Koenig Report, after its author, Israel Koenig, Northern District (Galilee) commissioner of the Ministry of Interior. The lengthy report warned against growing Palestinian nationalism and suggested a number of ways Palestinians with Israeli citizenship could be thwarted. These included examining "the possibility of diluting existing Arab population concentrations"; "giving preferential treatment [in the economic sector, including jobs] to Jewish groups or individuals rather than to Arabs"; encouraging Arab students to enroll in difficult scientific studies because "these studies leave less time for dabbling in nationalism and the dropout rate is higher"; and encouraging Arab students to study abroad "while making the return and employment more difficult—this policy is apt to encourage their emigration."[26]

The government announced that the report was one man's opinion and not official policy, a claim not generally accepted by the Arabs or other observers.[27] As proof, critics of the policy noted that Koenig remained in his post as district commissioner for Galilee, and the memorandum's coauthor, Zvi Aldoraty, was recommended by Prime Minister Yitzhak Rabin as his candidate for appointment as director of the Labor party's Arab Department.[28]

However, in his inaugural address in 1992, when he returned as prime minister, Rabin vowed: "Today, almost 45 years after the foundation of the state, there are quite large gaps between the Jewish and the Arab sectors in many areas. On behalf of the new government, I would like to promise the Arab, Druze and Bedouin population to make every possible effort to close those gaps."[29] Whether his words can be taken seriously, given his past record, remains to be seen.

THIRTEEN

THE
ISRAELI LOBBY

Israel's influence on the U.S. government has become legendary, primarily because of what is called the Israeli lobby.
Despite modest disclaimers about its power, virtually all
politicians, newspeople, and others who have experienced the
lobby firsthand attest to the overwhelming influence of Israel's
supporters in the Congress and in the formulation of U.S.
foreign policy. Of the myriad pro-Israel groups, none is better
organized, more active, or more powerful than AIPAC, the
American Israel Public Affairs Committee, the major lobby
supporting Israel in the United States since 1951.[1] Its influence
on Congress is such that for more than two decades Israel has
enjoyed extraordinary levels of financial aid and special benefits, all of them granted with barely a word of serious discussion. AIPAC is the envy of other lobbies for its easy access to
the highest levels of government.[2] Today AIPAC has an annual
budget of $15 million, about fifty thousand dues-paying
members, and, in addition to its headquarters in Washington,
D.C., offices in eight cities. Its endorsement of a political
candidate usually results in contributions from the nearly one
hundred pro-Israel political action committees around the
country.[3]

FALLACY

"In the final analysis, it is self-interest that sustains the close U.S.-Israeli relationship, and not the exercise of raw power by any lobbying group."

—*Representative Stephen J. Solarz,*
Democrat of New York, 1985[4]

FACT

The New York Times reported in 1987 that AIPAC "has become a major force in shaping United States policy in the Middle East. . . . [T]he organization has gained power to influence a presidential candidate's choice of staff, to block practically any arms sale to an Arab country and to serve as a catalyst for intimate military relations between the Pentagon and the Israeli army. Its leading officials are consulted by State Department and White House policy makers, by senators and generals." The *Times* report concluded that AIPAC "has become the envy of competing lobbyists and the bane of Middle East specialists who would like to strengthen ties with pro-Western Arabs."[5]

A year later, freelance reporter Eric Alterman examined AIPAC and came up with a similar judgment. He reported: "Without a doubt, AIPAC is the most powerful ethnic lobby to emerge in recent American history. A case can be made that it is, in fact, the most powerful Washington lobby of any kind. . . . AIPAC's influence is felt not merely on the Hill but in the White House, the Pentagon, the state department, the treasury and in a host of buildings in between. And its influence doesn't depend on the assistance of a friendly administration; more often than not, it's the other way around."[6]

Kathleen Christison, a former CIA analyst, wrote in 1988: "Under [President] Reagan, AIPAC has become a partner in policy-making. . . . [T]he American Israel Public Affairs Committee is so pervasive at the White House as well as in Congress that it is impossible to ascertain where lobby pressure ends and independent presidential thinking begins."[7]

FALLACY

"Another myth pertained to the extent of [AIPAC's] influence and its alleged invincibility."
—*I. L. Kenen, a founder of AIPAC, 1981*[8]

FACT

AIPAC reached a new height of power and influence during the Reagan years. Its power had grown so great that veteran correspondent Hedrick Smith reported in *The New York Times* that it was a "superlobby. . . . AIPAC gained so much political muscle that by 1985, AIPAC and its allies could force President Reagan to renege on an arms deal he had promised [Jordan's] King Hussein. By 1986, the pro-Israel lobby could stop Reagan from making another jet-fighter deal with Saudi Arabia; and Secretary of State George Shultz had to sit down with AIPAC's executive director—not congressional leaders—to find out what level of arms sales to the Saudis AIPAC would tolerate."[9]

AIPAC so dominated the Reagan administration that AIPAC Executive Director Thomas A. Dine reported at AIPAC's twenty-seventh annual policy conference in 1986 that relations had never been better between the United States and Israel—and, implicitly, better for AIPAC.[10] Dine said that in the process of this development "a whole new constituency of support for Israel is being built in precisely the area where we are weakest—among government officials in the state, defense and treasury departments, in the CIA, in science, trade, agriculture and other agencies."

He added that President Reagan and Secretary of State Shultz were among Israel's two best friends and were going to "leave a legacy that will be important to Israel's security for decades to come." Shultz, he said, had vowed to him to "build institutional arrangements so that eight years from now, if there is a secretary of state who is not positive about Israel, he will not be able to overcome the bureaucratic relationship between Israel and the U.S. that we have established."[11]

Later in 1986, former AIPAC staffer Richard B. Straus wrote in *The Washington Post* that "American Middle East policy has shifted so dramatically in favor of Israel" that now it could only be described as "a revolution." He quoted Dine as saying the special relationship "is a deep, broad-based partnership progressing day-by-day toward a full-fledged diplomatic and military alliance." Straus added: "State Department Arabists acknowledge that Arab interests hardly get a hearing today in Washington. 'We used to have a two-track policy,' says one former State Department official. 'Now only Israel's interests are considered.'"[12]

In fact, relations became so close during the Reagan administration that it was not unusual for high-ranking State Department officials and AIPAC's Dine to privately discuss Middle East policy issues and how to handle them in Congress.[13] Dine even received a personal telephone call from President Reagan thanking him personally for AIPAC's support in gaining congressional approval for keeping U.S. Marines in Lebanon in 1983.[14] AIPAC was informed twelve hours before Assistant Secretary of State for Near Eastern Affairs Richard Murphy learned about the Reagan administration's 1984 decision to drop arms sales to Jordan and Saudi Arabia.[15]

The relationship cooled off during the Bush administration, but not entirely. Secretary of State James A. Baker III called Dine to plead for his help during the administration's effort to convince Israel to delay its demand for $10 billion in loan guarantees in 1991. Dine rejected the request.[16]

"No justification exists for selling the Saudis the most sophisticated aircraft in the American arsenal."

—*AIPAC, 1989*[17]

FACT

Saudi Arabia deserves whatever it needs to defend itself. The value of America's close special relationship with that kingdom, developed over half a century, is proven every day as Americans consume oil. Saudi Arabia, a major producer and price-setter of oil, is also a strategic ally, as was dramatically demonstrated in 1990–1991 when American troops and aircraft used Saudi—not Israeli—territory to force Iraq out of Kuwait. Another little-noted advantage to selling weapons to Saudi Arabia is that Riyadh pays cash, unlike Israel, which receives U.S. weapons without cost—compliments of the American taxpayer.

Despite the U.S. interest in helping Saudi Arabia provide for its own defense, Israel and its supporters have consistently opposed weapons sales to the kingdom. Such opposition to the proliferation of weapons would make sense if Washington had a coherent arms control program that applied to everyone. But given Israel's repeated aggressions and its unlimited demand on U.S. weapons supplies, it is the height of hypocrisy for Israel to challenge arms sales to Saudi Arabia and other Arab states at the same time that it is being gorged with American weaponry.

The biggest, longest, and harshest fight between AIPAC and the White House over arms sales came in 1981 when President Reagan decided to sell for $8.5 billion five sophisticated AWACS (airborne warning and control system) planes to Saudi Arabia.[18] AIPAC and Israel applied pressure on congressional representatives and senators to defeat the deal. They were nearly successful. It was only after a lengthy and difficult fight that Reagan finally prevailed with a Senate vote of 52 to

48. In doing so he reminded the lawmakers and the country that "it is not the business of other countries to make American foreign policy."[19]

At the end, one observer described the fight as "among the most intense [lobbying efforts] ever experienced by Congress."[20] But while the administration had won the battle, Israel and AIPAC had made a potent point: if the administration bucked Israel's wishes, it would have to pay dearly in time, effort, and, ultimately, political prestige. For legislators, its message was equally grim. As Professor Cheryl A. Rubenberg, a perceptive critic of U.S.-Israeli relations, noted: "[T]hereafter how a senator voted on this issue became the most important factor in the [Israeli] lobby's determination of an individual's 'friendship' toward Israel. Those who were labeled 'unfriendly' faced serious problems at reelection."[21]

Indeed, it was largely because of his support for the AWACS sale that highly respected Republican Senator Charles Percy was defeated in 1984. After the election, Thomas Dine of AIPAC declared: "All the Jews in America, from coast to coast, gathered to oust Percy. And American politicians—those who hold public positions now, and those who aspire—got the message."[22]

Since the AWACS defeat, AIPAC has completely overhauled its operation and expanded greatly. Hedrick Smith reported in *The New York Times* that "its budget shot up eight-fold [to $6.1 million] in nine years, its membership multiplied from nine thousand households in 1978 to fifty-five thousand in 1987, its staff grew from twenty-five to eighty-five. By the mid-eighties, its leadership was steering roughly $4 million in campaign contributions to friendly candidates and punishing political foes."[23]

As Dine later said: "The AWACS fight was the bench mark. We lost the vote but won the issue."[24]

FALLACY

"When I needed information on the Middle East, it was reassuring to know that I could depend on AIPAC for professional and reliable assistance."
    —Senator Frank Church, Democrat of Idaho, 1982[25]

FACT

AIPAC has the fastest handout in Washington. Any representative or senator who expresses any desire to know anything about the Middle East is immediately flooded with "position papers" by AIPAC.

As former Democratic senator Charles Mathias of Maryland wrote: "When an issue of importance to Israel comes before Congress, AIPAC promptly and unfailingly provides all members with data and documentation, supplemented, as circumstances dictate, with telephone calls and personal visits. Beyond that, signs of hesitation or opposition on the part of a Senator or Representative can usually be relied on to call forth large numbers of letters and telegrams, or visits and phone calls from influential constituents."[26]

The problem with depending on AIPAC for information is that the information is certain to contain only Israel's point of view. Its publications tend to such scholarly titles as *A US-Israel Free Trade Area: How Both Sides Gain*, and they are filled with footnotes and citations to academic works. But no reader can escape the fact that they are strictly aimed at promoting Israeli interests.

AIPAC also oversees the *Near East Report*, a weekly newsletter that goes to about sixty thousand persons and is sent free to all members of Congress, high-ranking government officials, academics, and many media representatives. Although the newsletter is legally separate from AIPAC, it was founded by Sy Kenen, one of AIPAC's founders, and it strictly follows Israel's policy line. It regularly prints stories about legislators' voting patterns, thereby alerting lawmakers that their votes are being noted, and the disposition of new legislation affecting Israel.

The newsletter staff also distributes a supplement called *Myths and Facts*, which purports to dispel such "myths" about the Arab-Israeli conflict as the plight of the Palestinian refugees. The supplement is widely distributed on campuses as a "study aid" and to Israel's many friends in Congress and the media.

AIPAC does not limit its activities to legitimate propaganda. In 1974 it joined with the American Jewish Committee and other Jewish groups to form a "truth squad" to counter what it called pro-Arab propaganda. According to investigative reporter Robert I. Friedman, the truth squad turned into "a kind of Jewish thought police. Investigators—sometimes overzealous Jewish college students, sometimes sources with access to U.S. intelligence agencies—were used to ferret out critics of Israel, Jew or Gentile, wherever they might be. . . . Their speeches and writings were monitored, as were, in some cases, their other professional activities. And they were often smeared with charges of anti-Semitism or with the pernicious label of self-hating Jew. The intention was to stifle debate on the Middle East within the Jewish community, the media and academia, for fear that criticism of any kind would weaken the Jewish state."[27]

It was only a small step from truth squad to blacklist. In 1983, AIPAC published *The Campaign to Discredit Israel*. AIPAC Executive Director Thomas Dine wrote in the preface that the pamphlet was issued as a way to provide a "more complete and convenient analysis" of anti-Israel activity. Despite his words, the pamphlet was nothing more than an old-fashioned blacklist.

The Campaign to Discredit Israel listed such Americans as George Ball, a former under secretary of state who has been critical of Israel, and Alfred Lilienthal, an anti-Zionist Jew who as early as 1954 had written a book warning of the U.S.-Israeli relationship: *What Price Israel?* Altogether, the pamphlet listed twenty-one organizations and thirty-nine individuals "who are active in the effort to weaken the bonds between the United States and Israel, who seek to enhance U.S.-Arab relations at the expense of Israel, or who perform paid services to Arab governments pursuing these goals."[28] The Anti-Defamation League of B'nai B'rith also published its own blacklist called *Arab Propaganda in America: Vehicles and Voices*.

Scholar Cheryl Rubenberg charged that both pamphlets employed "techniques reminiscent of the McCarthy era . . . smear[ing] their opposition with the label 'pro-PLO.'"[29] With the reaction to the blacklists so negative, AIPAC dropped plans to publish an annual updated version. Instead, AIPAC took its efforts underground. It continued monitoring "anti-Israel" individuals and groups, but disseminated the results secretly. According to Gregory D. Slabodkin, a young scholar who was once an AIPAC researcher: "To date, revelations about AIPAC's blacklisting and smear tactics have barely scratched the surface of the pro-Israel lobby's secret activities. . . . AIPAC operates a covert section within its research department that monitors and keeps files on politicians, journalists, academics, Arab-American activists, Jewish liberals, and others it labels 'anti-Jewish.' AIPAC selects information from these files and secretly circulates lists of the 'guilty,' together with their alleged political misdeeds, buttressed by their statements, often totally out of context."[30]

For instance, the secret research department provided Steve Emerson, a pro-Israel investigative reporter for Cable News Network, with information on *Nation* columnist Alexander Cockburn, a frequent critic of Israel, and also gave *The Wall Street Journal* derogatory information about Georgia banker Bert Lance and Arab banking interests. Other targets have included Jewish liberals such as Woody Allen, Richard Dreyfuss, Rita Hauser, and Barbra Streisand.[31]

AIPAC's new blacklist is a weekly publication called *Activities* devoted to naming individuals and organizations critical of Israel. AIPAC tries to hide its connection with *Activities*, warning readers to use its material "subject only to the proviso that AIPAC not be attributed as its source." *Activities* is distributed to AIPAC's Washington and regional staff, the major Jewish organizational leaders, Jewish Federations and Community Relations Councils nationwide, pro-Israel activists, and academics, as well as the Israeli embassy and selected Israelis.

AIPAC's stealth section is currently headed by Michael Lewis, son of Princeton University Orientalist Bernard Lewis. Michael Lewis has said of *Activities*: "Ultimately, of all the information disseminated from AIPAC, *Activities* may well be the most eagerly sought, read and used to good advantage."[32]

According to Slabodkin, such "good advantage" included a smear campaign to try to paint anti-Israel activists as practitioners of the "new anti-Semitism"—criticism of Israel's policies. Slabodkin revealed that Lewis keeps locked up in his office "literally hundreds and hundreds of such files on people and organizations that AIPAC deems 'anti-Israel.' Among politicians upon whom such files exist are former Chief of Staff John Sununu, former Reagan administration Secretaries of Defense Caspar Weinberger and Frank Carlucci, former President Jimmy Carter and former Democratic presidential candidate George McGovern, Senate Minority Leader Robert Dole, Republican Senator John Chafee, House Majority Whip David Bonior, and Democratic Representatives John Conyers, John Dingell, Mervyn Dymally, Mary Rose Oakar, Nick Joe Rahall, James Traficant, Jr., and many others."

Nor are politicians the only ones named in Lewis's collection of dossiers. Members of the media, entertainers, and academics are also listed in AIPAC's secret files as among the enemies of Israel—even Peggy Say, sister of former hostage Terry Anderson.

FALLACY

"We have not abandoned our concerns for the best America or best world while engaged in efforts on behalf of a secure Israel."

—Hyman Bookbinder, former representative of the American Jewish Committee, 1987[33]

While Jewish activists address issues as varied as human rights and poverty around the globe, Israel is the one and only issue for AIPAC and the pro-Israel political action committees that distribute money. This has been true since the emergence in the 1950s of organized lobbying in behalf of Israel. As AIPAC President David Steiner said in 1992: "I believe in political loyalty, and if someone has been good for Israel, no matter who—if my brother would run against them—I would support them because they'd been good to Israel."[34]

President Richard Nixon noted in his memoirs: "One of the main problems I faced . . . was the unyielding and shortsighted pro-Israeli attitude in large and influential segments of the American Jewish community, Congress, the media and in intellectual and cultural circles. In the quarter century since the end of World War II this attitude had become so deeply ingrained that many saw the corollary of not being pro-Israel as being anti-Israeli, or even anti-Semitic. I tried unsuccessfully to convince them that this was not the case."[35]

A similar complaint was registered as early as 1956 by Secretary of State John Foster Dulles. He complained to friends: "I am aware how almost impossible it is in this country to carry out a foreign policy [in the Middle East] not approved by the Jews. [Former Secretary of State George] Marshall and [former Defense Secretary James] Forrestal learned that." Dulles later remarked about the "terrific control the Jews have over the news media and the barrage which the Jews have built up on congressmen. . . . I am very much concerned over the fact that the Jewish influence here is completely dominating the scene and making it almost impossible to get Congress to do anything they don't approve of. The Israeli Embassy is practically dictating to the Congress through influential Jewish people in the country."[36]

Such influence is not accidental. AIPAC's forerunner, the American Zionist Committee for Public Affairs, first polled all 750 candidates for the House and Senate in 1954. The only question asked of each candidate was his or her views on Israel and the Middle East.[37] That has continued to be the sole criterion for determining AIPAC's attitude toward candidates. AIPAC Executive Director Thomas Dine is proud of the focus on Israel. He has said: "We are single-minded about being single issue."[38]

Such single-mindedness explains AIPAC's astonishing success in helping strong supporters of Israel get elected to Congress. It stems largely from its targeting of vast sums of campaign money to politicians voicing support for Israel. Although AIPAC cannot legally give money to candidates, many pro-Israel political action committees take their lead from AIPAC's rating of candidates and funnel their funds accordingly.

A 1991 study by the Center for Responsive Politics showed that pro-Israel political action committees donated $4 million to congressional candidates in the 1990 elections, and individual contributors to the PACs also contributed $3.6 million to the same candidates. All the recipients were strong supporters of Israel. Sixteen Senate incumbents received more than $100,000 each from the two sources; among the top recipients were Carl Levin (Democrat of Michigan), $563,073; Paul Simon (Democrat of Illinois), $449,417; Tom Harkin (Democrat of Iowa), $344,650; Claiborne Pell (Democrat of Rhode Island), $225,811; and Mitch McConnell (Republican of Kentucky), $213, 900. The top House recipients were Mel Levine (Democrat of California), $89,779; Sidney R. Yates (Democrat of Illinois), $72,250; David R. Obey (Democrat of Wisconsin), $57,949; Ron Wyden (Democrat of Oregon), $53,340; and Wayne Owens (Democrat of Utah), $52,450.[39]

The Wall Street Journal reported that eighty pro-Israeli PACs spent $6,931,728 in the 1986 elections, making them the largest contributors of narrow-issue PACs in the country. Second were realtor PACs at $6,290,108, followed by the American Medical Association at $5,702,133.[40] Another study showed that senators who voted for pro-Israel legislation in 1985–1986 received an average of $54,223 from pro-Israel PACs; those who voted the other way averaged $166. Senators elected or reelected in 1986 received $1.9

million from pro-Israel PACs, nearly three times as much as they raised from PACs of all other ideological groups.[41]

As author Edward Tivnan has written: "Few ambitious American politicians could even dream of higher office without the prospect of Jewish money."[42]

Vice President Dan Quayle declared: "As Americans you have every right to voice your support for the State of Israel. . . . [A]ccess to the political process is not a privilege. It is a right."[43] But in Israel's case, that right sometimes leads to startling consequences.

During the 1973 war, there occurred a tense encounter between Admiral Thomas Moorer, chairman of the Joint Chiefs of Staff, and Israeli military attaché Mordecai Gur. Gur demanded that the United States give Israel warplanes equipped with the Maverick air-to-land antitank missile. Moorer explained that the United States had only one squadron of such planes and that Congress "would raise hell" if it was given away. Moorer recalls: "Gur told me, 'You get the airplanes; I'll take care of Congress.'" Moorer adds: "And he did. I've never seen a President—I don't care who he is—stand up to them [the Israelis]. It just boggles your mind. They always get what they want."[44]

Another example occurred in the same war when Israel felt the United States was not providing it with adequate supplies. Israel's ambassador to the United States, Simcha Dinitz, threatened Secretary of State Henry Kissinger that "if a massive American airlift to Israel does not start immediately then I'll know that the United States is reneging on its promises and its policy, and we will have to draw very serious conclusions from all this." The Kalb brothers, who interviewed Dinitz extensively for their biography of Kissinger, observed of this remark: "Dinitz did not have to translate his message. Kissinger quickly understood that the Israelis would soon 'go public' and that an upsurge of pro-Israeli sentiment could have a disastrous impact upon an already weakened administration."[45]

Another instance of intimidation involved President Carter and Israeli Foreign Minister Moshe Dayan. During a 1977 meeting on the peace process, Carter suddenly changed the subject and said: "Let's talk politics." Carter admitted he was in political trouble with Congress and Jewish Americans. This naive admission put in Dayan's hands a significant negotiating advantage. Dayan made the most of the blunder. He laid down to President Carter a number of conditions for agreeing to peace with Egypt: there should be no American pressure to impose a settlement, no cut in economic and military aid to Israel, and, finally, a statement by the United States that Israel does not have to return to the 1967 boundaries. If these conditions were embraced by Carter, then "Dayan could tell the American Jews that there was an agreement and they would be happy." Dayan added: "But if he was obliged to say that Israel would have to deal with the PLO on a Palestinian state, then there would be screaming in the United States and Israel."[46] This verged on blackmail, in the opinion of some U.S. diplomats, but Carter did not protest beyond making the mild observation that a confrontation would not be good for Israel either.[47]

In 1972, Yitzhak Rabin did not hesitate to give his public endorsement to Richard Nixon's reelection campaign while Rabin served as Israel's ambassador in Washington. In an interview on Israeli national radio, Rabin said: "While we appreciate the support in the form of words which we are getting from one camp, we must prefer the support in the form of deeds which we are getting from the other."[48] *The Washington Post* was so offended by what it called Rabin's meddling in American domestic politics that it harshly criticized Rabin in an editorial titled "The Undiplomatic Diplomat."[49]

At AIPAC's 1992 meeting, Executive Director Dine directly challenged President Bush for his remarks the previous September criticizing AIPAC's lobbying efforts for $10 billion in loan guarantees to Israel. Dine claimed that Bush had "questioned the right of American citizens . . . to lobby on this issue. September 12, 1991, will be a day that lives in infamy for the American pro-Israel community. Like the Indian elephant, we shall not forget. We are not going away. We are here. And we will not be intimidated." Dine said that the $10 billion loan guarantee issue was not over: "We cannot and will not give up until we succeed. Ultimately, we will succeed in securing these guarantees. Our work just begins. We need to find new friends to bring to Congress."[50]

During 1992 AIPAC suffered a series of heavy blows. In August Yitzhak Rabin, newly installed as Israeli prime minister, publicly rebuked the organization. Eager to smooth the way for Bush's expected approval of the $10 billion in U.S. loan guarantees for Israel and at the same time strengthen his personal control of U.S.-Israeli relations, Rabin directed harsh words at the AIPAC leaders: "You have failed at everything. You waged lost battles. You created too much antagonism." In November AIPAC President David Steiner resigned when newspapers publicized his claims of strong lobby influence within the staff of President-elect Clinton.[51] During the year's primary and general elections, several of the lobby's most dependable and vocal supporters were defeated, chief among them Senator Robert W. Kasten, Jr., and Representatives Stephen J. Solarz of New York, Mel Levine of California, and Lawrence J. Smith of Florida.

Despite the setbacks, predictions of a "meltdown" at AIPAC are unfounded.[52] With an annual budget of $15 million and more than 55,000 energized supporters, many of them skilled at political influence, the lobby's robust survival is assured.

FOURTEEN

U.S. AID TO ISRAEL

Each year, U.S. aid to Israel exceeds that given to any other country. Since 1987 direct economic and military aid has annually totaled $3 billion or more. In addition, financial arrangements worked out solely for Israel bring the total to about $5 billion a year. This does not include such generous programs as the $10 billion loan guarantee granted Israel in 1992.[1] U.S. law provides for the termination of all aid, economic and military, to any nation that develops nuclear weapons or "engages in a consistent pattern of gross violations of internationally recognized human rights." For years the U.S. government has been aware of Israel's development of a nuclear arsenal and its persistent human rights violations. But no president or Congress has ever taken steps to terminate aid, as required by law, or even reduce it.[2]

FALLACY

"Comparatively speaking, aid to Israel is a bargain."
—*AIPAC, 1983*[3]

FACT

Between 1949 and the end of 1991, the U.S. government provided Israel with $53 billion in aid and special benefits. That is equal to 13 percent of all U.S. economic and military aid given worldwide during that period. From the 1979 Egyptian-Israeli peace treaty through 1991, the amount totaled $40.1 billion, equal to 21.5 percent of all U.S. aid, including all multilateral as well as all bilateral aid.[4]

Considering that Israel is a nation of little more than five million people, these figures are grossly out of proportion to U.S. aid to other countries, or even to other regions of the world. As scholar Cheryl Rubenberg observes: "The magnitude of U.S. support for Israel—militarily, politically, economically, and diplomatically—goes beyond any traditional relationship between states in the international system."[5]

Yet these figures barely begin to tell the whole story of U.S. aid to Israel. Some of the less known details were revealed for the first time in early 1992 on the Senate floor by the former majority leader Democratic Senator Robert Byrd of West Virginia. He said on the Senate floor: "We have poured foreign aid into Israel for decades at rates and terms given to no other nation on earth. And we are the only nation to have done so. Our European allies provided, by comparison, nearly nothing."

His well-researched speech received almost no attention in the media. Here are a few of Byrd's revelations:[6]

■ "Israel's assistance for fiscal year 1979 was $4.9 billion, almost $5 billion; 1980 saw the aid level drop back to just over $2.1 billion, but it has increased steadily since then to $3.7 billion in 1991. In 1985, we responded to an economic crisis in Israel by converting all military and economic support assistance to cash grants instead of loans, and by passing a $1.5 billion supplemental aid package bringing the total appropriated in 1985 to $4.1 billion in grants."

■ "Nor have we forgotten Israel in times of crisis. . . . [I]n 1990, the United States responded to the increased immigration of Soviet and Ethiopian Jews by providing $400 million in housing loan guarantees. The United States also rushed to provide additional assistance during the Persian Gulf war."

▌ "Additionally, items of assistance or special treatment that were contained in fiscal years 1991 and 1992 legislation are: Continued participation in the American Schools and Hospitals Grant Program, representing $2.7 million for 1991; $7 million for Arab-Israeli cooperative programs, of which approximately half is spent in Israel; $42 million for joint research and development on the Arrow antitactical ballistic missile follow-on program. This amount increased to $60 million in the fiscal year 1992 Defense Appropriations Act; also, authority to use up to $475 million of its military aid in Israel instead of spending it in the United States . . . additionally a major new petroleum reserve of 4.5 million barrels, worth $180 million, which is available for Israel's use in the case of an emergency; furthermore, $15 million to improve military facilities at the Israeli port of Haifa in 1991 and another $2 million in 1992 to study the costs of further improving the facilities to allow for full-scale maintenance and support of an aircraft carrier battle group; in addition thereto, specific inclusion in the Overseas Workload Program, allowing Israel to bid on contracts for the repair, maintenance, or overhaul of United States equipment overseas; and additionally $1 million in investment insurance in Israel, provided by the Overseas Private Investment Corporation."

▌ "Other, earlier legislative initiatives that provide continuing benefits to Israel include: Immediate transfer each year of the $1.2 billion Economic Support Fund grant and the $1.89 billion military assistance grant. Thus, our grants to Israel are turned into interest bearing assets for Israel while our own budget deficit is increased, resulting in higher interest charges to us. This immediate transfer created approximately $86 million in interest income for Israel in fiscal year 1991. Such an arrangement has been in place for the Economic Support Fund since 1982 and was extended to military aid in fiscal year 1991 and applies to no other country; moreover, debt restructuring that took place in the late 1980s allowed Israel to lower interest payments by an estimated $150 million annually; additionally, the fair pricing initiative within the Foreign Military Sales Program that allows Israel to avoid certain administrative fees normally charged on foreign military sales. This benefit saved Israel an estimated $60 million in 1991."

▌"Since 1984, Israel has been allowed to use a portion of its foreign military financing credits for procurement of Israeli-made military items. Unlike other countries that receive United States military assistance, Israel does not have to spend all of those funds to purchase United States equipment. In 1991, of a $1.8 billion military assistance grant, we allowed Israel to use $475 million to buy the output of its own defense industry instead of American-made products. Moreover, Israel was allowed to spend an additional $150 million of the 1991 grant for its own research and development in the United States. We also have provided $126 million in funding for the development of the Arrow antimissile defense system in Israel, with another $60 million appropriated for the Arrow follow-on in fiscal year 1992, and the prospect of several hundred million more dollars in the future."

FALLACY

"A significant portion of the U.S. aid to Israel has been in the form of loans paid with interest, and Israel, unlike many other nations, pays its debts—and on time."

—AIPAC, 1989[7]

FACT

For years Israel has paid its entire debt service on loans from the United States with funds granted from the U.S. Treasury.

Since 1985 all U.S. aid to Israel has been a grant, meaning that not a penny of it has to be repaid. When Israel pays interest and principal on loans given before 1985, it does so with U.S. tax dollars. This curious process began in 1984 when Democratic Senator Alan Cranston of California sponsored what became known as the Cranston amendment. It stipulates that economic aid to Israel each year will be at least equal to its annual repayments (principal and interest) of its debt to the United States.[8] In the wry words of then Secretary of State James A. Baker III in testimony before the Senate in 1992, the Cranston amendment provided that "we can always pay ourselves back with the money that we appropriate for Israel to do so."[9]

The effect of this amendment is to guarantee that Israel will always receive enough U.S. aid to cover its debt obligations. In actual practice, Congress always awards Israel funds far in excess of these obligations. No other country enjoys such an arrangement.

FALLACY

"Many aspects of U.S. policy favored the Arabs."
—AIPAC, 1989[10]

FACT

U.S. aid to Arab states, except for Egypt, is small, and most is in the form of repayable loans. Substantial aid to Egypt began as a reward when that government concluded its 1979 peace agreement with Israel. Dispersal of the aid is carefully monitored and Egypt must account for its use on specific projects.

Israel, by contrast, receives all of its economic aid as a contribution that goes directly into its general budget without any accountability at all. It is free to use it as it pleases. America's aid to Israel, moreover, extends well beyond economic assistance. Washington has made Israel a "strategic ally," designated it a non-NATO ally, granted it free trade status, and allowed it to participate in the most advanced technical research in the U.S. Strategic Defense Initiative. Nor is that the end of it. The United States protects Israel's diplomatic interests around the world and particularly at the United Nations. Only public warnings that the United States would refuse to pay its share of UN costs has kept the rest of the nations from expelling Israel from the world body as "not a peace-loving state."[11] And only the repeated use in recent years of the once rare U.S. veto has protected Israel from stiff UN sanctions aimed at making it comply with Security Council resolutions.[12]

FIFTEEN

LOAN GUARANTEES FOR ISRAEL

One of Israel's most bitter struggles with the United States arose over its demand in 1991 for $10 billion in loan guarantees to expand housing and other infrastructure for new immigrants. Because of its poor credit rating, Israel could not find lenders at attractive rates without U.S. guarantees.[1] The confrontation lasted more than a year, with President Bush insisting that construction of all Jewish housing in the occupied territories must stop. Prime Minister Yitzhak Shamir rejected such linkage. After Yitzhak Rabin came to power in June 1992, Bush essentially dropped any linkage. Congress approved the guarantees on October 1, 1992.

FALLACY

"The loan guarantees to Israel are humanitarian assistance at no cost to American taxpayers."
—Senator Robert W. Kasten, Jr.,
Republican of Wisconsin, 1992[2]

The congressional bill authorizing $10 billion in loan guarantees to Israel specifically says that Israel will pay for all costs of administration and other expenses incurred by the guarantees. However, another provision of the bill says that Israel could pay these costs with funds it receives as economic aid from the United States.[3] The message is that ultimately, regardless from which budget it comes, the American taxpayer will pay for the guarantees, including "scoring costs," whatever the final total.

Moreover, the U.S. government by law must "set aside" a certain amount of its own budget to offset possible default by any borrower receiving U.S. guarantees. In the case of Israel's guarantees, the amount of the offset could range from several million dollars to more than $800 million. The actual amount depends on how the risk factor of default is finally calculated.[4] American taxpayers would be required to cover all defaults.

Whatever the amount, the money set aside to cover the risk of the loan guarantees will come from the unified international, defense, and domestic discretionary budget. That means it will compete with domestic and defense spending as well as international projects.

The guarantees, moreover, include favorable features for Israel not usually part of such arrangements. This includes Congress's decision to guarantee 100 percent of Israel's loans and interest payments.[5] The February 11, 1993, issue of *Washington Jewish Week* announced that the loan guarantees will serve purposes in Israel that are strikingly nonhumanitarian: "investing in infastructure, bolstering foreign currency reserves, and making cheap loans available to the business community."

FALLACY

"Never has there been such an outright and blatant exploitation of humanitarian aid in order to force Israel to adopt a particular path."

—*Yitzhak Shamir, Israeli prime minister, 1992*[6]

FACT

It was not primarily humanitarian aid that Israel was seeking under Prime Minister Yitzhak Shamir's demand for gaining U.S. loan guarantees. It was mainly money to finance, directly or indirectly, its illegal settlements in the occupied territories and support its failing socialist economy. The Bush administration repeatedly made clear that it was willing to grant the guarantees to house Soviet Jews immigrating to Israel—if Israel halted construction of settlements in the occupied territories. This Shamir refused to do.

Though many Jewish Americans opposed Bush's insistence on linkage, it was notable that a number of influential Jewish spokespersons did not. One was Michael Lerner, Jewish editor of *Tikkun*, a liberal magazine, who wrote: "This is the fault of Shamir, not Bush. . . . Shamir is trying to create facts on the West Bank that would make a land for peace exchange impossible. Now he is demanding that the United States give him the money to subvert American policy. What kind of chutzpah is that?"[7]

Two Israeli journalists sarcastically commented on Shamir's arrogance in seeking the guarantees: "Our message to the Americans is true-to-type Israeli: 'Give us money and have confidence in us! Everything will be OK. And besides, why should you worry? What does $10 billion really matter between friends?' As long as the Americans so desire, they will continue to swallow all deceptions."[8]

Shamir also asserted that the United States had a "moral obligation" to give Israel loan guarantees.[9] Such a contention has an ironic twist, since it was Israel's own policies that had resulted in so many Soviet Jews moving to Israel in the first place. For years Israel had pressed the United States to limit its acceptance of Soviet Jewish immigrants so they would go instead to Israel.[10] The reason for Israel's concern was that as many as 91 percent of the Jews leaving the Soviet Union were going to countries other than Israel in 1988; the previous year the figure had been 70 percent, and Israelis feared the trend would soon be 100 percent.[11]

Washington finally acceded to Israel's wishes and on October 1, 1989, restricted immigration of Soviet Jews to America to 50,000 a year. This had the effect of forcing most Jews leaving the Soviet Union to go to Israel, which was exactly what the Israelis sought.[12]

Nonetheless, Israel's failure to provide jobs and adequate plans to accommodate the new immigrants significantly reduced early predictions that a million Soviets would arrive in Israel in three to five years. Between September 1989, when the wave of immigration began, and the end of 1991, a total of 328,187 arrived.[13] In January 1992 the monthly figure dropped to 6,237, the lowest total in two years.[14] By May 1992 it declined to 3,360, and thousands were reported returning in disillusionment to the former Soviet Union.[15] Cato Institute scholar Sheldon L. Richman estimated in August 1992 that "outflow exceeds immigration . . . [because] almost half the immigrants from the former Soviet Union are unemployed."[16]

Thus the early estimates of immigration on which the $10 billion loan guarantees were based appear to be off by at least half. It seems likely that less than half a million Soviet Jews will have immigrated to Israel by 1994. On that basis the U.S. guarantee—if justified at all, which I question—should have been for no more than $5 billion.

In the end Israel could not do without U.S. loan guarantees. Israeli voters confirmed this by voting out of office Israeli Prime Minister Yitzhak Shamir after his defiance of President Bush held up the guarantees. Despite frequent statements by Israeli officials that they really did not need America's help, Israel did not have the resources to continue settling the occupied territories at an unprecedented rate without U.S. aid. Nor did Shamir have the support he needed among Israelis to be reelected in 1992.

Nonetheless, Shamir had tried everything. The Israeli Hebrew daily *Hadashot* reported that major Jewish organizations in America made an attempt to find loan guarantors among wealthy Jewish Americans after the Bush administration insisted on a settlement freeze. However, these Jewish Americans would not accept Israel as a credit risk. *Hadashot* reported that the Jewish group "approached twenty Jewish billionaires in the U.S. selected from the list of the 500 richest persons in the world, asking them to guarantee Israel's loans for Soviet immigrant absorption. All twenty, who support Israel politically, flatly refused. They claimed that as businessmen motivated solely by considerations of profitability, they could not guarantee loans to a state considered such a risk case in respect to its repayment ability."[17]

FALLACY

"I believe that the executive branch's position [of linking loan guarantees to an Israeli settlement freeze] is especially troublesome with the Mideast peace talks underway, because it has the consequence of undermining the position of the U.S. as an honest broker."

—*Senator Arlen Specter,*
Republican of Pennsylvania, 1992[18]

FACT

The fact is that by granting the loan guarantees Congress and the Bush administration proved again that the United States basically is not an honest broker in the Middle East. Since Israel's 1967 occupation of Arab lands, U.S. policy—along with that of the rest of the world—has officially been to oppose Jewish settlements in the occupied territories, including Arab East Jerusalem. Yet Congress has continued to finance Israel with lavish aid. Israel routinely promises not to use this aid in the occupied territories, but it just as routinely breaks its promise as Washington turns a blind eye.[19] There is no way Israel could continue its colonization of the occupied territories without U.S. aid.

FALLACY

"Under existing guidelines, no U.S. foreign assistance to Israel can be used beyond Israel's pre-1967 borders. Israel strictly adheres to these guidelines and each year provides a full, detailed report on the expenditure of all U.S. assistance."

—AIPAC, 1992[20]

FACT

The Bush administration found that promises by Israel under Likud Prime Minister Yitzhak Shamir were not reliable. This became clear after the White House released $400 million in loan guarantees in 1991 with the Israeli promise that it would not use the money in the occupied territories. But Israel reneged.

A 1992 report by the General Accounting Office on Israel's pledges found that Israel had failed to provide any of the promised information on government spending in the occupied territories. The report concluded: "We found that the $400 million guaranty program had no discernible effect on Israel's housing policies and did not influence the Israeli government's decisions on where to build new housing or on how much settlement activity to undertake in the occupied territories. The primary effect of the loan guaranty was to give the Israeli government access to borrowed funds at a lower interest rate."[21]

The study also found wide discrepancies between Israeli and State Department figures on the number of new immigrants moving into the occupied territories. It noted that Israeli officials estimated that 1,500 of the new immigrants who had entered the country in 1990 had chosen to live in the territories. However, it said, "The State Department's estimate is much higher; the Department believes that about 8,800 of the 185,000 Soviet immigrants who entered Israel in 1990 live in the occupied territories. We were unable to reconcile this disparity."[22]

Democratic Senator of West Virginia Robert C. Byrd, chair of the Senate Appropriations Committee, said that Israel's pledges not to use the money in the occupied territories were like "an exercise in building a paper dam. The money that Israel borrowed under the guarantee program went straight into the Israeli treasury and immediately lost its identity."[23] Byrd later added: "Unfortunately, this linkage was not enough to influence Israeli policy in any way. . . . Indeed, the number of settlers in the occupied territories has risen from 75,000 in 1989 to 104,000 in 1991."[24]

At the beginning of 1992 there were 242,000 Jews living in Arab territory occupied in 1967, 129,000 Jews in Arab East Jerusalem, 97,000 in 180 settlements in the West Bank, 14,000 in 20 settlements in the Golan Heights, and 5,000 in 16 settlements in the Gaza Strip. The Palestinian population numbered 1 million in the West Bank, 750,000 in the Gaza Strip, and 150,000 in East Jerusalem. In addition, there were 15,000 Syrians in the Golan Heights. Ariel Sharon, Shamir's hawkish housing minister, said in late 1991 that his current building plans envisioned construction of units in the occupied territories to accommodate between 40,000 and 120,000 more Jewish settlers annually for the next three years.[25]

On January 22, 1992, a study by Israel's Peace Now group showed that Israel had started 13,650 housing units in the occupied territories in 1991 at a cost of $1 billion. The new units represented 65 percent growth in one year of all the units established over the previous twenty-three years in the territories.[26] The figures did not include more than 10,000 units under construction in Arab East Jerusalem or on the Golan Heights.[27]

In the words of *Washington Post* correspondent Jackson Diehl in early 1992: "In the last 18 months, [Prime Minister

Yitzhak] Shamir's government has launched the biggest housing construction campaign in the 24-year history of its rule of the territories."[28] Diehl added: "Shamir's government has appeared to pursue a policy of obscuring the true scale and cost of its campaign."[29]

In a speech in the Senate, Senator Byrd said the total cost of Israel's settlement program in 1991 in the occupied territories, including Arab East Jerusalem, totaled $3 billion.[30]

Francis A. Boyle, an expert in international law, argues that the loan guarantees aid and abet Israel in its violation of Palestinian rights.

The $10 billion in new loan guarantees perpetuates America's collusion in Israel's occupation. Although the authorizing bill stipulates that the loans will not be used outside the frontiers of pre–June 5, 1967 Israel, this provision is meaningless. Prime Minister Yitzhak Rabin publicly declared that Israel would permit the completion of some 11,000 uncompleted housing units on the West Bank and would not restrict new Jewish housing construction in Arab East Jerusalem or at new "security settlements" in the Jordan Valley and the Golan Heights.[31] He said the Israeli government would reserve the right to decide which settlements are necessary for "security." This policy lets Israel continue the expansion of Jewish housing in the occupied territories with no serious limitation. As testament to the influence of pro-Israel interests, the Rabin announcement elicited no protest from either end of Pennsylvania Avenue and little from the countryside.

SIXTEEN

ISRAEL'S SPYING ON AMERICA

Israel has routinely spied on the United States for decades. The arrest and conviction of U.S.-born Israeli spy Jonathan Jay Pollard and his wife in the mid-1980s is only the most dramatic evidence of Israel's activities against the United States. In the words of *The Washington Post*: "Israeli intelligence agencies have blackmailed, bugged, wiretapped and offered bribes to U.S. government employees in an effort to gain sensitive intelligence and technical information."[1]

FALLACY

"Spying on the United States stands in total contradiction to our policy."
—*Shimon Peres, Israeli prime minister, 1985*[2]

FACT

The Washington Post revealed the breadth of Israel's spying on the United States on the basis of a forty-seven-page secret

CIA report, "Israel: Foreign Intelligence and Security Services," issued in March 1979. It was seized along with other secret documents in November 1979 by militants occupying the U.S. embassy in Tehran. Although Israel and its supporters have cast doubts on the document's authenticity, no U.S. official has.

According to the report, Arab countries were Israel's top intelligence targets but "collection of information on secret U.S. policy or decisions . . . concerning Israel" and "collection of scientific intelligence in the U.S. and other developed countries" ranked second and third in priority. "The Israelis devote a considerable portion of their covert operations to obtaining scientific and technical intelligence," the report continued. "This . . . included attempts to penetrate certain classified defense projects in the United States and other western nations."

It was later revealed that during the late 1960s and early 1970s the FBI and military counterintelligence conducted a program called Scope to prevent Israel from recruiting Americans to steal sophisticated military technology. The operation involved wire taps and electronic surveillance of the Israeli embassy. Scope was halted in the early 1970s when it was determined that it might be violating the constitutional rights of Americans.[3]

Since then, Victor Ostrovsky, a former Israeli intelligence agent, has revealed in a 1990 book that Israel kept in the United States twenty-four to twenty-seven Mossad agents belonging to a supersecret intelligence division known as *Al*, which in Hebrew means "above" or "on top." Reports Ostrovsky: "[Israeli intelligence is] actively spying, recruiting, organizing and carrying out covert activities, mainly in New York and Washington, which they refer to as their playground." He writes that Israel influences Congress by trying to recruit Jewish aides to representatives and senators serving on key committees.[4]

Another researcher writes that between the mid-1960s and mid-1980s Israel conducted so many operations inside the United States that there were forty official U.S. investigations of Americans working for Israel. She added: "[U.S. officials] say that the Israelis have become supremely confident of their ability to spy on the U.S. and get away with it."[5]

FALLACY

"Immediately upon Pollard's arrest, Israel apologized and explained that the operation was unauthorized."

—*AIPAC, 1992*[6]

FACT

On March 4, 1987, American citizens Jonathan Jay Pollard and Anne Henderson Pollard both pleaded guilty to spying for Israel. He was sentenced to life imprisonment and his wife to five years; she was released after serving two and a half years.[7] Author Seymour Hersh labeled Pollard as "Israel's first nuclear spy," claiming that Pollard passed on to Israel intelligence about U.S. nuclear targeting and that Prime Minister Yitzhak Shamir personally decided to give some of the information to the Soviet Union at a time when Washington was engaged in the cold war with Moscow in the early 1980s.[8]

During his eighteen months of self-admitted spying for Israel, Pollard stole more than a thousand classified documents, more than eight hundred of them classified top secret.[19] Some of the documents ran to more than one hundred pages each. Most of them were detailed analytical studies with technical calculations, graphs, and satellite photographs. Other documents contained messages providing details about U.S. ship positions and naval tactics and training operations. Also involved were analyses of Soviet missile systems that revealed how the United States collects information, including clues to the identity of U.S. agents or agents working for the United States. The documents also revealed the identity of the American authors of the studies, leaving them vulnerable targets of other intelligence services.[10]

The sheer mass of the material stolen has raised suspicions that Pollard had two or more Americans in high positions aiding him.[11] However, no other American citizen was charged in the case.

Defense Secretary Caspar Weinberger later said: "It is difficult for me . . . to conceive of greater harm to national security than that caused by the defendant, in view of the breadth, the critical importance to the United States and high sensitivity of the information he sold to Israel."[12] The thefts were so extensive that it was estimated it would cost $3 billion to $4 billion to correct security systems and neutralize exposed operations.[13]

FALLACY

"As promised to the U.S. Government, the spy unit that directed Pollard was disbanded, his handlers punished and the stolen documents returned."

—AIPAC, 1992[14]

FACT

No American can be sure what happened to Israel's LAKAM spy unit, which enlisted the Pollards, but former Israeli agent Victor Ostrovsky was in a position to know. His report: "All they did was change the mailing address and attach LAKAM to the foreign affairs department."[15]

Despite Israel's promise to punish the spies, it actually promoted the two Israeli principals involved.

Veteran intelligence operative Rafael Eitan,[16] director of Israel's LAKAM technology intelligence agency, was later put in charge of Israel Chemicals, the largest of Israel's state-owned companies. There he had enough free time to serve as an adviser to Colombia's President Virgilio Barco Vargas.[17]

Air Force Colonel Aviem Sella, who was Pollard's contact and had been indicted in the United States on charges of espionage, was promoted to brigadier general and given command of one of Israel's most sophisticated air bases, Tel Nof, a position usually considered a stepping-stone to the top command of the air force.[18]

In 1988 Israeli officials began seeking the Pollards' release by suggesting various deals to the White House and the State Department.[19] A campaign was started in Israel calling the Pollards "prisoners of Zion." More than 70 members of the 120-member Knesset signed a petition asking President Reagan for the Pollards' release, and both of Israel's chief rabbis also wrote to the president on their behalf.[20] The appeals continued into 1989 when Israel's health minister, Yaacov Tsur, asked U.S. Ambassador to Israel William Brown that Pollard's wife be released on medical grounds because she suffered a rare stomach ailment; a group of Israeli women's organizations issued similar calls. The groups included representatives from the Labor party, the religious parties, the prime minister's adviser on women's affairs, and Ruth Rasnic, manager of the Herzliya Women's Center. Rasnic sent a telegram directly to Barbara Bush seeking her help.[21]

Anne Pollard was released in 1990 after serving two and a half years of her sentence; she is now living in Israel. One of her first trips was to Israel, where she was warmly greeted on August 1, 1990, at Ben-Gurion Airport. Among the greeters were Deputy Prime Minister Geula Cohen of the right-wing Tehiya party and Knesset member Edna Solar of the Labor party.[22] A Public Committee for the Pollards had been established in Israel to raise money and work for the Pollards' release. In addition, an Israeli insurance company was reportedly paying Anne Pollard's medical bills "as a humanitarian gesture."[23]

Jonathan Pollard has not been released so far. His life sentence was upheld on March 20, 1992, after an appeal argued by Harvard lawyer Alan Dershowitz in Federal Appeals Court in Washington, D.C.[24] The U.S. Supreme Court later declined to review the case.[25] Nonetheless, in the heat of the presidential campaign, Democrat Bill Clinton promised Jewish groups that he would personally and promptly review the Pollard case if elected president,[26] and a large number of

U.S. rabbis took a full-page ad in *The New York Times* on October 23, 1992, calling on President Bush to release Pollard forthwith.[27]

As for returning the stolen documents, Israel sent back only 163 of the stolen documents. It was an empty promise anyway, since Israel had had more than enough time to copy them all.[28] Nor was Israel's promise of full cooperation in the Pollard investigation ever honored. In June 1986, FBI Director William H. Webster took the unusual action to complain in public that Israel had provided only "selective cooperation" in the U.S. investigation. He called on Israel to provide "full cooperation."[29] There was no answer from Israel.

SEVENTEEN

ISRAEL'S NUCLEAR WEAPONS

Israel's program to produce nuclear weapons is almost as old as the Jewish state. Its early sponsor was France, which helped construct Israel's secret nuclear facility Dimona in the Negev Desert in the late 1950s and early 1960s. Israeli officials have never officially admitted that Israel has nuclear weapons. Instead, they have confined themselves to the phrase that Israel would "not be the first" to introduce them in the Middle East. Nonetheless, ample evidence exists that Israel has had such weapons since the mid-1960s.[1]

FALLACY

"Israel has no intention of producing nuclear weapons and its [nuclear] program is concerned exclusively with the peaceful uses of atomic energy."
—*Israeli government statement, 1960*[2]

FACT

After officially assuring Washington on December 19, 1960, that Israel had no nuclear weapons program, Israeli Prime

Minister David Ben-Gurion two days later went before the Knesset and admitted that a nuclear reactor was under construction in the Negev at Dimona. But, he insisted, it was solely for peaceful purposes.[3] Ben-Gurion vowed that the Dimona facility would "serve the needs of industry, agriculture, health and science," adding that it would be open to trainees from other countries.[4] None of these statements has proved true.

Ben-Gurion's 1960 admission that Dimona was a nuclear facility was a major turning point, since before that time the official Israeli explanation about the construction at Dimona, undertaken with French help, was that it was a textile factory or a pumping station.[5] Israel's previous denials to the United States about Dimona's real purpose infuriated some members of Congress.

At a secret session of the Senate Foreign Relations Committee early in 1961, Senator Bourke Hickenlooper exploded: "I think the Israelis have just lied to us like horse thieves on this thing. They have completely distorted, misrepresented, and falsified the facts in the past. I think it is very serious, for things that we have done for them to have them perform in this manner in connection with this very definite production reactor facility which they have been secretly building, and which they have consistently, and with a completely straight face, denied to us they were building."[6]

Despite such sentiments, the United States never took any serious action to prevent Israel from continuing to develop nuclear weapons. The only half-serious effort was made by President Kennedy in the early 1960s. He insisted that Israel allow U.S. inspectors into Dimona. But Israeli technicians built a completely false control room at the Dimona installation in order to deceive the Americans about the actual type of research going on. The ruse worked and the inspections came to an end in 1969—a year after the CIA reported that Israel had nuclear weapons—without finding anything suspicious.[7]

Through the years Israel has moderated its public statements. At first its statements were limited to the formulation uttered by Prime Minister Levi Eshkol in the mid-1960s: "I have said before and I repeat that Israel has no atomic arms and will not be the first to introduce them into our region."[8] Since then it has dropped its denials of having a nuclear program or nuclear weapons and asserted simply that Israel will not be "the first to introduce nuclear weapons into the Middle East."[9]

The CIA and other experts around the world believe that Israel has not only nuclear weapons but the means to deliver them over long distances. A five-page CIA report dated September 4, 1974, said its conclusion that Israel is a nuclear power was "based on Israeli acquisition of large quantities of uranium, partly by clandestine means; the ambiguous nature of Israeli efforts in the field of uranium enrichment; and Israel's large investment in a costly missile system designed to accommodate nuclear warheads."[10] Israel can deliver nuclear warheads on its 260-mile ballistic missile Jericho; on its advanced Jericho, which has a range of over 500 miles; or by artillery, naval guns, or airplanes.[11] In September 1988 Israel launched an experimental satellite, *Ofek-1* (Horizon), into an elliptical 250-by-1,000-kilometer orbit. An American analyst said data indicated that the rocket that launched the satellite was powerful enough to carry a nuclear weapon to Moscow or Libya.[12]

According to reporter Seymour Hersh, who conducted a major study of Israel's program: "By the mid-1980s, the technicians at Dimona had manufactured hundreds of low-yield neutron warheads capable of destroying large numbers of enemy troops with minimal property damage. The size and sophistication of Israel's arsenal allows men such as Ariel Sharon to dream of redrawing the map of the Middle East aided by the implicit threat of nuclear force."[13]

None of Israel's major steps to develop nuclear weapons went undetected by U.S. intelligence. Yet the United States did nothing to keep the Israeli nuclear genie in the bottle. Hersh concludes: "America's policy toward the Israeli arsenal . . . was not just one of benign neglect: it was a conscious policy of ignoring reality."[14]

General Amnon Shahak-Lipkin, deputy chief of staff of the Israel Defense Forces, declared in April 1992: "I believe that the state of Israel should from now on use all its power and direct all its efforts to preventing nuclear development in any Arab state whatsoever. . . . In my opinion, all or most available means serving that purpose are legitimate."[15]

Israel's threats about development of such weapons by the Arabs are hypocritical. After all, the Israelis were the first to develop nuclear weapons in the region.

What's more, guarding against the proliferation of nuclear weapons is the function of the International Atomic Energy Agency in Vienna, operating under international supervision delegated by the Treaty on the Non-Proliferation of Nuclear Weapons. Most Arab nations have signed that treaty. Israel has not.

Yet Israel has acted as the region's nuclear policeman, with disastrous results. Its 1981 bombing of Iraq's Osirak nuclear research facility near Baghdad, more than 600 miles from Israel's borders, with U.S.-made warplanes and direct U.S. assistance helped radicalize Iraq.[16] The Osirak facility was the most advanced technological project in the Arab world, and its loss was a major blow to Iraq. The loss was especially painful since Iraq was a signatory to the nuclear Non-Proliferation Treaty while Israel was not.[17]

Israel's American supporters later congratulated the Jewish state during the 1991 Persian Gulf war for this attack as representing an early blow to Saddam's militancy. There can be little doubt, however, that its effect was to make Saddam resentful of the United States's relations with Israel, add to his suspicions of the West, and encourage his lawlessness. However irrational as a leader, Saddam had suspicions of U.S.-Israeli attempts to destabilize Iraq that were well founded.[18] A *New York Times* editorial noted at the time that the Israeli raid was an act of "inexcusable and shortsighted aggression."[19]

The raid likely helped goad Saddam into a number of significant actions, none of them in the interests of the United States. These included increased meddling in the civil war in

Lebanon and support of some of the most radical of the region's terrorists, such as Abu Nidal.[20] The Israeli raid may also have encouraged Saddam to make renewed efforts to acquire Western technology, including a clandestine operation to develop nuclear facilities. These efforts were overall successful in adding sophisticated technology to Iraq's military machine.[21]

In reality, the Israeli raid was the culmination of a secret Israeli terror campaign called Operation Sphinx against Iraq's nuclear program.[22] The operation began as early as April 6, 1979, when three bomb explosions in the nuclear facility of the French firm Constructions Navales et Industrielles de la Méditerranée in La Seyne-sur-Mer near Marseilles blew up the reactor cores about to be shipped to Iraq's facility. This sabotage set back Iraq's program by half a year.[23] Bombs also were set off at the offices and homes of officials of Iraq's key suppliers in Italy and France during the year.[24] Then on June 13, 1980, Dr. Yahya Meshad, an Egyptian nuclear physicist working for Iraq's Atomic Energy Commission, was killed in his Paris hotel room. Meshad had been in France checking on enriched uranium that was about to be shipped as the first fuel for Iraq's reactor. According to Israeli Mossad defector Victor Ostrovsky, Meshad was the victim of Israel's secret agents.[25]

In the United States Israel's supporters have been willing to hamper government efforts to stem proliferation in other countries if such acts threatened Israel. In 1981 Democratic Representatives Stephen J. Solarz and Jonathan B. Bingham, both of New York, dropped their amendment to ban U.S. aid to countries manufacturing nuclear weapons after the State Department informed them that Israel might be affected. After a private briefing by Under Secretary of State James L. Buckley, Solarz said: "We didn't want to find ourselves in a position where we had inadvertently and gratuitously created a situation that might lead to a cutoff of aid for Israel. They left us with the impression that such a requirement might well trigger a finding by the administration that Israel has manufactured a bomb."[26]

"Israel's decision not to be bound by the Non-Proliferation Treaty is based largely on the grounds that the treaty has done little to stem nuclear proliferation in the region."
—*AIPAC, 1992*[27]

FACT

Israel was well on its way to producing nuclear weapons before the nuclear Non-Proliferation Treaty was promulgated in 1968. No Arab nation was even close to developing a nuclear device at the time. Yet Israel has resisted all international and U.S. efforts to sign the treaty or to open its nuclear facilities to international inspection. The reason is obvious: since 1968, according to the CIA, Israel has possessed nuclear weapons.[28]

A series of leaked intelligence reports and news stories have since then reported on the progress of Israel's ambitious nuclear program.[29] But authentic details of Israel's program only became public on October 5, 1986, when Mordechai Vanunu, a disaffected worker at Dimona, talked to the *Sunday Times* of London. Vanunu reported that Israel had "at least 100 and as many as 200 nuclear weapons." He revealed that Israel had been producing the weapons for twenty years and that it now was a leading nuclear power. No American official or nuclear physicist has disputed that description.

EIGHTEEN

ISRAEL
AND
SOUTH AFRICA

The relationship between Israel and South Africa is deep and strong, and has been for many years. The two countries' isolation in the international community because of their repressive policies toward their indigenous populations led to a common concern about security, which in turn developed into an active military relationship. Israel supplies South Africa with a vast array of military technology in exchange for South African raw materials, especially uncut diamonds. The cooperation is widely reported to include joint efforts in developing nuclear weapons.[1]

FALLACY

"Opposition to apartheid is so strong in Israel that even the present modest relationship [with South Africa] is being reconsidered."

—*Hyman Bookbinder, former representative of the American Jewish Committee, 1987*[2]

Israel's relationship with South Africa remains largely hidden, in part because any reporting inside Israel on military cooperation between the two countries is "strictly forbidden by the military censors."[3] But reporter Seymour Hersh has disclosed that cooperation between the two countries on nuclear matters "began in earnest" in 1967, and Israeli scholar Benjamin Beit-Hallahmi has reported that Israel sold South Africa small arms as early as 1955.[4]

Despite such cooperation, media coverage of the relationship was so lax that it was only in 1971 that *New York Times* foreign affairs columnist C. L. Sulzberger scored an exclusive by reporting that friendly relations existed between Israel and South Africa, including military cooperation.[5] Such attention resulted in 1975 in the UN General Assembly's condemnation of Israel's "relations and collaboration [with] the racist regime of South Africa . . . in the political, military, economic and other fields."[6]

By 1982 Yoel Marcus, the leading Israeli political commentator of *Ha'aretz*, Israel's most important newspaper, called South Africa "Israel's second most important ally, after the U.S."[7] After being briefed by the CIA in 1989, Democratic Representative Stephen Solarz, an ardent supporter of Israel, said: "Israel's military relations with South Africa . . . are much larger than has been rumored or suggested."[8] Nothing has occurred since then to change Solarz's assessment.

The first dramatic signal that relations between the two countries had progressed significantly came in April 1976 when South African Prime Minister John Vorster publicly visited Israel. Although Israel described the visit as a religious pilgrimage, Vorster, a World War II Nazi sympathizer, was treated with the pomp of a visiting foreign leader.[9]

At a dinner for Vorster, Prime Minister Yitzhak Rabin explained Israel's reasons for the closeness between the two countries: "I believe both our countries share the problem of how to build regional dialogue, coexistence and stability in the face of foreign-inspired instability and recklessness. . . .

This is why we here follow with sympathy your own historic efforts to achieve détente on your continent, to build bridges for a secure and better future, to create coexistence that will guarantee a prosperous atmosphere of cooperation of all the African peoples, without outside interference and threat."[10]

Several months after Vorster's visit, relations between Israel and South Africa became closer than ever, mainly as a result of Israel's willingness to provide the apartheid country with weapons. Israel was reported to have sold South Africa two to six long-range gunboats armed with missiles and two dozen Kfir fighter planes; fifty South African naval personnel were being trained in Israel; and Israel provided South Africa with advanced military electronics equipment in return for coal, including an estimated one million tons a year to support Israel's steel industry.[11]

During the 1980s Israel provided South Africa with the technology and the blueprints to build its own advanced warplane. This major addition to South Africa's armory came as a result of the cancellation of Israel's failed Lavi fighter plane project. Despite $1.5 billion in U.S. financing to Israel to develop the warplane, Israel was unable to keep the project within budget and, under American pressure, dropped it in 1987. Israel then concluded a deal to help South Africa produce a version called Simba. Israeli technicians laid off from the Lavi project flocked to South Africa to work on the Simba.[12]

Although the United Nations in 1977 imposed a worldwide arms embargo against South Africa because of its racist policies, Israel continued to cooperate with South Africa. This infuriated members of the Congressional Black Caucus. When Israeli Prime Minister Yitzhak Shamir visited Washington in 1988, members of the Black Caucus presented him with a letter stating: "The United States provided Israel with nearly $1.5 billion in assistance in developing the Lavi fighter aircraft. We have since learned that . . . the Israeli engineers who worked on the Lavi project are taking the benefits of U.S. foreign assistance to South Africa. We consider this an unconscionable use of our aid." Shamir ignored the note, and no further action was taken.[13]

In November 1991 South African President F. W. de Klerk paid a four-day official visit to Israel assuring the Jewish state that "the new South Africa will be as trustworthy a friend as we have always been." The two countries signed a memorandum of understanding extending their cooperation in economic, scientific, and cultural affairs and, according to *The Jerusalem Post*, "other areas." Reports at the time revealed that the two countries had $317 million in nonmilitary trade in 1990, mainly in raw materials from South Africa in return for manufactured goods from Israel. Military trade was estimated to run as much as $800 million annually in 1987, when Israel officially promised not to undertake any new military contracts with South Africa. However, there were reports that the military trade actually increased.[14]

FALLACY

"Despite sensationalist stories of nuclear cooperation between Israel and South Africa, no proof has been produced to substantiate the claim."

—*AIPAC, 1992*[15]

FACT

Both Israel and South Africa have refused to sign the nuclear Non-Proliferation Treaty. As a result, their nuclear facilities have not been examined by international authorities for decades. The CIA learned as early as 1968 that Israel possessed nuclear weapons, and it was widely believed by the mid-1970s that South Africa was capable of assembling its own.[16]

Well before that, South Africa was selling Israel uranium to fuel its Dimona nuclear reactor.[17] In fact, it was South Africa's large reserves of uranium ore that made that country a natural ally for Israel. As reporter Seymour Hersh has commented: "Israel was trading its expertise in nuclear physics for the uranium ore and other strategic minerals that existed in abundance in South Africa."[18]

The evidence of the Israeli–South African nuclear connection comes from a September 22, 1979, detection by a U.S. *Vela* satellite of the unique light signature of a nuclear explosion halfway between South Africa and Antarctica. A committee appointed by the White House concluded that the *Vela* sighting "was probably not from a nuclear explosion," but critics since then have taken serious exception to the report and charged that it was a whitewash prompted by political considerations.[19]

The critics' case is that the committee was severely circumscribed in its work because it was given only limited information. The CIA, however, saw all the intelligence, and its conclusion in 1979 was unequivocal: "Technical information and analysis suggest that: An explosion was produced by a nuclear device detonated in the atmosphere near the earth's surface."[20] Director of Central Intelligence Stansfield Turner later pointed out that no one from the White House panel had requested information from the CIA and without that information the panel's conclusions were "absurd."[21]

Israeli–South African cooperation has extended beyond nuclear weapons to missile systems to deliver them.[22] On October 25, 1989, NBC-TV News provided an in-depth report on the Israeli–South African nuclear connection. Said the report: "Intelligence sources tell NBC News that Jerusalem is in a 'full-blown partnership' with Pretoria to produce a nuclear-tipped missile for South Africa." The report said that a missile secretly launched July 5 by South Africa over a nine-hundred-mile range had been constructed by the state-owned South African conglomerate Armscorp on the basis of Israeli technology.[23] Although Israel denied the NBC reports, *The Washington Post* quoted unidentified U.S. officials as confirming major parts of it, specifically Israeli aid to South Africa's missile program. One U.S. official said that the ambassador in Tel Aviv and other American officials attempting to pursue the matter with Israel were bluntly told it was none of America's business.[24]

Two years later, in October 1991, U.S. intelligence determined that Israel within the past year had shipped key ballistic missile components to South Africa with substantial parts of U.S. technology. However, President Bush decided to waive sanctions called for under U.S. law. Such sanctions could have included a prohibition on all trade with Israel.[25]

NINETEEN

ISRAEL
AND THE
THIRD WORLD

Israel has active relations with many Third World countries, mainly because of its vigorous sales of military equipment and its close ties to the United States, which small countries seek to exploit. Israel at times also acts as a surrogate for the United States in activities in which Washington wishes to conceal its involvement. A dramatic example is the Iran-Contra affair in which Israel shipped weapons to Iran and the profits were used to finance the Nicaraguan Contras in contravention of congressional restrictions.

FALLACY

"We do not sell arms to Iran. . . . The reports are completely unfounded."

—Shimon Peres, Israeli prime minister, 1986[1]

FACT

Israel's relations with Iran continued even after the assumption of power by Ayatollah Ruhollah Khomeini in 1979.

Though the relationship cooled under Khomeini's anti-Zionist policy, Israel continued to supply Iran with military equipment. There is little doubt that Israel operated under approval from Washington.

The humiliation of Iran's taking fifty-two Americans hostage in late 1979 (and holding them until the end of his presidency in January 1981) caused President Jimmy Carter to clamp an embargo on arms sales to Iran. The newly installed Reagan administration officially continued the embargo, yet throughout Reagan's presidency Israel sent massive amounts of materiel to Iran. Despite Israel's official denials in 1986 by Prime Minister Peres, other Israeli officials repeatedly declared in public that the shipments were made with Washington's approval. The Reagan administration at the time denied giving such approval.[2]

However, when *The New York Times* reported in 1991 that the Reagan administration had secretly allowed Israel to sell several billions of dollars worth of U.S.-made weapons to Iran starting in the spring of 1981, Secretary of State James Baker essentially confirmed the story by saying the United States "might very well have" approved such sales but he did not know the specifics.[3] *Times* reporter Seymour M. Hersh said he could find no former Reagan official to offer a rationale for the policy.[4]

There are a number of possibilities.

Conspiracy buffs immediately cited the arrangement as proof of the so-called October Surprise conspiracy. This is the alleged plot by which some critics claimed Reagan campaign officials secretly promised Iran a supply of arms in exchange for not freeing the hostages until after the 1980 presidential election. The conspiracy was supposedly motivated by fears of the Reagan people that release of the American hostages in October would help Carter's chances for reelection. Such a conspiracy has been by no means proved, but tantalizing bits of evidence inspired calls for a formal investigation.[5]

There are, however, several other explanations, mainly involving Israel's intimate relations with Iran.

Foremost, Iran has long been the key state in Israel's "periphery strategy." This was Israel's strategic plan developed in the late 1940s and early 1950s for combating the Arab nations by creating friendly relations with non-Arab nations on the edge of the Arab Middle East and with minorities within the region. In broad terms, the strategy called for Israel's support of any such minorities as the Kurds, the Druze, and the Maronites within the Middle East and, on its periphery, such nations as Ethiopia, Turkey, and, most of all, Iran.[6]

As a result of this strategy, Iran was the first Muslim nation to give de facto recognition to Israel in 1950. Over the years relations became extremely close: Iran became one of Israel's main suppliers of oil, and Israel joined with the United States in the early 1970s to help the shah of Iran destabilize Iraq by supporting the Kurds.[7]

Israel's friendly relations with Iran were specifically aimed at keeping Iraq weak and its attention diverted from the Arab-Israeli conflict. As *Ha'aretz* columnist S. Schweitzer wrote: "Iran destabilizes the Arab camp and neutralizes one of the strongest and most venomous of our potential enemies, Iraq. . . . There is truth in the laws of geopolitics: whoever rules Tehran becomes, willy-nilly, an ally of whoever rules Jerusalem."[8]

Israel worried that Iraq might turn its attention from the Persian Gulf and throw its massive military machine against Israel. As Defense Minister Yitzhak Rabin noted in 1988, if Iraq sent just half of its battle tanks to Jordan and Syria against Israel, the Jewish state would face on its eastern front more tanks than NATO had deployed in Europe.[9] Thus despite the public anti-Zionism of Iran's new Shi'ite regime under Ayatollah Khomeini, Israel continued to see a strong Iran as serving Israel's interests for years to come.

Israeli leaders repeatedly sought to influence U.S. policy away from Iraq and toward Iran during the 1980s.[10] This effort helps explain why Israel was so interested in promoting what became the Iran-Contra scandal of the mid-1980s under which the Reagan administration sold weapons through Israel to Iran. Such a pivotal intermediary role reinforced Israel's influence in Tehran, continued the enervating war between Iran and Iraq, which Israel saw in its national interests, and preserved a hugely profitable business.[11]

Even after exposure of the Iran-Contra scandal, Defense Minister Rabin in 1987 publicly criticized U.S. policy for leaning too far in support of Iraq. Rabin charged that U.S. assistance of Iraq and the Arabs in the gulf had resulted in the Soviet Union becoming "the only superpower that can talk to both parties in the war, while the United States cannot do it." Rabin said that Iran was currently Israel's enemy, adding: "But at the same time, allow me to say that for twenty-eight of thirty-seven years Iran was a friend of Israel. If it could work for twenty-eight years . . . why couldn't it once this crazy idea of Shi'ite fundamentalism is gone?"[12]

A final reason for Israel to supply weapons to Iran in the face of the U.S. arms embargo was its concern with the Jewish community there. There were some seventy thousand Jews in Iran, many of whom fled in the first few months of Khomeini's revolution. But at least thirty thousand remained, and Israel sought to protect them by currying favor with Tehran.[13]

FALLACY

"Black African nations did not break relations with Israel because of any concerns about racism; most severed ties with the Jewish State because of pressure from the Arab oil-producing nations in 1973."

—*AIPAC, 1992*[14]

FACT

The friendly days of Israel's flirtation with sub-Saharan Africa were brief, and their end had at least as much to do with Israel's aggressive policies as with Arab oil money.

The friendly period began in 1956 with the establishment of diplomatic relations with Ethiopia. It soon included formal relations between Israel and most of the new countries emerging from colonialism. But by the mid-1960s disillusionment with Israel's aggressive policies toward its Arab neighbors and its not too secret alliance with the CIA in Africa began to grow. The CIA was reported to have paid Israel as much as $80 million during the 1960s for "political penetration of newly independent states in black Africa."[15] As early as 1966, the Tricontinental Solidarity Conference in Havana passed a strong anti-Israel resolution that included a denunciation of Israeli technical assistance (supported by the CIA) as a form of imperialism.[16]

All but three African nations had broken their ties with Israel by 1976.[17] The exceptions were Malawi, Swaziland, and Lesotho, the latter two both essentially protectorates of South Africa.[18]

The break with Israel began before the Arab oil embargo of 1973. The severing of ties actually began in 1972. At that time Israeli diplomats more accurately identified the reasons as a "general radicalization of the African continent and growing disillusion with the West among many African leaders."[19]

There were other compelling, more specific reasons. The emerging Third World countries began to recognize the oppressive nature of Israel's treatment of the Palestinians. After the 1967 war, Israel was revealed as an occupying power much like the Western colonialists Africa had so recently shed. Moreover, Israel's friendly relations with the white racist regimes in Rhodesia and South Africa were resented, as was its support of Portugal's efforts to retain colonies in Angola, Guinea-Bissau, and Mozambique. Its voting record in the United Nations generally supporting the West also was resented by Africans.[20] In addition, many Africans were disillusioned by Israel's support of some of Africa's most repugnant regimes including those of Idi Amin in Uganda, Mobutu in Zaire, and Bokassa in the Central African Republic.[21]

"Now that the coercive power of the Arab oil-producers has eroded, African countries have begun to reestablish relations with Israel and to seek new cooperative projects."

—AIPAC, 1992[22]

FACT

The most likely motive for African countries to resume relations with Israel these days is the expectation that such a move will pay off because of Israel's influence in the U.S. Congress. There is a belief among many leaders of the world—not just African—that good relations with Israel automatically assure good relations with the United States.[23]

Zaire, for example, began the resumption of relations with Israel in 1982.[24] Although Zairian dictator Mobutu Sese Seko was widely recognized as one of Africa's most corrupt leaders, the resumption immediately paid off. All U.S. aid to Zaire had been cut off, but after its renewal of ties with Israel Congress quickly reestablished an aid program for Zaire.[25] In fact, an Israeli newspaper reported that one of Mobutu's specific requests when resuming relations was that Israel improve his image in the United States.[26] Israeli Prime Minister Yitzhak Shamir reportedly promised: "Israel will aid Zaire through its influence over Jewish organizations in the United States, which will help in improving [Zaire's] image."[27]

Romania is an example beyond Africa. Despite the monstrous character of Nicolae Ceausescu's rule, the Romanian tyrant nonetheless enjoyed a fairly good reputation in the United States as a result of his refusal to follow the Soviet Union and other Eastern European nations during the 1967 war by breaking off relations with Israel. Thus Ceausescu was generally treated softly by the U.S. media and Congress. Israel and its friends encouraged Congress to continue Romania's most favored nation status during Ceausescu's rule, a reduced tax category worth millions of dollars annually to Romania.[28]

One of the secrets underlying Israel's ties with Romania was a clandestine operation whereby Israel paid Romania to allow Romanian Jews to immigrate to Israel. The operation began around the mid-1950s and lasted over the next thirty years. Israel reportedly paid more than $1 billion to buy the release of more than 300,000 Jewish Romanians. Part of the deal included Israel's promise to lobby Congress on Romania's behalf, an action that contributed to the distortion of America's view of the country's dictator.[29]

The Philippines' Imelda Marcos candidly told an Israeli newspaper in 1981 that her husband, President Ferdinand Marcos, wanted to improve relations with Israel and Jewish Americans as a way "to improve the tainted image [of the Philippines] in the American media, and to combat its unpopularity in the American Congress."[30]

FALLACY

"The extent of Israel's activities in the Third World is baffling and disquieting to both friends and foes of Israel."
—*Benjamin Beit-Hallahmi, Israeli scholar*[31]

FACT

No one should be surprised by Israel's large involvement in the Third World. Certainly intelligence circles are not. They are well aware that part of Israel's perceived value to the United States is its willingness to act as a surrogate, thus giving Israel an enormous cachet in opening doors in countries many times the size of the Jewish state.[32]

Central and Latin America—as well as Africa—provide illuminating examples. There is no doubt that when the Reagan administration sought to bypass congressional opposition to aiding the Nicaraguan rebels known as the Contras it enlisted the help of the Israelis.[33] As former Israeli General Mattiyahu Peled said in the mid-1980s: "In Central America, Israel is the 'dirty work' contractor for the U.S. administration. Israel is acting as an accomplice and arm of the United States."[34]

Like leaders of other nations, Latin American rulers appreciate Israel's influence with Congress. *Washington Post* reporter Edward Cody reported in 1983 that there were "hopes in the Salvadoran government that the influential pro-Israel lobby in the United States [would] lend a discreet hand in congressional debates over the wisdom of administration policy on Central America."[35]

It was in part the Reagan administration's effort to bypass the Boland amendment outlawing aid to the Contras that motivated Israel to suggest that profits gained from selling arms to Iran be diverted to buying arms for the Contras.[36] This was the heart of the scandal involving Colonel Oliver North and Admiral John Poindexter known as the Iran-Contra affair.

Israeli Foreign Minister Shimon Peres declared at the time that "Israel didn't earn one red cent from this. This is not an Israel operation, this is a matter for the United States, not for Israel. Our purpose was to help a friendly country save lives. Israel was asked to help and it did."[37]

However, the final report of the Tower Commission investigation of the scandal concluded: "It is clear . . . that Israel had its own interests, some in direct conflict with those of the United States, in having the United States pursue the initiative. For this reason, it had an incentive to keep the initiative alive. It sought to do this by interventions with the NSC staff, the National Security Advisor, and the President."[38]

Israeli scholar Aaron S. Klieman notes that Central America has become a major market for Israeli weapons and security services: "Israel has offered to share stocks of arms captured in Lebanon, assisted intelligence activities in Costa Rica and Guatemala, and reportedly trained government forces in both of those countries as well as in Honduras and El Salvador to combat antigovernment insurgents. . . . Israel reportedly is among the largest secondary suppliers to Central America."[39]

Israelis have found lucrative work advising some of South America's most loathsome characters. In Panama, former

Israeli Mossad agent Mike Harari eluded U.S. invasion forces as they swept into Panama in search of dictator Manuel Noriega in December 1989. After retiring in 1980, he had gone into the arms business and other ventures in Panama and became Noriega's closest adviser. Harari later turned up in Israel while Noriega was captured and put in a U.S. prison.[40]

In Colombia, former Israeli Lieutenant Colonel Yair Klein, owner of Spearhead Ltd., a Tel Aviv–based security firm, was charged with training drug dealers known as *sicarios*—assassins—in sophisticated military tactics and use of explosives. Klein fled to Israel and claimed he thought he was training Colombian farmers to protect themselves from rebels.[41] Israel later charged Klein with illegally exporting weapons, and he pleaded guilty to three counts of selling arms and his military expertise.[42] On January 3, 1991, he was sentenced to pay a $75,000 fine and given a one-year suspended jail term. Colombia's Foreign Minister Luis Fernando Jaramillo Correa protested the leniency of the sentence.[43]

Besides drug dealers and small-time crooks like Noriega, Israel has courted and befriended such brutal despots as General Augusto Pinochet Ugarte of Chile, Roberto D'Aubuisson of El Salvador, General Romeo Lucas Garcia of Guatemala, Jean-Claude Duvalier of Haiti, Anastasio Somoza Debayle of Nicaragua, and General Alfredo Stroessner of Paraguay.[44] It must be acknowledged, sadly, that the United States has also been intimately involved with these same unsavory characters.

PART THREE

PERILS
TO
PEACE

TWENTY

YITZHAK RABIN'S GOVERNMENT

Yitzhak Rabin's record offers no optimistic clues that Israel's current government will be forthcoming in achieving peace. Rabin is one of Israel's most experienced officials. He became Israel's first native-born leader when he took power as prime minister in 1974. His rule lasted until 1977, when Menachem Begin's Likud party took over and dominated Israel's political scene for the next fifteen years. Rabin again became prime minister when Likud was voted out of office on June 23, 1992.

Rabin was born in Jerusalem on March 1, 1920, and was among the first volunteers in 1941 to join the new Jewish underground military units call Palmach (assault companies). As a Palmach commander he was instrumental in forcing thousands of Palestinians from their homes. His army career culminated with his appointment in 1964 as chief of staff, Israel's highest military command. Under his guidance, Israel launched the 1967 war, which resulted in the conquest of the West Bank, Gaza, the Golan Heights, and the Sinai Peninsula and the creation of hundreds of thousands more Palestinian refugees. He left military service in 1968 to begin five years as Israel's ambassador to the United States. In 1984 he became defense minister and fashioned Israel's brutal suppression of the Palestinian intifada. Rabin was replaced as defense minister in June 1990.

FALLACY

"I am willing to travel today, tomorrow, to Amman, Damascus, Beirut on behalf of peace, because there is no greater triumph than the triumph of peace."
—Yitzhak Rabin, Israeli prime minister, 1992[1]

FACT

If Prime Minister Rabin's record is any indication, his words portraying himself as an active seeker of peace must be taken with caution.

Over the years Rabin has repeatedly made clear that he does not favor returning all or even most of the occupied territories. He opposes Palestinian statehood. In his inaugural address, he explicitly ruled out any discussion, much less compromise, on the status of Jerusalem. He implicitly laid claim to major parts of the occupied West Bank, the Golan Heights, and, presumably, the Gaza Strip by stating that he would continue establishing "security" settlements. He made no mention at all of UN Resolution 242, which established the formula of trading land for peace, or of the Palestine Liberation Organization, the Palestinians' sole legitimate representative. He opposes Israeli citizenship for Palestinians in the occupied territories.

All this amounts to a hard-line position.

Nor does Rabin's record provide much hope that he has earned the trust of the Palestinians. As defense minister from the start of the intifada in late 1987, Rabin approved the variety of cruel measures used by Israel to suppress the Palestinians in the occupied territories. These included round-the-clock curfews imposed on hundreds of thousands of Palestinians, the cutting off of power and telephones to the refugee camps, and the blockading of badly needed food supplies.[2] When Defense Minister Yitzhak Rabin was asked if Israel would continue to deny food to the refugee camps, he said: "No doubt about it. We will not allow any support from the outside of commodities, not by countries, not by organizations."[3]

Rabin was also the official who announced the notorious policy of "broken bones," saying that Israel would use "force, power and blows" to suppress the intifada.[4] Shortly afterward, Israeli press accounts reported that 197 Palestinians had been treated in a three-day period in the Gaza Strip for fractures as a result of beatings; *The New York Times* added that the toll in all of the occupied areas "clearly runs well into the hundreds and perhaps higher."[5]

Rabin also increased the number of expulsions of Palestinians and suspended judicial procedures for "administrative detention" in order to allow easier jailing of suspects; defendants could now be held without charge or trial for indefinite periods.[6] The suspects included doctors, lawyers, journalists, union leaders, university officials, and students.[7] Under Rabin, all Palestinian schools were closed, depriving young Palestinians of education.[8] *The New York Times* commented in a headline: "For West Bank Arabs, Education Has Been Deemed a Criminal Act."[9]

Rabin forbade residents of the occupied territories from traveling inside Israel or between major West Bank towns. Reporters were barred from the occupied territories. Only the Jewish settlers there were permitted free movement.[10] Rabin announced prison terms of five years for stone throwers causing serious damage and fines of $1,000 against parents of children under fourteen caught throwing stones.[11]

As the Palestinian uprising continued, Rabin said that Israeli civilians could shoot on sight anyone carrying a Molotov cocktail, a policy protested by the U.S. State Department.[12] He increased the destruction or sealing of homes of suspects, even when it denied habitation for other members of a family.[13]

When the use of plastic bullets by Israeli troops dramatically increased casualties among Palestinians, Rabin said that was "precisely our aim. . . . our purpose is to increase the number [of wounded] among those who take part in violent activities but not to kill them." A UN official likened the new tactics to "open season" on the Palestinians.[14]

Such brutality was not new for Rabin. In 1948 he was the brigade commander in charge of the captured of the Palestinian cities of Lydda and Ramle, both all-Arab towns designated as part of the Arab state in the UN Partition Plan. Under David Ben-Gurion's orders, Rabin forced at least 50,000 and perhaps 60,000 Palestinians to flee their homes and become refugees.[15]

During the 1967 war, Rabin was chief of staff and oversaw the destruction of numerous Palestinian villages and the turning of 323,000 Palestinians into refugees. Of these, 113,000 were second-time refugees from the 726,000 who were made homeless by the 1948 war, another human flood of the wretched dispersed into their own diaspora.[16]

When he first became prime minister in 1974, Rabin initiated a new Israeli retaliatory policy against Palestinian guerrilla bases in southern Lebanon. The policy included liberal use of warplanes. In the first air strikes under Rabin's new policy at least 100 Arabs were killed and 200 wounded.[17]

Under Rabin, Israel was so inflexible in the 1975 negotiations with Egypt over the Sinai Peninsula that President Gerald Ford felt it necessary to announce a major "reassessment" of U.S. policy for the Middle East. It was a thinly veiled effort to pressure Israel into making compromises to Egypt in Secretary of State Henry Kissinger's strategy to achieve a second accord between the two nations.[18] But Rabin refused to give in. When Israel's lobby secured the signatures of seventy-six Senators on a protest letter, Ford dropped the reassessment.

It was only when Kissinger promised Rabin record levels of financial, diplomatic, and technological support that Israel finally agreed to the Sinai II partial withdrawal agreement.[19]

If that precedent is any guide to what Rabin's current "peace proposals" might cost the United States, it is a sobering message. Sinai II was one of the most expensive agreements Washington has ever undertaken. Kissinger promised aid to Israel at about $2 billion annually for the next five years. This was later increased to $3 billion. But that was only the beginning of the cornucopia of U.S. assets given to Israel.[20]

Additional benefits included a series of secret understandings providing a broad array of commitments signed in September 1975. In the major secret memorandum of understanding (MOU) with Israel, Kissinger committed the United States to "make every effort to be fully responsive . . . on an on-going and long-term basis to Israel's military equipment and other defense requirements, to its energy requirements and to its economic needs."[21] The memorandum officially committed American support against threats by a "world power," meaning the Soviet Union. Among other promises to the Rabin regime:

■ The United States would guarantee for five years that Israel would be able to obtain all its domestic oil needs, from the United States if necessary.

■ The United States would pay for construction of facilities capable of storing a one-year's supply of reserve oil needs.

■ The United States would conclude contingency planning to transport military supplies to Israel during an emergency.

■ The United States agreed to share Israel's position that any negotiations with Jordan would be for an overall peace settlement; that is, there would be no attempt at step-by-step diplomacy on the West Bank.

■ The United States promised in a secret addendum to the secret MOU that the administration would submit every year to Congress a request for both economic and military aid for Israel. It also declared that the "United States is resolved to continue to maintain Israel's defensive strength through the supply of advanced types of equipment, such as the F-16 aircraft." In addition, the United States agreed to study the transfer of "high technology and sophisticated items, including the Pershing ground-to-ground missile," which is usually used to deliver atomic warheads. When the agreement was revealed in public, Washington later turned down the Pershing transfer.

■ In another secret memorandum, Kissinger committed the United States not to "recognize or negotiate with the Palestine Liberation Organization as long as the Palestine Liberation Organization does not recognize Israel's right to exist and does not accept Security Council Resolutions 242 and 338."[22] This language was passed into law by Congress in 1985. The United States also promised to coordinate fully on strategy for any future meetings of the Geneva Conference. Thus, with Israel refusing to recognize the PLO and with powerful groups within the PLO at that time refusing to accept Resolutions 242 and 338, the stalemate on the West Bank was set in concrete.

■ President Ford signed a letter promising Rabin that the United States would not put forward any peace proposals without first discussing them with the Israelis. This was a significant concession since it gave Israel, in effect, a direct input to formulation of U.S. policy in the Middle East.[23]

■ In addition, President Ford signed a letter promising that the United States "will lend great importance to Israel's position that any peace treaty with Syria must be based on Israel's remaining on the Golan Heights."[24]

For this commitment of U.S. wealth, technology, prestige, and diplomatic support, Rabin agreed to withdraw Israel's occupation forces twenty to forty miles east of the Suez Canal, still leaving well over half of Sinai under its control.[25]

Kissinger remarked once of Rabin: "If he had been handed the entire United States Strategic Air Command as a free gift he would have (a) affected the attitude that at last Israel was getting its due, and (b) found some technical shortcoming in the airplanes that made his accepting them a reluctant concession to us."[26]

"We would like to emphasize that the government will continue to strengthen and build up Jewish settlement along the confrontation lines, due to their security importance."
—*Yitzhak Rabin, Israeli prime minister, 1992*[27]

A persuasive number of Israeli generals and others have asserted over the years that Jewish settlements in the occupied territories have no security value at all. Even such a dedicated ideologue as Binyamin Ze'ev Begin, son of the former prime minister and a prominent voice in the Likud party, wrote in 1991: "In strategic terms, the settlements (in Judea, Samaria, and Gaza) are of no importance." What makes them important, he added, was that "they constitute an obstacle, an unsurmountable obstacle to the establishment of an independent Arab state west of the river Jordan."[28]

The Israeli supreme court has ruled that the seizure of Palestinian land to locate a Jewish settlement overlooking Nablus in the occupied West Bank was not justified on grounds of security. The 1979 court ruling essentially meant that settlements did not offer enough security value to justify the confiscation of Palestinian land. The court's decision was based in part on a strong affidavit filed by former Chief of Staff Haim Bar-Lev, who stated: "The Jewish settlements in the populated areas of Judea and Samaria have nothing whatever to contribute to ongoing security. On the contrary, they interfere with security. . . . Any attempt to attribute motives of security to these settlers is misleading and distorted. These settlements are detrimental to security."[29]

Prime Minister Yitzhak Rabin now makes a distinction between "security" settlements and "political" settlements. By security settlements he means outposts established along the Jordan Valley frontier with Jordan and Syria's Golan Heights. Political settlements are those settlements in the midst of Palestinian population centers, except in East Jeru-salem. At the time of Rabin's reelection, there were about 90 "security" settlements with a population of 51,000 in the West Bank—half of the total of about 180 West Bank settle-ments with nearly 100,000 settlers.[30]

Former Defense Minister Ezer Weizman supports settle-ments but has had the candor to admit: "Security reasons—that term is negotiable currency in the state of Israel. The lesson to be learned from all the wars we have suffered is the reverse: border settlements have never been a substitute for the army. Even those settlements that held out against the Arab armies in 1948 usually did so with the help of the army. Moreover, Israel was obliged to evacuate its Golan Heights settlers during the Yom Kippur War when they were stranded in the middle of the battlefield. . . . Weak and isolated settle-ments are a burden and a nuisance in military terms."[31]

Rabin makes no security pretense about settlements in and around Jerusalem. The purpose of Jewish settlements there is simply to lay claim to the entire city as the capital of Israel. Rabin said in his 1992 inaugural address: "This government, just like all its predecessors, believes there are no differences of opinion within this House concerning the eternalness of Jerusalem as the capital of Israel. Jerusalem, whole and united, has been and will remain the capital of the Israeli people under Israeli sovereignty, the place every Jew yearns [for] and dreams of. The government is resolute in its position that Jerusalem is not a negotiable issue. The coming years, too, will witness expansion of construction in metropolitan Jerusalem. Every Jew, both religious and secular, vows: 'If I forget thee, O Jerusalem, let my right hand wither! This vow unites all of us and certainly applies to me, being a native of Jerusalem.'"[32]

"As a first step on the way to the permanent solution, we will discuss the implementation of autonomy in Judea, Samaria, and the Gaza district."
—*Yitzhak Rabin, Israeli prime minister, 1992*[33]

While Prime Minister Rabin sounded forthcoming in his 1992 inaugural address in declaring Israel's willingness to grant autonomy to occupied Palestinians, there was no celebrating among Palestinians. The reason: Rabin was proposing the same autonomy plan offered nearly fifteen years earlier by Menachem Begin. It has long since been discredited as merely another delaying tactic enabling Israel to retain the occupied territories.

Begin's autonomy plan granted the occupied Palestinians only a narrow range of self-rule over such matters as trash collection and street repairs but not over essentials such as water or the land they lived on. At the same time it allowed for the continued presence of Israeli occupation troops and offered no deadline for resolution of the central issue of who held sovereignty over the territories.[34]

As Israeli Defense Minister Ezer Weizman observed: "[Begin's] unshakable adherence to the perpetuation of Israeli rule over the West Bank and Gaza Strip led him into the autonomy plan."[35] It was, in other words, a clever ploy to retain Israeli control while making it appear that Israel was offering major concessions to the Palestinians. Outgoing Prime Minister Yitzhak Shamir's justice minister, Dan Meridor, admitted as much in early 1992: "The autonomy plan is presently the most efficient means to ensure the maintenance of Israeli control over Judea, Samaria, and Gaza."[36]

The Begin plan was condemned even by some Israelis, most notably Professor Jacob Talmon of Hebrew University in Jerusalem, one of Israel's most respected authorities on Zionism and modern nationalism. In a long letter to Begin, Talmon wrote: "Mr. Prime Minister, the idea of autonomy as you present it is archaic, a trick to shut up the Gentiles. Whoever knows something of the history of multinational empires at the close of the last century . . . can but shake his head at this bargain scrounged from these historical junk piles. . . .

"Mr. Prime Minister, with all due respect to the head of the government and a fellow historian, allow me to inform you on the basis of decades of research into the history of nationalism, that however ancient, special, noble, and unique our subjective motives are, the striving to dominate and rule, at the end of the twentieth century, a hostile foreign population which is different in its language, history, culture, religion, national consciousness and aspirations, economy, and social structure—is like the attempt to revive feudalism."[37]

FALLACY

"Already in its initial steps, the government—possibly with the cooperation of other countries—will give its attention to the foiling of every possibility that any of Israel's enemies should get a hold of nuclear weapons."
—Yitzhak Rabin, Israeli prime minister, 1992[38]

FACT

There is something absurd about the pretense that Israel stands as some kind of guardian against the proliferation of nuclear weapons when it is in reality the only state in the region to have them. But even more disturbing is the hint by Prime Minister Rabin that "other countries" may join Israel in that role. Rabin almost certainly is referring to the United States, meaning the establishment of another area of covert collusion by the two countries against the Arabs. President Bush seemed to acknowledge the effort when he met with Rabin several weeks after Rabin's inauguration and said in their joint news conference on August 11: "We thus committed ourselves to work to stem the proliferation of conventional arms as well as weapons of mass destruction."[39] If so, it is one more instance of entwining U.S. policy with Israel's.

An example of how America's embrace of Israel distorts U.S. policy against proliferation came in June 1992 with the publication of a Commerce Department guide to the Third World's most dangerous rocket projects. The point of the list was to provide industrial firms with the identities of such projects and thereby prevent sales that would aid them. Amazingly, the list omitted some of the most dangerous rocket projects in the Middle East. The reason, in the words of nuclear expert Gary Milhollin: "The Israelis fought the administration's 1991 version of the list because it did name the Jericho, their premier missile. After caving in to Israeli demands that the Jericho be excluded, the administration felt forced to exclude projects underway in Egypt, Libya, and Syria because, administration officials told me privately, it would have been politically embarrassing to do otherwise."[40]

In other words, to accommodate Israel's desire that its own Jericho missile, capable of carrying nuclear weapons to any Arab capital, not be named, the United States turned a blind eye to all missile projects in the Middle East.

TWENTY-ONE

THE FATE
OF THE
PALESTINIANS

The basic nature of the Arab-Israeli conflict has been misunderstood for many years because Israel successfully portrayed it as a struggle between Jews and Arabs. In fact, at its core it is a much more limited and more personal conflict. It centers on the Zionist effort to wrest from the native Palestinians their land and their homes, a relentless campaign that continues to this day. This is the basic nature of the conflict. The larger Arab dimension is a by-product. Peace efforts are likely to remain ineffectual until the basic nature of the conflict is understood—and acknowledged—in the United States.

FALLACY

"In reality, the Palestinian Arab question is the result of the conflict, which stems from Arab unwillingness to accept a Jewish State in the Middle East."

—*AIPAC, 1992*[1]

The Palestinians are the heart and the soul of the Arab-Israeli conflict. It was the Palestinians who in 1948 and again in 1967 lost their homes and land, their businesses and farms, their olive and citrus groves to the Israelis.[2] Many of them and their progeny remain refugees today.

It is these desperate and angry people who formed the original core of Israel's "problem" in the Middle East. They have been joined in their resentment of Israel by nearly 2 million other Palestinians who have been living under Israeli military occupation since 1967.[3]

The centrality of the Palestinians was well recognized by the pioneering Zionists. As David Ben-Gurion, Israel's first prime minister, said as early as 1936: "We and they [the Palestinians] want the same thing: we both want Palestine. And that is the fundamental conflict."[4]

FALLACY

"The degeneration of the [UN General] Assembly has reached such depths that any proposal, even the most absurd, can receive its blessing. . . . When the Arab-Soviet votes do not suffice, they are supplemented by the votes of those trying to curry favor with the Arabs and those yielding to oil-blackmail."

—*Yigal Allon, Israeli foreign minister, 1974*[5]

FACT

Israel has fought hard over the years to discredit the United Nations largely because the UN has been the leader in recognizing the fundamental nature of the Israeli-Palestinian conflict. In 1969 the UN General Assembly took the first major step in changing the world's perception of the conflict. It passed a resolution recognizing the Palestinians as a separate people and affirming their "inalienable rights." Resolution

2535 noted that the assembly recognized "that the problem of the Palestine Arab refugees has arisen from the denial of their inalienable rights under the Charter of the United Nations and the Universal Declaration of Human Rights." The United States was among twenty-two nations that voted against the resolution.[6]

Passage of the resolution marked the beginning of the world's recognition of the Palestinians as a dispossessed people with basic rights under international law.[7] Previously the assembly and most non-Arab governments had concentrated on Palestinians as individuals who were refugees and war victims. This was an attitude strongly fostered by Israelis, who long had insisted on treating the Palestinians as individuals instead of part of a community—just as Jews had been refused recognition as a community in Eastern Europe at the turn of the century.[8]

Subsequent assembly resolutions between 1970 and 1974 laid down the Palestinians' fundamental rights. The assembly recognized that the "people of Palestine are entitled to equal rights and self-determination, in accordance with the Charter of the United Nations" (Resolution 2672);[9] affirmed "the legitimacy of the struggle of peoples under colonial and alien domination [who are] entitled to the right of self-determination to restore to themselves that right by any means at their disposal" (Resolution 2649);[10] and declared that the Palestinians' inalienable rights included the linkage of their self-determination with the refugees' right of return (Resolution 3089).[11]

Passage of these resolutions formed the legal and moral basis for the Palestinian struggle as we know it today. In the words of Palestinian scholar Ghayth Armanazi: "Palestinians were now fully backed by the world community with four major rights: the right of return, the right of self-determination, the right of struggle and the right to receive aid in their struggle."[12]

The United States joined Israel in voting against all the preceding resolutions. However, Washington did routinely support resolutions offering Palestinians return or compensation, as first formulated in General Assembly Resolution 194 in 1948. That resolution resolved that "the refugees wishing to return to their homes and live at peace with their neighbors should be permitted to do so at the earliest practicable date, and that compensation should be paid for the property of those choosing not to return and for loss of or damage to property."[13] The United States reaffirmed its support of the return-or-compensate formula as late as May 12, 1992.[14] The difference between that formulation and the one used in Resolution 3089 is that the latter asserts that the Palestinians had a "right" to return.

The final buttress in the Palestinian position was the 1974 recognition by the General Assembly of the Palestine Liberation Organization as "the representative of the Palestinian people."[15] The United States also opposed this resolution.[16] Two weeks later, the Arab states meeting at Rabat, Morocco, designated the Palestine Liberation Organization as "the sole legitimate representative" and voice of the Palestinians.[17]

The State Department finally broke with Israel on November 12, 1975, by declaring publicly that "in many ways, the Palestinian dimension of the Arab-Israeli conflict is the heart of that conflict. Final resolution . . . will not be possible until agreement is reached defining a just and permanent status for the Arab peoples who consider themselves Palestinians."[18] This declaration by Deputy Assistant Secretary of State for Near Eastern Affairs Harold H. Saunders was the first official extensive U.S. statement about Palestinians.[19]

The Israeli cabinet expressed "grave criticism" at Saunders's statement, charging that it contained "numerous inaccuracies and distortions."[20] The uproar in Israel over the statement was so great that Secretary of State Henry Kissinger discounted the Saunders Document, as it became known, as an "academic and theoretical exercise"—even though Kissinger himself had carefully reviewed it.[21] The Arabs briefly were buoyed by the statement but soon concluded that it represented no serious shift in the U.S. position.[22]

The Saunders Document became a significant landmark in the Arab-Israeli conflict. After this, for the first time, U.S. analysts began identifying Palestinians as a people, not by their function or situation such as that of refugees, terrorists, or occupied Arabs.

FALLACY

"The charge of anti-Arab 'racism' is a cheap shot."
—Hyman Bookbinder, former representative of the American Jewish Committee, 1987[23]

FACT

As the world began to perceive that the Palestinians were the heart of the Arab-Israeli conflict, Israeli leaders and propagandists tried to marginalize and dehumanize the Palestinians. This trend accelerated after the right-wing Likud party came to power in 1977, when even the vocabulary of Israel's leaders became studded with public racist remarks about Palestinians.

Prime Minister Menachem Begin likened Palestinians to "two-legged animals."[24] His successor, Yitzhak Shamir, compared a Palestinian to a "fly"[25] and a "grasshopper."[26] Shamir went so far as to call Palestinians, a people who had lived for many centuries on the land of Palestine, "brutal, wild, alien invaders in the Land of Israel that belongs to the people of Israel, and only to them."[27] Added Rafael Eitan, Israel's military chief of the staff during the 1982 invasion of Lebanon: "When we have settled the land, all the Arabs will be able to do about it will be scurry around like drugged roaches in a bottle."[28]

Eitan later founded the far-right Tsomet (Junction) party, devoted to "transferring" the Palestinians, whom he labeled as good and bad—"the bad ones should be killed, the good deported."[29] Eitan's Tsomet faction soared in popularity in the 1992 elections, quadrupling its representation to an impressive total of eight seats in the Knesset.

The leaders of the long dominant Labor party had also repeatedly attempted to deny the Palestinians' existence. In 1969 Prime Minister Levi Eshkol asserted: "What are Palestinians? When I came here—there were 250,000 non-Jews—mainly Arabs and Bedouins. It was desert—more than underdeveloped. Nothing."[30]

A few months later Golda Meir, who succeeded Eshkol, said: "When was there an independent Palestinian people with a Palestinian state? It was either southern Syria before the First World War, and then it was a Palestine including Jordan. It was not as though there was a Palestinian people and we came and threw them out and took their country away from them. They did not exist."[31]

Shimon Peres, prime minister in the mid-1980s, similarly wrote in a book published in 1970: "The country was mostly an empty desert, with only a few islands of Arab settlement."[32]

A number of Israelis still maintain this position. In 1988 extremist Rabbi Meir Kahane, founder of the militant Jewish Defense League and now deceased, wrote in an ad in *The New York Times*: "There is no such thing as 'Palestinian people.' . . . There are no Palestinians."[33]

By painting Palestinians as less than human, Israel implies that no matter how harshly it has acted the Palestinians do not deserve better.[34]

TWENTY-TWO

ISRAEL'S CLAIMS TO JERUSALEM

A major obstacle to achieving peace remains the struggle over the status of Jerusalem. The fact that Jerusalem is revered by Christians, Jews, and Muslims means that its status concerns the international community. The 1947 UN Partition Plan recognized this worldwide interest in Jerusalem by designating the city as *corpus separatum*, a city that stands apart and is to be ruled by neither Arab nor Jew but by an international regime under the United Nations. Israel accepted this arrangement when it endorsed the partition plan and again when it was admitted into the United Nations in 1949. However, Israel has consistently acted otherwise, claiming that Jerusalem is the eternal capital of Jews. Since 1967, Israel has ruled over all of Jerusalem. On July 30, 1980, it formally annexed the city and declared that "Jerusalem united in its entirety is the capital of Israel."[1] It continues to maintain that position today.

"Jewish Jerusalem is an organic and inseparable part of the State of Israel."
—*David Ben-Gurion, Israel's first prime minister, 1949*[2]

FACT

In approving the 1947 UN Partition Plan, the Jews accepted the world body's designation of Jerusalem as a *corpus separatum* under international control with neither Arab nor Jew claiming sovereignty. This pledge was reconfirmed when Israel was finally admitted to the United Nations on May 11, 1949, after its third application for membership. Its earlier applications had been turned down in part because of international suspicions about Israel's intentions toward Jerusalem.[3]

Israel moved early to claim Jerusalem as its own in defiance of the world community.[4] On December 5, 1949, Israeli leader David Ben-Gurion declared: "Jerusalem is the heart of hearts of the State of Israel. . . . We do not imagine that the United Nations Organization will try to tear Jerusalem out of the State of Israel, or to prejudice Israeli sovereignty in the eternal capital of Israel."[5]

In reaction, the UN General Assembly four days later reconfirmed the partition plan's designation of the entire city of Jerusalem as a *corpus separatum*, rejecting Israel's claim. But Israel responded boldly. It ignored the world body and on December 11 formally declared that Jerusalem had been Israel's capital since the first day of Israel's existence.[6]

On December 16, Ben-Gurion defied the world community by moving the prime minister's office to Jerusalem. He declared the beginning of the new year of 1950 as the date for the transfer of all government offices to Jerusalem with the exception of the foreign and defense ministries and the national police headquarters.[7] Israel's transfer of government offices to Jerusalem continued undeterred by a December 20

UN Trusteeship Council demand that Israel remove the offices from Jerusalem as being incompatible with its commitments to the United Nations.[8] On December 31, Israel formally informed the council it would not remove the government from Jerusalem.[9]

Israel's defiance of the United Nations proved successful. From December 1949 onward, Israel has acted as though its legitimate and recognized capital is Jerusalem.

FALLACY

"The term 'annexation' . . . is out of place. The measures adopted [at the end of the 1967 war] relate to the integration of Jerusalem in the administrative and municipal spheres, and furnish a legal basis for the protection of the Holy Places in Jerusalem."

—Abba Eban, Israeli foreign minister, 1967[10]

FACT

At the end of the 1967 war, Israel moved rapidly to expand the city limits and to annex all of Jerusalem as its "eternal capital."[11] Up to 1967, Jerusalem had consisted of the historic walled Old City, divided into Armenian, Christian, Jewish, and Muslim quarters, and the surrounding city, which was divided with Arabs in the east and Israelis in the west.

In the predawn darkness on June 11, the day after the fighting ended, Israeli troops gave Palestinians living in the Mughrabi section of the Old City of Jerusalem, next to the Western (Wailing) Wall of the Temple Mount/Haram al-Sharif, three hours' notice to vacate their homes. Then Israeli bulldozers crushed the residences and two mosques, leaving 135 families—650 men, women, and children—homeless. It was the first confiscation of Palestinian property following the war.[12]

A week later, on June 18, Israeli soldiers began ordering Palestinians to leave the Old City's Jewish quarter. At first the expulsions were only a few hundred but over the years they totaled the entire Palestinian population of the quarter, about 6,500 persons. Jews began moving into the quarter as early as October 1967.[13]

Israel moved decisively to tighten its grip on Arab East Jerusalem two weeks after the war by passage in the Knesset on June 27 of two basic ordinances: the Law and Administration Ordinance and the Municipal Corporations Ordinance. The corporations law enabled the interior minister to change the boundaries of Jerusalem, and the administration ordinance allowed him to extend Israeli law to the enlarged municipality.[14] The interior minister did both one day later, on June 28. He more than doubled Jerusalem's size by extending the boundaries north nine miles and south ten miles, increasing Jerusalem's municipal limits from forty square kilometers to one hundred square kilometers.[15]

Jerusalem's new boundaries were carefully laid out to ensure, as Deputy Mayor Meron Benvenisti later reported, "an overwhelming Jewish majority" within the new boundaries.[16] Areas densely populated by Palestinians were omitted while the land abutting Arab villages was incorporated into the enlarged city.[17] The result was that the enlarged city limits of Jerusalem now contained 197,000 Jews and 68,000 Palestinians[18]—a dramatic change from the pre-partition days in 1947 when there were some 105,000 Palestinians and 100,000 Jews in Greater Jerusalem. Within the city limits of the old municipality the proportion now was 60,000 Palestinians and 100,000 Jews.[19]

The UN General Assembly on July 14, 1967, deplored Israel's refusal to abide by the Assembly's resolution of July 4, which called for Israel to rescind all measures to change the status of Jerusalem and called those measures invalid. It also asked the secretary-general to report on the situation in Jerusalem.[20]

Ambassador Ernesto Thalmann of Switzerland was chosen as the secretary-general's special representative. He reported that "it was made clear beyond any doubt that Israel was taking every step to place under its sovereignty those parts of

the city which were not controlled by Israel before June 1967.
. . . The Israeli authorities stated unequivocally that the
process of integration was irreversible and not negotiable."[21]

Although Israeli Foreign Minister Abba Eban assured the
United Nations that Israel was not annexing Arab East Jerusalem, annexation was the practical effect of its actions.
Henceforth, Arab East Jerusalem was linked to Israel's water
supply and the whole city was treated by Israel as an integral
part of the Jewish state.

It was not until July 30, 1980, that Israel formally and
publicly annexed all of Jerusalem by declaring that "Jerusalem
united in its entirety is the capital of Israel." By designating
the ordinance a "basic law," Israel's Knesset gave it quasi-
constitutional rank.[22] The action came one day after the UN
General Assembly voted for a Palestinian state and Israeli
withdrawal from all occupied territories, including Arab East
Jerusalem.[23]

The annexation was a landmark in the long struggle by
Israel against the world community's opposition to all of
Jerusalem being an Israeli-controlled city. Although the annexation provoked an immediate international uproar, Israel
refused to retreat and still retains its grip on the Holy City.[24]

FALLACY

"[The year 1967] inaugurated a new American policy which
remains essentially unchanged to this day; namely, the implicit
acceptance of Israel's de facto control of a unified Jerusalem."
—*Yossi Feintuch, Israeli scholar, 1987*[25]

FACT

The United States has consistently opposed Israel's claim to
the entire city. It has, along with most other nations, maintained its embassy in Tel Aviv rather than Jerusalem as a
symbol of its opposition to Israel's defiant assertion of sovereignty over all of Jerusalem.

In the early 1950s the Eisenhower administration went so far as to prohibit American diplomats from doing business with Israeli officials in Jerusalem. That drastic move came in reaction to Israel's transfer of its Foreign Ministry from Tel Aviv to Jerusalem on July 13, 1953. In response the United States, Great Britain, and other countries boycotted all functions in Jerusalem and refused to visit the Foreign Ministry, whose move to Jerusalem was seen as an effort to support Israel's claim to Jerusalem as its capital.[26]

Secretary of State John Foster Dulles maintained the boycott for a year and a half before yielding to Israel's determination and the practical inconveniences of the situation. On November 12, 1954, he allowed America's new ambassador to Israel, Edward Lawson, to present his credentials in Jerusalem, effectively ending the boycott.[27]

The State Department, however, was determined, in the words of an internal memo, "to keep the Jerusalem question an open one and to prevent its being settled solely through the processes of attrition and fait accompli."[28] Thus when Israel opened its new Knesset building in Jerusalem on August 30, 1966, no U.S. diplomats attended, although a group of congressional representatives did.[29]

Nonetheless, Washington's policy on Jerusalem has weakened over the years. As early as 1949 the administration deserted the designation of Jerusalem as an international city that it had approved in the 1947 Partition Plan, opting instead for the proposal that there be Arab and Israeli zones of local government with a UN commissioner in charge of the holy places and international affairs while Jerusalem remained the capital of no country.[30]

Another U.S. policy retreat came in 1969 under the Nixon administration when the United States dropped any mention of a UN commissioner, abandoned its insistence that Jerusalem was an international city, and reduced its position to the simple formula that Jerusalem remain an undivided city whose future was to be decided by the parties involved.[31] However, the administration also declared in 1969 that Arab East Jerusalem, which Israel had captured in 1967, was "occupied territory [similar] to other areas occupied by Israel."[32]

President George Bush publicly reaffirmed this policy on March 3, 1990, as well as the designation of Arab East Jerusalem as occupied territory.[33]

FALLACY

"Jerusalem is and should remain the capital of Israel."
—U.S. Senate and House of
Representatives resolution, 1990[34]

FACT

While U.S. policy has consistently opposed Israel's claim to Jerusalem as its capital, Congress has routinely passed non-binding resolutions calling for recognition of Jerusalem as Israel's capital. In 1988 Republican Senator Jesse Helms of North Carolina went so far as to add an amendment to the Department of State Appropriations Act calling for the construction of two separate diplomatic facilities in Israel, one in Tel Aviv and one in Jerusalem "or the West Bank." Critics claimed the amendment was yet another effort by Israel's supporters to try to have the U.S. embassy moved to Jerusalem.[35] Republican minority leader Robert Dole of Kansas complained in 1990 that Congress was acting irresponsibly in passing such resolutions that "sail through in about 15 seconds [without] debate." Dole pointed out that the 1990 resolution "declares Jerusalem the capital of Israel—the position of the Israeli government; a position 180 degrees contrary to the views of the Arab states and the Palestinians. Most important, the resolution declares on an issue that our government—and many outside observers—see as better left to negotiations among the parties involved, rather than decided by unilateral action."[36]

At the same time, the Democratic party has officially endorsed Israel's position in its political platform, calling for transfer of the U.S. embassy to Jerusalem. The 1984 Democratic plank said: "The Democratic Party recognizes and supports the established status of Jerusalem as the capital of Israel. As a symbol of this stand, the U.S. Embassy should be moved from Tel Aviv to Jerusalem."[37]

That same year, the House Foreign Affairs subcommittees on international operations and on Europe and the Middle East passed a nonbinding resolution saying it was a sense of Congress that the embassy should be moved to Jerusalem "at the earliest possible date."[38] This was one of the top goals of the American Israel Public Affairs Committee (AIPAC), Israel's official lobbying arm.[39] Even Secretary of State George Shultz, one of Israel's warmest supporters, warned Congress that such a move would not be prudent.[40]

Nonetheless, the Democratic party has continued to support Israel's policy on the matter of Jerusalem. In 1988 Democratic presidential candidate Michael Dukakis indicated his willingness to move the embassy to Jerusalem, as did Bill Clinton in 1992. The 1992 Democratic platform called Jerusalem Israel's capital, but it did not go so far as to urge that the U.S. embassy be moved there.

TWENTY-THREE

JEWISH
SETTLEMENTS

Jewish settlements established on the land of Palestinians in the occupied territories pose a serious impediment to the search for peace. The charter of the United Nations specifically outlaws the acquisition of territory by force, and the 1949 Fourth Geneva Convention Relative to the Protection of Civilian Persons in Time of War specifically prohibits an occupying power from transferring part of its own population to the territory it occupies. Israel has routinely violated both of these international covenants. Since 1967 it has forcefully occupied Arab East Jerusalem, the West Bank, the Golan Heights, and the Gaza Strip and at the same time has continued to establish Jewish settlements in all of these territories.[1]

The United States shares equal guilt with Israel because it has colluded with Israel in the military occupation and colonization of Palestinian land. Although U.S. policy officially opposes Jewish settlements, no effort has ever been made to withhold the $3 billion in annual U.S. economic and military aid to Israel in order to make the Jewish state stop its colonization of the occupied territories. Without U.S. aid, Israel would not have the resources to establish and maintain settlements or to continue its military occupation.

"Our right to [the occupied] land is indisputable."
—*Yitzhak Rabin, Israeli prime minister, 1974*[2]

Until the strongly pro-Israel Reagan presidency, every U.S. administration, Democratic and Republican, had challenged Israel's claim to the territories occupied in 1967, calling the occupation a violation of the UN charter and the Fourth Geneva Convention Relative to the Protection of Civilian Persons in Time of War and therefore illegal. The United Nations has taken the same position.

U.S. policy was first voiced by President Richard Nixon's U.S. ambassador to the United Nations, Charles W. Yost. He said in 1969, "The part of Jerusalem that came under the control of Israel in the June war, like other areas occupied by Israel, is occupied territory and hence subject to the provisions of international law governing the rights and obligations of an occupying power."[3]

President Gerald Ford's U.S. ambassador to the United Nations, William W. Scranton, declared in the Security Council on March 23, 1976, that Israel's settlements in the occupied territories were illegal and that its claim to all of Jerusalem was void.[4] Said Scranton: "My government believes that international law sets the appropriate standards [governing Israel's settlements]. An occupier must maintain the occupied areas as intact and unaltered as possible, without interfering with the customary life of the area, and any changes must be necessitated by the immediate needs of the occupation and be consistent with international law. The Fourth Geneva Convention speaks directly to the issue of population transfer in Article 49: 'The occupying power shall not deport or transfer parts of its own civilian population into the territory it occupies.' Clearly then substantial resettlement of the Israeli civilian population in occupied territories, including East

Jerusalem, is illegal under the convention and cannot be considered to have prejudged the outcome of future negotiations between the parties or the location of the borders of states of the Middle East. Indeed, the presence of these settlements is seen by my government as an obstacle to the success of the negotiations for a just and final peace between Israel and its neighbors."[5]

The speech brought an official protest from Israel. The State Department responded by noting that Scranton was merely restating long-standing U.S. policy.[6]

It was the Carter administration that issued the most frequent statements on U.S. opposition to settlements. Both President Carter and his secretary of state, Cyrus Vance, spoke out publicly declaring Israel's settlements illegal.[7] On April 21, 1978, State Department legal adviser Herbert Hansell officially rendered Washington's legal position, saying settlements were "inconsistent with international law." The opinion also asserted that the Fourth Geneva Convention applied to the West Bank and Gaza, despite Israeli claims that it did not because sovereignty over those areas was in dispute.[8]

It was not until Ronald Reagan's presidency starting in 1981 that U.S. policy suddenly was muted by his astonishing declaration on February 2 that "I disagreed when the previous administration referred to [Israeli settlements] as illegal—they're not illegal."[9] Just what the legal status of the settlements was in Reagan's policy was never clear. But as time passed it became obvious to him that they were a major "obstacle to peace," as he repeatedly said, and that Israel's "rush" to establish settlements was "unnecessarily provocative."[10]

Meanwhile, the rest of the world continued to consider them illegal and said so. The European Community has consistently maintained that "Jewish settlements in the territories occupied by Israel since 1967, including East Jerusalem, are illegal under international law" and that Israel's settlement policy presented "a growing obstacle to peace in the region."[11]

After Reagan had issued his "not illegal" declaration, George Bush chose not to turn back the clock during his own presidency. But Bush administration officials implied that the administration considered settlements not only obstacles to peace but illegal as well. As Secretary of State James Baker noted in 1991, "we used to characterize [Israeli settlements] as illegal [but] we now moderately characterize [them] as an obstacle to peace."[12]

Prime Minister Yitzhak Shamir was guided by another philosophy. Shortly after his defeat for reelection in 1992, Shamir said: "The Likud never concealed its intention to demand sovereignty over Judea and Samaria during the negotiations for their final status. It implemented the principle that the right of the Jews to settle in all parts of Eretz Yisrael would be upheld during the entire course of negotiations. The only guarantee against Arab sovereignty west of the Jordan River is Jewish urban and rural settlement throughout Judea and Samaria."[13]

FALLACY

"The Jewish people [have a] right to settle the occupied territories."

—*Menachem Begin, Israeli prime minister, 1980*[14]

FACT

Jews enjoy no "right" to establish settlements in the occupied territories, as both the United States and the United Nations have repeatedly warned. Yet Israel has defied world opinion by colonizing the occupied territories almost from the day the 1967 war ended. Less than three weeks later, on June 27, Israel had effectively annexed Arab East Jerusalem, and on July 15 it established the first Israeli settlement in the territories—Kibbutz Merom Hagolan near Quneitra on the Golan Heights.[15]

Prime Minister Levi Eshkol waited until September 24 before he made the first public announcement of Israel's settlement plans, which he said would be limited.[16] Even this mild statement brought criticism from the United States, which said Eshkol's announcement amounted to a change in Israel's previous position against settlements. The U.S. statement also said that Israel had failed to notify Washington of the change. In amplifying the statement, a State Department spokesperson said the new Israeli policy conflicted with President Johnson's June 19 declaration of U.S. support of territorial integrity throughout the region.

The criticism was the second public rebuke of Israel by Washington in four days. U.S. Ambassador to the United Nations Arthur Goldberg had warned that peace could not be served "if military success blinds a member state to the fact that its neighbors have rights and interests of their own."[17] Nonetheless, by the end of 1967 Israel had established Jewish settlements in all the occupied lands of Egypt, Jordan, and Syria.[18] Israel's establishment of settlements has proceeded at an accelerating pace since 1967.[19]

Prior to 1948 there had been only seven Jewish communities in the lands occupied in 1967, and Jewish land ownership was at most 1 percent in those areas.[20] A quarter century later, in May 1992, the State Department reported there were 129,000 Jews in Arab East Jerusalem (compared with 155,000 Palestinians); 97,000 Jews in 180 settlements in the West Bank with half of the land under exclusive Jewish control; 3,600 in 20 settlements in the Gaza Strip; and 14,000 in 30 settlements in the Golan Heights.[21] According to another report, Israel during that quarter century had confiscated or otherwise alienated from Palestinian ownership 55 percent of the land of the West Bank, 42 percent of the Gaza Strip, and all of the Golan Heights, which it had annexed along with Arab East Jerusalem. All of the water resources were under Israeli control and 30 percent of the water in the West Bank was diverted to Israel or its settlers.[22]

In addition, Jewish ultranationalists such as members of Ateret Kohanim, which seeks to take over the Temple Mount/Haram al-Sharif in the Old City of Jerusalem, were aggressively settling within the Old City. In 1992, encouraged by the Shamir government, some 600 Jewish settlers, mainly seminary students, were living in some 55 sites outside the traditional boundaries of the Old City's Jewish quarter—in the Christian, Armenian, and Muslim quarters.[23]

Shamir's housing minister, Ariel Sharon, a leader of the far right, acquired an apartment in the Muslim quarter in 1987.[24] Sharon has said: "We have set a goal for ourselves of not leaving one neighborhood in East Jerusalem without Jews. This is the only thing that can assure a united city under Israeli sovereignty."[25]

TWENTY-FOUR

ISRAEL
AND THE
UNITED NATIONS

There is not likely to be peace as long as Israel continues to violate the charter of the United Nations and defy the world body's resolutions. No nation has been the subject of as much and as frequent official criticism by the UN General Assembly and the Security Council as Israel has, and none has been defended and shielded more often by the United States. Like all members of the United Nations, Israel solemnly vowed to act in accordance with the UN charter and to pursue "no policies on any question which were inconsistent with . . . the resolutions of the Assembly and the Security Council." Israel has observed neither of these commitments, yet the United States has repeatedly supported Israel in UN votes—even to the point of threatening in 1983 to withdraw from the General Assembly if it suspended Israel for its refusal to abide by UN resolutions.[1]

"Thus the UN had become a mosque, sounding the call to deny Israel sovereignty and survival—to treat her as a pariah, to deny her legitimacy, while Islam trumpeted the ancient shibboleth for Israel's disappearance."

—*I. L. Kenen, a founder of AIPAC, 1981*[2]

FACT

Israel's isolation in the world community derives from resolutions critical of Israel that were approved by the UN Security Council. Because of council rules, all such resolutions have to receive either the open approval of the United States or its acquiescence through abstention in the voting. The United States, as one of the five permanent Security Council members, has the right to veto any resolution placed before the council.

Despite Washington's unwavering support of Israel, the United States over the years has supported, actively or passively, an unprecedented sixty-nine resolutions that find fault with the Jewish state. These range from fairly mild calls urging Israel to take or refrain from certain actions to sharper messages demanding action and strongly condemning its behavior. (See list of resolutions at the end of this section.)

The official record would be more reflective of the depth of international opprobrium of Israel's behavior except for U.S. intercession. Washington has cast twenty-nine vetoes to protect Israel from council criticism.

In the General Assembly, where no nation has veto power and resolutions are usually adopted by a simple majority, the scope and number of resolutions passed against Israel have been even greater. The assembly has repeatedly condemned Israel's occupation of Arab land, its attacks on Lebanon, its violations of the human rights of Palestinians under occupation, its violations of the Fourth Geneva Convention, its claim to Jerusalem as its unified capital, its relations with South Africa, and its nuclear program.

At the same time, the General Assembly has officially affirmed the rights of the Palestinians. It has recognized Palestinians as a separate people with inalienable rights, which include the right of self-determination, the right to their own homeland, the right of return to their homes or compensation, and the fundamental right to struggle "by any means at their disposal."[3]

FALLACY

"It is doubtful the UN has any useful role to play in solving the Arab-Israeli dispute . . . [because of its] continuing anti-Israel bias."

—AIPAC, 1992[4]

FACT

The United Nations has a fundamental role to play in solving the Arab-Israeli conflict. It was the United Nations that first recommended partition of Palestine in 1947. And it is the United Nations that remains responsible for the humanitarian effort to care for the refugees dispossessed in 1948 and 1967.

The United Nations remains the most complete repository of open and accessible factual data involving the conflict. Its archives document the conflict from its beginning to its current impasse. The United Nations was the institution that officially determined the number of original Palestinian refugees (726,000) created in 1948 and it has documented, almost daily, the violations committed by Israeli troops against the human rights of the Palestinians living under occupation.

Israel, with Washington's collusion, has been successful over the decades in keeping the United Nations on the sideline in efforts to find peace. The reason for Israel's opposition to the United Nations is that the nations of the world have repeatedly shown they oppose Israel's occupation. In the words of Resolution ES-9/1 of 1982, "Israel's record and actions establish conclusively that it is not a peace-loving

Member State and that it has not carried out its obligations under the Charter."[5] If the United Nations were allowed to preside over a final settlement of the conflict, Israel would be obligated to abide by the UN charter and the various resolutions of the Security Council. In other words, it would have to cease its occupation, compensate or accept back the refugees, and give up its claim to all of Jerusalem.

FALLACY

"[What happens in the Security Council] more closely resembles a mugging than either a political debate or an effort at problem-solving."

—*Jeane Kirkpatrick,*
U.S. ambassador to the United Nations, 1983[6]

FACT

Despite attempts by Israel and its supporters to discredit the United Nations, there has been a remarkable consensus over the years in the world body about the Arab-Israeli conflict. This consensus is evident in the Security Council. Its first critical resolution (59) on Israel came on October 19, 1948, when the council unanimously expressed its "concern" that Israel had "to date submitted no report to the Security Council or the Acting Mediator regarding the progress of the investigation into the assassination" of UN Special Representative Count Folke Bernadotte.[7] The second resolution (93) was on May 18, 1951, when, by a vote of 10 to none with one abstention (Soviet Union), the council called on Israel to stop draining the marshes and lake of Huleh in the Upper Galilee and to allow the return of Palestinians evicted by Israeli forces from the demilitarized zone shared with Syria.[8]

The first outright condemnation of Israel came on November 24, 1953, when the council in Resolution 101 expressed its "strongest censure" of Israel's attack on the Palestinian village of Qibya, which killed sixty-six and wounded seventy-five, most of them women and children.

In addition to these three early resolutions, the following are sixty-six other critical Security Council resolutions, each supported or tacitly accepted by the United States:

Resolution 106, March 29, 1955: "condemns" Israel for Gaza raid.

Resolution 111, January 19, 1956: "condemns" Israel for raid on Syria that killed fifty-six people.

Resolution 127, January 22, 1958: "recommends" Israel suspend its "no-man's zone" in Jerusalem.

Resolution 162, April 11, 1961: "urges" Israel to comply with UN decisions.

Resolution 171, April 9, 1962: "determines flagrant violation" by Israel in its attack on Syria.

Resolution 228, November 25, 1966: "censures" Israel for its attack on Samu in the West Bank, then under Jordanian control.

Resolution 237, June 14, 1967: "urges" Israel to allow return of new 1967 Palestinian refugees.

Resolution 248, March 24, 1968: "condemns" Israel for its massive attack on Karameh in Jordan.

Resolution 250, April 27, 1968: "calls" on Israel to refrain from holding military parade in Jerusalem.

Resolution 251, May 2, 1968: "deeply deplores" Israeli military parade in Jerusalem in defiance of Resolution 250.

Resolution 252, May 21, 1968: "declares invalid" Israel's acts to unify Jerusalem as Jewish capital.

Resolution 256, August 16, 1968: "condemns" Israeli raids on Jordan as "flagrant violation."

Resolution 259, September 27, 1968: "deplores" Israel's refusal to accept UN mission to probe occupation.

Resolution 262, December 31, 1968: "condemns" Israel for attack on Beirut airport.

Resolution 265, April 1, 1969: "condemns" Israel for air attacks on Salt in Jordan.

Resolution 267, July 3, 1969: "censures" Israel for administrative acts to change the status of Jerusalem.

Resolution 270, August 26, 1969: "condemns" Israel for air attack on villages in southern Lebanon.

Resolution 271, September 15, 1969: "condemns" Israel's failure to obey UN resolutions on Jerusalem.

Resolution 279, May 12, 1970: "demands" withdrawal of Israeli forces from Lebanon.

Resolution 280, May 19, 1970: "condemns" Israeli attacks against Lebanon.

Resolution 285, September 5, 1970: "demands" immediate Israeli withdrawal from Lebanon.

Resolution 298, September 25, 1971: "deplores" Israel's changing of the status of Jerusalem.

Resolution 313, February 28, 1972: "demands" that Israel stop attacks against Lebanon.

Resolution 316, June 26, 1972: "condemns" Israel for repeated attacks on Lebanon.

Resolution 317, July 21, 1972: "deplores" Israel's refusal to release Arabs abducted in Lebanon.

Resolution 332, April 21, 1973: "condemns" Israel's repeated attacks against Lebanon.

Resolution 337, August 15, 1973: "condemns" Israel for violating Lebanon's sovereignty.

Resolution 347, April 24, 1974: "condemns" Israeli attacks on Lebanon.

Resolution 425, March 19, 1978: "calls" on Israel to withdraw its forces from Lebanon.

Resolution 427, May 3, 1978: "calls" on Israel to complete its withdrawal from Lebanon.

Resolution 444, January 19, 1979: "deplores" Israel's lack of cooperation with UN peacekeeping forces.

Resolution 446, March 22, 1979: "determines" that Israeli settlements are a "serious obstruction" to peace and calls on Israel to abide by the Fourth Geneva Convention.

Resolution 450, June 14, 1979: "calls" on Israel to stop attacking Lebanon.

Resolution 452, July 20, 1979: "calls" on Israel to cease building settlements in occupied territories.

Resolution 465, March 1, 1980: "deplores" Israel's settlements and asks all member states not to assist Israel's settlements program.

Resolution 467, April 24, 1980: "strongly deplores" Israel's military intervention in Lebanon.

Resolution 468, May 8, 1980: "calls" on Israel to rescind illegal expulsions of two Palestinian mayors and a judge and to facilitate their return.

Resolution 469, May 20, 1980: "strongly deplores" Israel's failure to observe the council's order not to deport Palestinians.

Resolution 471, June 5, 1980: "expresses deep concern" at Israel's failure to abide by the Fourth Geneva Convention.

Resolution 476, June 30, 1980: "reiterates" that Israel's claims to Jerusalem are "null and void."

Resolution 478, August 20, 1980: "censures [Israel] in the strongest terms" for its claim to Jerusalem in its "Basic Law."

Resolution 484, December 19, 1980: "declares it imperative" that Israel readmit two deported Palestinian mayors.

Resolution 487, June 19, 1981: "strongly condemns" Israel for its attack on Iraq's nuclear facility.

Resolution 497, December 17, 1981: "decides" that Israel's annexation of Syria's Golan Heights is "null and void" and demands that Israel rescind its decision forthwith.

Resolution 498, December 18, 1981: "calls" on Israel to withdraw from Lebanon.

Resolution 501, February 25, 1982: "calls" on Israel to stop attacks against Lebanon and withdraw its troops.

Resolution 509, June 6, 1982: "demands" that Israel withdraw its forces forthwith and unconditionally from Lebanon.

Resolution 515, July 29, 1982: "demands" that Israel lift its siege of Beirut and allow food supplies to be brought in.

Resolution 517, August 4, 1982: "censures" Israel for failing to obey UN resolutions and demands that Israel withdraw its forces from Lebanon.

Resolution 518, August 12, 1982: "demands" that Israel cooperate fully with UN forces in Lebanon.

Resolution 520, September 17, 1982: "condemns" Israel's attack into West Beirut.

Resolution 573, October 4, 1985: "condemns" Israel "vigorously" for bombing Tunisia in attack on PLO headquarters.

Resolution 587, September 23, 1986: "takes note" of previous calls on Israel to withdraw its forces from Lebanon and urges all parties to withdraw.

Resolution 592, December 8, 1986: "strongly deplores" the killing of Palestinian students at Bir Zeit University by Israeli troops.

Resolution 605, December 22, 1987: "strongly deplores" Israel's policies and practices denying the human rights of Palestinians.

Resolution 607, January 5, 1988: "calls" on Israel not to deport Palestinians and strongly requests it to abide by the Fourth Geneva Convention.

Resolution 608, January 14, 1988: "deeply regrets" that Israel has defied the United Nations and deported Palestinian civilians.

Resolution 636, July 6, 1989: "deeply regrets" Israeli deportations of Palestinians.

Resolution 641, August 30, 1989: "deplores" Israel's continuing deportation of Palestinians.

Resolution 672, October 12, 1990: "condemns" Israel for violence against Palestinians at the Haram al-Sharif/Temple Mount.

Resolution 673, October 24, 1990: "deplores" Israel's refusal to cooperate with the United Nations.

Resolution 681, December 20, 1990: "deplores" Israel's resumption of the deportation of Palestinians.

Resolution 694, May 24, 1991: "deplores" Israel's deportation of Palestinians and calls on it to ensure their safe and immediate return.

Resolution 726, January 6, 1992: "strongly condemns" Israel's deportation of Palestinians.

Resolution 799, December 18, 1992: "strongly condemns" Israel's deportation of 413 Palestinians and calls for their immediate return.

At the same time that Washington joined or acquiesced in these sixty-nine resolutions, it used its veto twenty-nine separate times to prevent the Security Council from passing resolutions against Israel.[9]

The following are resolutions vetoed by the United States:

September 10, 1972: condemned Israel's attacks against southern Lebanon and Syria; vote: 13 to 1, 1 abstention.

July 26, 1973: affirmed the rights of the Palestinian people to self-determination, statehood, and equal protections; vote: 13 to 1, China absent.

December 8, 1975: condemned Israel's air strikes and attacks in southern Lebanon and its murder of innocent civilians; vote: 13 to 1, 1 abstention.

January 26, 1976: called for self-determination of Palestinian people; vote: 9 to 1, 3 abstentions.

March 25, 1976: deplored Israel's altering of the status of Jerusalem, which is recognized as an international city by most world nations and the United Nations; vote: 14 to 1.

June 29, 1976: affirmed the inalienable rights of the Palestinian people; vote: 10 to 1, 4 abstentions.

April 30, 1980: endorsed self-determination for the Palestinian people; vote: 10 to 1, 4 abstentions.

January 20, 1982: demanded Israel's withdrawal from the Golan Heights; vote: 9 to 1, 4 abstentions.

April 2, 1982: condemned Israel's mistreatment of Palestinians in the occupied West Bank and Gaza Strip and its refusal to abide by the Geneva Convention protocols of civilized nations; vote: 14 to 1.

April 20, 1982: condemned an Israeli soldier who shot eleven Moslem worshipers on the Haram al-Sharif/Temple Mount near the Al-Aqsa Mosque in the Old City of Jerusalem; vote: 14 to 1.

June 8, 1982: urged sanctions against Israel if it did not withdraw from its invasion of Lebanon; vote: 14 to 1.

June 26, 1982: urged sanctions against Israel if it did not withdraw from its invasion of Beirut; vote: 14 to 1.

August 6, 1982: urged cutoff of economic aid to Israel if it refused to withdraw from its occupation of Lebanon; vote: 11 to 1, 3 abstentions.

August 2, 1983: condemned continued Israeli settlements in occupied territories in the West Bank and Gaza Strip, denouncing them as an obstacle to peace; vote: 13 to 1, 1 abstention.

September 6, 1984: deplored Israel's brutal massacre of Arabs in Lebanon and urged its withdrawal; vote: 14 to 1.

March 12, 1985: condemned Israeli brutality in southern Lebanon and denounced the Israeli "Iron Fist" policy of repression; vote: 11 to 1, 3 abstentions.

September 13, 1985: denounced Israel's violation of human rights in the occupied territories; vote: 10 to 1, 4 abstentions.

January 17, 1986: deplored Israel's violence in southern Lebanon; vote: 11 to 1, 3 abstentions.

January 30, 1986: deplored Israel's activities in occupied Arab East Jerusalem that threatened the sanctity of Muslim holy sites; vote: 13 to 1, 1 abstention.

February 6, 1986: condemned Israel's hijacking of a Libyan passenger airplane on February 4; vote: 10 to 1, 1 abstention.

January 18, 1988: deplored Israeli attacks against Lebanon and its measures and practices against the civilian population of Lebanon; vote: 13 to 1, 1 abstention.

February 1, 1988: called on Israel to abandon its policies against the Palestinian intifada that violated the rights of occupied Palestinians, to abide by the Fourth Geneva Convention, and to formalize a leading role for the United Nations in future peace negotiations; vote: 14 to 1.

April 15, 1988: urged Israel to accept back deported Palestinians, condemned Israel's shooting of civilians, called on Israel to uphold the Fourth Geneva Convention, and called for a peace settlement under UN auspices; vote: 14 to 1.

May 10, 1988: condemned Israel's May 2 incursion into Lebanon; vote: 14 to 1.

December 14, 1988: deplored Israel's December 9 commando raids on Lebanon; vote: 14 to 1.

February 17, 1989: deplored Israel's repression of the Palestinian intifada and called on Israel to respect the human rights of the Palestinians; vote: 14 to 1.

June 9, 1989: deplored Israel's violation of the human rights of the Palestinians; vote: 14 to 1.

November 7, 1989: demanded that Israel return property confiscated from Palestinians during a tax protest and allow a fact-finding mission to observe Israel's crackdown on the Palestinian intifada; vote: 14 to 1.

May 31, 1990: called for a fact-finding mission on abuses against Palestinians in Israeli-occupied lands; vote: 14 to 1.

TWENTY-FIVE

ISRAEL AND THE PEACE PROCESS

Former Secretary of State James Baker was fond of saying that peace could come to the Middle East only when all parties to the conflict wanted it. But Israel's record clearly reveals that it has consistently favored land over peace. As Israel's first prime minister, David Ben-Gurion, wrote in his diary in 1949: "Peace is vital—but not at any price."[1] That has been the guiding principle of every Israeli leader since then.

Although Israel has been offered a number of peace plans in good faith over the years, it has rejected them all in favor of retaining territory acquired by force. This includes its refusal to accept back Palestinian refugees created in 1948 by the occupation of Palestinian land, its rejection of various land-for-peace proposals after its conquests of 1967, and its current insistence on continuing to occupy parts of the territory of Jordan, Lebanon, and Syria—as well as keeping under military occupation 1.7 million Palestinians. In nearly a half century, Israel has favored peace only with Egypt, thereby neutralizing the militarily strongest Arab nation adjacent to the Jewish state.

FALLACY

"Israel wants peace. Wants it more than any other nation."
—Menachem Begin, Israeli prime minister, 1979[2]

FACT

No less a friend of Israel than Henry Kissinger has acknowledged Israel's preference for land over peace. The former U.S. secretary of state wrote in 1992: "Israel adopted procrastination as the best strategy.... The way the peace process evolved seemed to confirm this judgment. In 1948 Israel's Arab neighbors went to war rather than accept the Jewish state. In the '50s and '60s, some of them began to move toward accepting the '47 frontiers but not those that existed. For example, in 1954 Egyptian President Gamal Abdel Nasser demanded that Israel retire to the frontier of the UN Partition Plan of 1947— that is, reduce Israel, as it then was, to about 40 percent of its size and leave Jerusalem an internationalized city surrounded by Arab territory. Similarly, Anthony Eden, speaking also for the United States, recommended a compromise between the 1947 frontier and that which existed (which we now describe as the '67 frontiers). In the '70s and '80s, the United States and some moderate Arab regimes accepted the '67 frontiers, but once again balked at those that existed. The PLO accepted them in 1988.

"In the face of these constantly improving offers, Israel had nothing to lose and much to gain from procrastination."[3]

Former Israeli Foreign Minister Abba Eban once confessed that Israel's preference for land was especially notable in the years before the 1973 war: "I will be honest: the collapse of Israel's diplomacy began under the Labor Government, not under the Likud.... It was true that Labor's official line was that the territories were a temporary bargaining card until peace was attained. But, at the same time, [Defense Minister Moshe] Dayan said, 'Sharm el Sheikh is more important than peace,' all the more so, the West Bank.

"Anyone who observed us in those years before the Yom Kippur War would have had the impression that we were really not interested in peace—we were a nation content without it. We felt that we held the trump cards in our hands and we were happy to hold them, but as time went on, we grew fond of them, and we were not ready to play them."[4]

FALLACY

"We are prepared to discuss peace with our neighbors, any day and on all matters."
—Golda Meir, Israeli prime minister, 1975[5]

FACT

Every U.S. president has been assured by Israeli leaders that Israel wants peace. But when the United States sought to find a peace formula, presidents learned over the decades that Israel had other priorities.

President Harry Truman was the first president to learn Israel's real attitude toward peace and land.[6] During the peace talks in Lausanne, Switzerland, in 1949, Truman was concerned that Israel was making "excessive claims" to territory. His message to Israel warned that the United States was "seriously disturbed by the attitude of Israel with respect to a territorial settlement in Palestine and to the question of Palestinian refugees. . . . The US Govt is gravely concerned lest Israel now endanger the possibility of arriving at a solution of the Palestine problem in such a way as to contribute to the establishment of sound and friendly relations between Israel and its neighbors. The Govt of Israel should entertain no doubt whatever that the US Govt relies upon it to take responsible and positive action concerning Palestine refugees and that, far from supporting excessive Israeli claims to further territory within Palestine, the US Govt believes that it is necessary for Israel to offer territorial compensation for territory which it expects to acquire beyond the boundaries" of the UN Partition Plan.[7]

President Dwight Eisenhower faced similar intransigence from Israel. The president had sent a secret emissary to the Middle East in early 1956 to encourage peace between Israel and Egypt. Instead, Eisenhower discovered that "the Israel officials are . . . completely adamant in their attitude of making no concessions whatsoever in order to obtain peace."[8]

Eisenhower recorded in his diary his impression of Israeli arrogance gained during a visit to him by two young Israelis: "The two of them belittled the Arabs in every way. . . . They boastfully claimed that Israel needed nothing but a few defensive arms, and they would take care of themselves forever and without help of any kind from the United States. I told them they were mistaken—that I had talked to many of the Arab leaders, and I was certain they were stirring up a hornet's nest and if they could solve the initial question peacefully and without doing unnecessary violence to the self-respect and interest of the Arabs, they would profit immeasurably in the long run."[9]

Eisenhower's administration was concerned enough about Israel's belligerence that it publicly warned Israel to "drop the attitude of conqueror and the conviction that force and a policy of retaliatory killings is the only policy that your neighbors will understand. You should make your deeds correspond to your frequent utterances of the desire for peace."[10]

Presidents John Kennedy and Lyndon Johnson made no serious efforts to find peace, largely because of Johnson's strong pro-Israel sympathies, and so did not encounter any serious conflicts with Israel.

President Richard Nixon in early 1973 wrote a note to National Security Adviser Henry Kissinger complaining: "We are now Israel's *only* major friend in the world. I have yet to see *one iota* of give on their part—conceding that Jordan and Egypt have not given enough on their side. . . . The time has come to quit pandering to Israel's intransigent position. Our actions over the past have led them to think we will stand with them *regardless* of how unreasonable they are."[11]

At another point Nixon proposed joining with the Soviet Union to impose a peace on the region. According to Kissinger, by then secretary of state, Nixon sent a message to him in the midst of the 1973 war while Kissinger was in Moscow. Kissinger, who partly paraphrased the message in his memoirs, wrote that Nixon proposed: "We would serve even Israel's best interests if we now used 'whatever pressures may be required in order to gain acceptance of a settlement which is reasonable and which we can ask the Soviets to press on the Arabs.' Nixon then listed the obstacles that had so far prevented a solution: Israel's intransigence, the Arabs' refusal to bargain realistically, and our own 'preoccupation with other initiatives.'" Nixon added: "I want you to know that I am prepared to pressure the Israelis to the extent required, regardless of the domestical [*sic*] political consequences."[12]

President Gerald Ford was so irritated by Israel's refusal to make concessions to reach a second Sinai agreement that he sent a sharp letter on March 21, 1975, to Prime Minister Yitzhak Rabin: "I am disappointed to learn that Israel has not moved as far as it might." Ford added that if Israel did not become more flexible, the United States would have to reassess its Middle Eastern policy, "including our policy towards Israel."[13]

The ploy backfired. The Rabin government merely became more intransigent and the talks collapsed the next day. Ford complained that although the United States had helped Israel become "stronger militarily than all [its] Arab neighbors combined" in the expectation that it would become more flexible, its position actually became more intransigent and "peace was no closer than it had ever been."[14]

Observed Kissinger: "I ask Rabin to make concessions, and he says he can't because Israel is too weak. So I give him arms, and he says he doesn't need to make concessions because Israel is strong."[15]

President Jimmy Carter's efforts to achieve the 1979 Egyptian-Israeli peace treaty caused him endless conflict with

Israel.[16] He recorded in his diary: "[Israeli Prime Minister Menachem Begin] was not willing to withdraw politically or militarily from any part of the West Bank; not willing to stop the construction of new settlements or the expansion of existing settlements; not willing to withdraw the Israeli settlers from the Sinai or even leave them there under UN or Egyptian protection; not willing to acknowledge that UN Resolution 242 applies to the West Bank–Gaza area; not willing to grant the Palestinian Arabs real authority, or a voice in the determination of their own future."[17]

At another point Carter said: "Whenever we seemed to be having some success with the Arabs, Begin would proclaim the establishment of new settlements or make provocative statements. This behavior . . . seriously endangered prospects for peace."[18]

President Ronald Reagan had sharp clashes with Israel, though he was the most pro-Israel president ever.[19] When Reagan in September 1982 put forward his plan for peace Prime Minister Begin instantly rejected it. When the idea of an international peace conference was suggested in 1987 to Israeli Prime Minister Yitzhak Shamir, he responded by calling it "this perverse and criminal idea," adding, "We reject this idea absolutely."[20]

President George Bush said publicly on July 1, 1991, that Israel's settlements were counterproductive and "the best thing for Israel to do is to keep its commitment . . . not to go in and build further settlements." The very next day Israeli cabinet members dedicated two new facilities at settlements in the West Bank.[21] When Bush's Secretary of State James Baker proposed in mid-1991 an international peace conference, Prime Minister Shamir turned him down on Israeli TV, saying he, Shamir, did not believe in returning territory and asking: "Where would you find among the nations of the world a people who would be ready to give up the territory of their homeland?"[22]

"Every Israeli government . . . has favored a comprehensive settlement and has stated a desire to talk peace with the leaders of any or all of the neighboring Arab states."

—AIPAC, 1989[23]

FACT

Israel has rejected every peace plan put forward by the Arabs and the United States except for the bilateral treaty with Egypt. (See more on the Egyptian-Israeli treaty below.)

The following are the major peace proposals and Israel's reaction:

▌ *The 1967–1971 UN Jarring Mission.* Swedish diplomat Gunnar Jarring was chosen as the UN's special mediator in the Middle East under the dictates of UN Security Council 242, which called for a trade of land for peace. His task was "to establish and maintain contacts with the [Middle Eastern] States concerned in order to promote agreement and assist efforts to achieve a peaceful and accepted settlement in accordance with the provisions and principles in this resolution." Jarring worked throughout 1968 without success and then in 1971 made a final effort by demanding that Israel at least express its support of Resolution 242's call for withdrawal from Arab territories it occupied in 1967. Israel's answer: "Israel will not withdraw to the pre–June 5, 1967, lines." With that, Jarring's mission came to an end and the United Nations made no further effort to implement Resolution 242.[24]

▌ *The 1969 Rogers Plan.* Secretary of State William P. Rogers on December 9 outlined a plan that called for implementation of UN Resolution 242. The plan involved withdrawal of Israeli forces from territory occupied in 1967 and Arab acceptance of a permanent peace with Israel as well as a "just settlement" of the Palestinian refugee problem.[25] This mild proposal sent the Israeli cabinet into a crisis session. When it emerged early in the morning of December 11, the cabinet released a statement flatly rejecting the proposal.[26]

■ *The 1977 Carter Comprehensive Peace Plan.* Slightly more than five months after assuming the presidency, Jimmy Carter put forth his ideas for a comprehensive peace. On June 27, his administration released a paper on its views of the elements of a comprehensive peace based on UN Resolution 242.[27] The paper said: "We consider that this resolution means [Israeli] withdrawal on all three fronts—that is, Sinai, Golan, West Bank–Gaza. . . . [N]o territories, including the West Bank, are automatically excluded from the items to be negotiated."[28] It added that there was a "need for a homeland for the Palestinians."[29]

In a meeting with Carter, Israeli Prime Minister Menachem Begin declared that Israel would never accept "foreign sovereignty" over "Judea and Samaria." He also refused to accept the usual interpretation that UN Resolution 242 meant withdrawal on all fronts. He insisted it meant only withdrawal on some fronts.[30] Carter then granted Begin a major concession. He acceded to Begin's request not to use in public the phrase "withdrawal with minor adjustments," arguing that Washington's use of such a formulation prejudiced future negotiations. Though withdrawal with minor adjustments was traditional U.S. policy, Carter agreed.[31]

Carter was frustrated at Begin's failure to respond with a gesture as generous as Egyptian President Anwar Sadat's dramatic visit to Jerusalem in late 1977. After nearly a year of deadlock Carter, Begin, and Sadat met at Camp David for thirteen days to find a formula for peace. When their talks ended September 17, 1978, Carter's vision of a comprehensive agreement lay in ashes, the Palestinians had been insulted by a bogus offer of "autonomy," Jerusalem was unmentioned, and Anwar Sadat got back only Egypt's own territories.[32] It was strictly a bilateral agreement, no more than Egypt probably could have had at any time since losing the Sinai in 1967.[33]

Israel finally accepted a peace treaty with Egypt in 1979 only after Egypt and the United States agreed essentially to ignore the Palestinians and the United States promised Israel up to $3 billion in extra aid beyond its annual sum of around $2 billion and substantial quantities of additional military equipment for the modernization of Israeli armed forces, including accelerated delivery of F-16 warplanes, the latest in America's air force.[34]

■ *The 1981 Prince Fahd Peace Plan.* Saudi Arabian Crown Prince Fahd bin Abdul Aziz put forward on August 8 a plan specifically "affirming the right of the states in the region to live in peace."[35] Fahd's plan called for Israel's withdrawal from all Arab land captured in 1967, including Arab East Jerusalem; removal of settlements established in the occupied territories since 1967; and establishment of a Palestinian state with East Jerusalem as its capital.

Israel immediately rejected the proposal, with Foreign Minister Yitzhak Shamir calling it "a poisoned dagger thrust into the heart of Israel's existence."[36] Israel announced it would counter the plan by establishing more settlements in the West Bank.[37]

■ *The 1982 Reagan Peace Plan.* The Reagan administration on September 1 offered a plan calling for Israeli withdrawal on all fronts under the guidelines of UN Resolution 242. The plan proposed a freeze on Israeli settlements, full autonomy for the Palestinians—but rejected the idea of an independent Palestinian state—and insisted that Jerusalem remain undivided and its future be negotiated between the parties. The proposal added that America's commitment to Israel's security was "ironclad." Despite the formal promise of a firm commitment to Israel's security and the retreat from Carter's offer of a "homeland" for the Palestinians, Prime Minister Menachem Begin instantly rejected the Reagan plan as a "serious danger" to Israel and labeled any Israeli who accepted it a "traitor."[38] Begin added: "We have no reason to get on our knees. No one will determine for us the borders of the Land of Israel."[39] The next day the Israeli cabinet formally rejected the Reagan plan and at the same time announced its intention to establish forty-two new settlements and revealed a thirty-year plan to settle 1.4 million Jews in the occupied territories.[40] Begin said: "Such settlement is a Jewish inalienable right and an integral part of our national security. Therefore, there shall be no settlement freeze."[41]

■ *The 1982 Arab Fez Peace Plan.* A summit meeting of the leaders of the Arab nations in Fez, Morocco, on September 9 adopted the Fez peace plan. It was largely based on Prince Fahd's proposal of a year earlier, differing mainly in its strong support of the Palestine Liberation Organization as the sole legitimate representative of the Palestinians.[42] The plan offered implicit recognition of Israel by calling for UN Security Council "guarantees for peace for all the states of the region."[43] The Israeli government rejected the Fez peace plan the next day, with Foreign Minister Yitzhak Shamir saying it amounted to a "renewed declaration of war on Israel . . . that has no weight, no value . . . and contains the same hate, the same war against peace."[44]

■ *The 1988 PLO Peace Plan.* The National Council of the Palestine Liberation Organization on November 15 renounced terrorism, accepted UN Security Council Resolutions 242 and 338, and called for an international peace conference. The council affirmed "the determination of the Palestine Liberation Organization to reach a comprehensive peaceful solution of the Arab-Israeli conflict and its essence, the Palestinian cause, within the framework of the United Nations Charter, the principles and provisions of international legitimacy, the rules of international law, the resolutions of the United Nations (the latest being United Nations Security Council Resolutions 605, 607, and 608), and the resolutions of the Arab summits in a manner that asserts the right of the Palestinian Arab people to return, exercise self-determination and establish its independent national state on its national territory, and creates arrangements of security and peace for all the states of the region."[45]

Israel immediately rejected the PLO's proposal: "Once again, the organization that claims to represent the Palestinian people proves unable or unwilling to recognize reality. In its new statements, ambiguity and double talk are again employed to obscure its advocacy of violence, resort to terrorism and adherence to extreme positions. Hence, any recognition or legitimation of the declaration will not be conducive to peace in the Middle East."[46]

U.S. reaction was lukewarm. Charles E. Redman, the State Department spokesperson, said that while the PLO statement was "encouraging," more concessions by the PLO would be necessary.[47] However, on the basis of the statement the United States finally agreed to hold official bilateral talks with the PLO for the first time. The talks continued without any serious progress for more than two years, when they were finally halted in May 1990 by the United States at the insistence of Israel.[48]

■ *The 1989 Bush Peace Plan.* The Bush administration embraced Resolution 242 as the basis for peace. On May 22 it urged all parties to moderate their behavior so a peace process could begin. Secretary of State James Baker advised Israel that "now is the time to lay aside, once and for all, the unrealistic vision of a greater Israel. Israeli interests in the West Bank and Gaza, security and otherwise, can be accommodated on a settlement based on Resolution 242. Forswear annexation. Stop settlement activity. Allow schools to reopen, reach out to the Palestinians as neighbors who deserve political rights."[49] Prime Minister Yitzhak Shamir immediately labeled the speech "useless."[50]

During 1990 frustration grew in the Bush administration at Israel's acceleration of its settlement activity. Baker on June 13 publicly deplored Israel's settlements and said: "I have to tell you that everybody over there [in Israel] should know what the [White House] telephone is: 1-202-456-1414. When you're serious about peace, call us."[51] Israel ignored Baker's remarks and continued its ambitious establishment of settlements for the rest of the year.

In 1991 Baker personally intervened by undertaking an arduous series of trips to Israel and Arab nations in search of a way to get the parties to agree to meet. After four trips, Baker reported on May 22 to the House Foreign Affairs Subcommittee on Foreign Operations: "Nothing has made my job of trying to find Arab and Palestinian partners for Israel more difficult than being greeted by a new settlement every time I arrive [in Israel]. I don't think that there is any bigger obstacle to peace than the settlement activity [by Israel] that continues not only unabated but at an enhanced pace. This does violate United States policy. . . . I've raised the issue on any number of occasions with the leadership of the government of Israel to no avail."[52]

Although on July 22, 1991, Baker received the unprecedented agreement of Egypt, Jordan, Lebanon, Saudi Arabia, and Syria to meet face to face with Israel, Prime Minister Shamir rejected the idea.[53] Said Baker: "For 43 years Israel has sought direct negotiations with its neighbors. . . . And now there is a real opportunity to get to those face-to-face negotiations. We will, for now, wait with great hope for a response from Prime Minister Shamir and his colleagues."[54] Shamir's reply: "I don't believe in territorial compromise."[55]

It took Baker three more trips to Israel to finally get Shamir's agreement to meet with Palestinians and the neighboring Arab states. The breakthrough came October 18, 1991, when the Soviet Union bowed to an Israeli demand and restored diplomatic relations with Israel, severed since 1967.[56] Arab and Israeli officials met in Madrid starting October 30 and later, in bilateral talks in Washington, Shamir made it clear that he was more interested in establishing settlements than in talking about peace. The peace talks dragged on inconclusively at a snail's pace, with Israel refusing to meet more than a few days every month or so. After Shamir was voted out of office in June 1992, he admitted that the lack of progress had been deliberate, a delaying tactic that he had been ready to employ for ten years in order to have time to colonize the occupied territories.[57]

New Prime Minister Yitzhak Rabin extended the talks to month-long sessions but did not fundamentally change Shamir's policies. As a result, after talks in September, October, and November 1992, no progress was reported in any of the bilateral negotiations except those with Jordan, with which Israel finally agreed to an agenda for holding future discussions. The talks with Lebanon and Syria were stalled, primarily because Israel insisted that its troops had to remain in southern Lebanon to protect Israeli frontier towns from guerrilla attacks and because Israel rejected the concept of total withdrawal of its troops from the Golan Heights. The Palestinian talks continued to be plagued by Israel's rejection of UN Resolution 242.[58]

Arab parties suspended both multilateral and bilateral talks in December 1992, when Israel expelled 413 Palestinians from the occupied territories to a hilltop north of the Israeli-controlled belt in southern Lebanon. Although the Bush administration voted for a UN Security Council resolution that condemned Israel for the action and demanded, in accordance with international law, that the Palestinians be returned home without delay, its successor in office quickly restored America's tradition of complicity in Israel's violations. Warren Christopher, President Clinton's secretary of state, welcomed Israeli Prime Minister Yitzhak Rabin's offer to take back one hundred of the Palestinians immediately and the rest a year later, saying that this offer removed any need for the Security Council to consider sanctions against Israel. Unmentioned in Christopher's announcement and overlooked by U.S. media was Israel's statement that the hundred would be jailed, not returned home. The remainder would likely face the same fate if returned a year hence.

Even in the absence of the expulsion controversy, the prospect of success in the peace talks was grim. The fact remains that no serious progress is likely unless the United States directly intervenes on substantive issues.

TWENTY-SIX

THE OTHER
COSTS
OF ISRAEL

The costs of U.S. support for Israel are enormous and varied. They go beyond the outpouring of dollars from the U.S. treasury and the moral price the American people pay as the result of our collusion in Israel's repression of human rights. Other losses to our nation result from direct, deliberate acts by Israeli authorities. These include the killing and harassment of U.S. military personnel, wide-scale and harmful espionage, corruption of our government institutions, and political pressures that cost our economy billions of dollars. Still other costs—including assassinations of U.S. civilians—are inflicted by Israel's enemies who resent America's pro-Israel bias.

FALLACY

"America's *own self-interest* has been well served by our Middle East policies."
—Hyman Bookbinder, former representative of
the American Jewish Committee, 1987[1]

208

The United States has been ill served by its close association with Israel. Because of this association, Americans have been tagged as legitimate targets by Israel's enemies. American diplomats from Italy to Lebanon to Sudan have been killed, and American travelers have been placed in peril, killed, or wounded in skyjackings and other acts of terror.

In the United States, Palestinian Sirhan Sirhan claimed he killed Senator Robert Kennedy because he resented Kennedy's support of Israel.[2] Arab American Alex Odeh, the western regional director of the American-Arab Anti-Discrimination Committee, was killed in 1985 by a bomb planted at his Santa Ana, California, office, victim of suspected members of the Jewish Defense League.[3]

American reporters and academics were held for years as hostages in Lebanon by groups protesting U.S. support for Israel, and 263 U.S. Marines and attached service personnel were killed and 151 wounded as they served in Lebanon in 1982–1984 to encourage the withdrawal of Israeli and Syrian forces from Lebanese territory.[4] In fact, Muslim anger at U.S. support of Israel resulted in driving out nearly all Americans during the last half of the 1980s from Lebanon, a country where Americans had prospered for the previous century.

Israel itself has even imperiled U.S. citizens. There are several documented instances in which Israel deliberately caused damage to U.S. property and injury or even death to Americans, among them the well-known Lavon Affair of 1954 when Israeli agents attacked American installations in Egypt in an effort to damage U.S.-Egyptian relations.[5]

Other examples are Israel's 1967 attack on the USS *Liberty* that killed 34 Americans and wounded 171[6] and the systematic pattern of Israeli harassment of U.S. Marine peacekeeping forces in Lebanon in 1983–1984.

The Israeli behavior in Lebanon became so provocative that Marine Commandant General R. H. Barrow complained about it in a public letter to Secretary of Defense Caspar Weinberger: "It is evident to me, and the opinion of the U.S.

commanders afloat and ashore, that the incidents between the Marines and the IDF [Israel Defense Forces] are timed, orchestrated, and executed for obtuse Israeli political purposes." Barrow detailed eight instances of Marine-IDF clashes that he characterized as "life-threatening situations, replete with verbal degradation of the officers, their uniform and country." His letter added: "It is inconceivable to me why Americans—serving in peacekeeping roles—must be harassed, endangered by an ally."[7]

FALLACY

"[W]e must never forget that Israel remains a strong, reliable friend and a stable, strategic ally."
—*Bill Clinton, Democratic presidential candidate, 1992*[8]

FACT

Beyond the Jonathan Pollard spy incident, which was exposed in 1985, there are a number of less publicized cases in which Israelis and their supporters have engaged in illegal acts against U.S. interests.

Cases involving Israel include arrests of suspects with ties to the Jewish state for trying to sell to Iran $2.5 billion worth of military equipment; illegally shipping to Israel devices to trigger nuclear bombs; attempting to acquire technology for the manufacture of tank cannon barrels and cluster bombs; and a massive fraud involving General Electric and an Israeli air force general in misappropriating more than $40 million in military aid to Israel.[9]

In the GE scheme, Israeli Brigadier General Rami Dotan was sentenced to thirteen years in prison, and on July 22, 1992, GE pleaded guilty in Cincinnati Federal District Court to charges of fraud, money laundering, and corrupt business practices. It agreed to pay fines and penalties of $69 million.[10] The case of massive fraud involves a number of other companies and includes continuing probes of Pratt & Whitney,

Textron Lycoming, General Motors, and Allison as well as a mysterious Swiss trading company, Ellis A.G. Also under investigation was Harold Katz, a dual U.S.-Israeli citizen with close ties to Ellis A.G. and the man whose Washington apartment was used by the Pollard spies in the mid-1980s to copy secret U.S. documents. The case even involves allegations of Dotan paying $50,000 in the United States to a hit man to intimidate or murder one of the witnesses against him.[11]

The Israeli government has refused to cooperate with the House oversight committee of the House Committee on Energy and Commerce chaired by Democratic Representative John D. Dingell of Michigan, including refusing to allow the United States to question Katz. Dingell complained publicly that Israel "has been markedly uncooperative."[12] Dingell added: "Here we give them engines, we give them technical assistance, we have a very extensive program to give them substantial funds, and they are alleging that their national security precludes us from looking into something that they admit is a crime."[13]

The corruption has even penetrated the higher levels of the Pentagon. In 1991 former Assistant Secretary of the Navy Melvyn R. Paisley pleaded guilty in Alexandria (Virginia) Federal District Court to massive fraud involving the awarding of defense contracts to the Israeli company Israeli Mazlat Ltd. and the U.S. firms Sperry Corporation and Martin Marietta Corporation. Paisley admitted he joined a conspiracy to help Mazlat win several defense contracts for making pilotless drones for battlefield reconnaissance in exchange for promises of $2 million in bribes. According to former Israeli Mossad spy Victor Ostrovsky, Mazlat was a subsidiary of the state-run Israeli Aeronautical Industries and Tadiran, and research for Mazlat's drone had been stolen by Mossad from U.S. firms.[14] On October 18 Paisley was sentenced to four years in prison and two years probation and fined $50,000.[15]

In addition, there is the Iran-Contra scandal in which Israel encouraged the Reagan administration to sell weapons to Iran in hopes of freeing American hostages in Lebanon and as a way to earn profits to help fund the Contras in Nicaragua in defiance of Congress. Senator David F. Durenberger, chairman of the Senate Intelligence Committee, later concluded that the administration had been exploited by "someone else's foreign policy and the avarice of arms dealers."[16] While that judgment fails to apportion the high level of guilt the administration bore, it does indicate how important Israel's role in the scheme was.

FALLACY

"More than 80 percent of U.S. military assistance is spent in the United States. This creates jobs and profits for American firms."

—*AIPAC, 1992*[17]

FACT

The Buy America Act requires foreign governments to spend in the United States at least 80 percent of the military aid they receive from U.S. taxpayers. The 80 percent rule, however, no longer applies to Israel. In an exemption adopted just for Israel, the Buy America Act is set aside. Israel is permitted to spend $475 million—26 percent of its annual U.S. grant of $1.8 billion for military purposes—to create "jobs and profits" in Israel, not the United States.[18]

Nor does the cost of Washington's bias toward Israel end there. Israel's supporters regularly pressure Congress into blocking military sales even to moderate Arab states that are prepared to pay cash to receive arms for their own defense. In 1985, Saudi Arabia expressed its interest in an unprecedented large purchase of F-15 warplanes from the United States. When fifty-one senators—a majority of the membership—signed a letter to President Reagan opposing the sale, the Saudis turned to Great Britain. The immediate sale was worth more than $7 billion and eventually reached about $30 billion, the biggest arms deal in history.[19]

The loss of such sales caused Secretary of Defense Frank C. Carlucci in 1988 to criticize "various interest groups and many in Congress" for opposing arms sales to Arab nations. He said such opposition was costing the United States a loss of political influence in the Arab world to other countries such as the Soviet Union, Great Britain, China, and France. Added Carlucci: "The notion that U.S. defense cooperation with moderate Arab states poses a danger to Israel is ill-founded and untrue."[20]

Carlucci's remarks raise a disturbing aspect of Israel's opposition to U.S. arms sales to the Arabs. It concerns the question of Israel's motives. Israel consistently claims it opposes such deals because of concern about its security. But the fact is that it continued to oppose sales to Saudi Arabia even when Washington worked out severe limits on the positioning of the weapons. For instance, in the case of the F-15s to Saudi Arabia, the Saudis agreed that the warplanes would not be stationed anywhere near Israel.[21] When they were finally bought from Great Britain, there were no similar restrictions.

The suspicion is that Israel is less concerned about its security in these cases than it is about showing the Arabs that Israel can dictate U.S. policy.[22]

FALLACY

"Our relationship with Israel is in our mutual self-interest."
—*President Ronald Reagan, 1988*[23]

FACT

A glaring example of how Israel took advantage of U.S. aid to work against U.S. interests is the Lavi airplane project of the 1980s. This vastly costly project was financed by the Reagan administration to provide Israel with its own warplane, designed and produced in Israel, with the U.S. paying 90 percent of the costs and providing half of the advanced technology. In return, Israel promised that it would not use the Lavi to compete with U.S. aircraft exports in the Third World, a pretense Israel's supporters maintain to this day. Said AIPAC in 1992: "The Lavi was never meant to compete with American-manufactured aircraft."[24] Yet *The Washington Post* discovered that Israel Aircraft Industries, the government-owned firm contracted to make the Lavi, distributed a marketing brochure in the early days of the project entitled "Lavi: The Affordable Fighter." The brochure projected that Israel would sell as many as 407 of the jets overseas.[25]

This left the United States in the bizarre position of financing and supporting with technology a foreign warplane that would compete directly with U.S. manufacturers, who were receiving no such level of support. In the end, U.S. manufacturers were saved by Israel's ineptness. Despite all the U.S. assistance, Israel proved unable to produce the plane, and the project had to be suspended because of cost overruns. The United States squandered $1.5 billion on the Lavi.[26]

Israeli State Comptroller Yaacov Maltz issued a withering criticism of Israel's handling of the Lavi project. His forty-page report said: "A great many of the significant and essential decisions were made with information that was without basis, inadequate, tendentious and lacking proper cost estimates." Maltz reported, in the paraphrase of *The Jerusalem Post*, that Israeli officials did not "consider the plane's purpose, size or cost. . . . Nor did they have details regarding cost, export potential and other aspects of the program."[27]

Nonetheless, after the Lavi's cancellation, Secretary of State George Shultz allowed Israel to use $450 million of its U.S. military aid to pay termination charges of contracts; approved continuation of Israel's "offset" practices in which U.S. companies had to buy up to $150 million of Israeli products in return for receiving Israeli contracts, which were paid by American aid; and allowed as much as $400 million in U.S. aid to be spent annually in Israel.[28]

Many of the Israeli technicians laid off from work on the Lavi moved to South Africa.[29] The transfer of such advanced U.S. technology came in the face of the embargo against trade with South Africa. In August 1988 South Africa unveiled its new Cheetah-E warplane, which had many features common to planes produced earlier in Israel.[30]

FALLACY

"The real story is who are these unnamed individuals who are floating these malicious rumors [about Israel's re-exporting U.S. technology]?"
—Moshe Arens, Israeli defense minister, 1992[31]

FACT

In March 1992 *The Wall Street Journal* reported that there was "no doubt in the U.S. intelligence community that Israel has repeatedly engaged in diversion schemes."[32] On April 1, 1992, the State Department's inspector general charged that Israel, identified in the report as a "major recipient" of U.S. military aid, was engaged in a "systematic and growing pattern" of selling secret U.S. technology in violation of U.S. law. The report said Israel's violations began about 1983 and that Israel sought to conceal the violations.[33]

One of the major charges against Israel was that it was selling secrets of America's Patriot antimissile missile to China.[34] A seventeen-member U.S. inspection team sent to Israel failed to find any proof of transfer of the Patriots or their technology.[35] Despite that, Defense Secretary Dick Cheney said: "We had good reason to believe there has been a diversion" of Patriot missiles.[36]

The charges sent a shock wave through Israel. Arms sales of about $1.5 billion annually account for 40 percent of Israel's exports and are based almost entirely on U.S. technology.[37] The subject of Israel profiting from classified U.S. technology was explored in detail by journalists Andrew and Leslie Cockburn in 1991 in their revealing book *Dangerous Liaison*. A year before, the *Los Angeles Times* had reported that Israel had become "the back door" for providing China with U.S. weapons technology.[38]

The transfer of American technology to Israel began in 1970 with the signing of the far-reaching Master Defense Development Data Exchange Agreement, which provides for the greatest transfer of technology to Israel or any other country ever undertaken.[39] Such a massive infusion of technology has been a boon to Israel's economy. By 1981 Israel emerged from being a technologically backward arms importer to the seventh largest exporter of military weapons in the world with overseas sales of $1.3 billion.[40]

An Israeli historian observes, "The Americans have made virtually all their most advanced weaponry and technology—meaning the best fighter aircraft, missiles, radar, armor, and artillery—available to Israel. Israel, in turn, has utilized this knowledge, adapting American equipment to increase its own technological sophistication, reflected tangibly in Israeli defense offerings."[41]

FALLACY

"Saudi Arabia is more dependent on the United States than the United States is on Saudi Arabia."

—AIPAC, 1989[42]

FACT

After Saudi Arabia imposed its devastating oil embargo in 1973, Secretary of State Henry Kissinger admitted too late: "I made a mistake."[43]

The Arab oil embargo of 1973–1974 came about because President Nixon ignored repeated warnings from the oil states that the United States should maintain a more evenhanded position in the 1973 Arab-Israeli war.[44] However, at Kissinger's urgings, Nixon brushed aside the pleas of Saudi Arabia and openly launched a major airlift of military weapons to Israel in the midst of the October war.[45]

Saudi Arabia's King Faisal and other Arab leaders had asked Washington no more than what the UN Security Council had demanded six years earlier—that Israel return to the 1967 ceasefire lines.[46] King Faisal had repeatedly passed this message to Washington since spring but without effect.[47]

Instead, Nixon, who was already badly weakened by the Watergate scandal, awarded Israel $2.2 billion in emergency aid on October 19.[48] The next day Saudi Arabia announced a total oil embargo against the United States in retaliation for its support of Israel. Other oil states quickly followed.[49]

TWENTY-SEVEN

ISRAEL AS A STRATEGIC ALLY

Israel is often cited as a strategic ally of the United States. This is a grossly inaccurate characterization that offends and tends to alienate nations and political movements whose cooperation is critical to peace. From both legal and practical standpoints, Israel is not an ally of the United States. There is no alliance treaty of any kind between the two nations. The Memorandum of Understanding of Strategic Cooperation that the Reagan administration signed with Israel on November 29, 1983, is not a treaty and has no force in international law. It merely binds the administration that signs it.

Israel lacks the land or population to support a role as a strategic ally of the United States. Even though it is the military superpower of the Middle East, its record of hostility toward neighboring populations makes it a serious burden from the standpoint of U.S. security interests. The United States is an asset of great strategic importance to Israel, but the reverse is not true.

"Americans have . . . come to recognize the enormous importance of Israel—as a partner in the pursuit of freedom and democracy, as a people who share our highest ideals, and as a vital strategic ally."

—George P. Shultz, secretary of state, 1985[1]

The claim that Israel is a "strategic asset" was successfully promoted in the 1980s by the Israeli lobby headed by AIPAC, the American Israel Public Affairs Committee. The essence of AIPAC's argument was that Israel is a strategic ally against Soviet incursion into the region because of its political stability, military skills, and intelligence services. To support its case, the lobby issued a series of monographs, *AIPAC Papers on US-Israeli Relations*, that sought to show the advantage of close U.S.-Israeli relations in the security field.[2]

Previous presidents and secretaries of state had avoided a formal alliance with Israel, although they often acted as if one existed. On the official level, however, Washington had consistently rejected Israel's efforts for formal ties. For instance, in the mid-1950s Israel had sought a formal security relationship with the United States but Secretary of State John Foster Dulles countered by noting that the United States could hardly be expected to "guarantee temporary armistice lines; it could only guarantee permanent agreed peace boundaries."[3] In other words, Dulles was telling Israel that it had to define its borders and live within them.

President Carter's secretary of defense, Harold Brown, rejected out of hand the idea of Israel as a strategic asset, saying: "The whole idea of Israel becoming our asset seems crazy to me. The Israelis would say, 'Let us help you,' and then you end up being their tool. The Israelis have their own security interests and we have our interests. They are not identical."[4]

President Ronald Reagan reversed this trend. On November 30, 1981, the United States, at Secretary of State Alexander Haig's urgings, concluded the Memorandum of Understanding on Strategic Cooperation with Israel. The agreement called for U.S.-Israeli cooperation against threats in the Middle East "caused by the Soviet Union or Soviet-controlled forces from outside the region."[5]

The UN General Assembly reacted by passing a resolution charging that the agreement would "encourage Israel to pursue its aggressive and expansionist policies and practices in the occupied territories" and would have "adverse effects on efforts for the establishment of a comprehensive, just and lasting peace in the Middle East and would threaten the security of the region."[6]

On December 14, 1981, Israel defied world opinion and essentially annexed Syria's Golan Heights. The United States joined in a UN Security Council resolution denouncing the action and declaring it "null and void."[7] Washington also suspended the strategic cooperation agreement with Israel.[8] However, on November 29, 1983, the Reagan administration resurrected the strategic cooperation agreement. On that date Israel and the United States again formally pledged jointly to fight Communist inroads to the Middle East.[9]

The policy had the strong backing of Secretary of State George Shultz, overriding opposition by Secretary of Defense Caspar Weinberger and some officials of the State Department and the CIA. They all warned against neglecting friendly ties with Arab states and allowing the United States to become a "hostage of Israeli policy."[10]

FALLACY

"Israel is our strongest ally and best friend, not only in the Middle East, but anywhere else in the world."

—*Senator Albert Gore,*
Democratic vice presidential candidate, 1992[11]

Scholar Cheryl A. Rubenberg has noted: "In the U.S.-Israeli relationship the United States has provided absolute support, but Israel has repeatedly engaged in actions that have contravened American interests—often significantly harming them."[12] Former Under Secretary of state George W. Ball adds: "[Israel] has never been prepared to deal with the United States in the manner and spirit expected of an ally. It does not share with us, as its primary objective, the establishment of enduring peace in the area, except on its own expansionist terms. It does not—and is not willing to—consult with us or seek to concert a common policy. It persistently deceives the United States as to its intended moves, often to the detriment of United States plans and interests."[13]

Complicating the relationship is the fact that successive administrations have secretly colluded with Israel against the Arabs, often in violation of official U.S. policy. Nonetheless, Israel has repeatedly spurned U.S. advice, flaunted its transgressions of U.S. policy, failed to consult with Washington before such grave actions as annexing Jerusalem, and, as noted earlier, spied on the United States. Its policies and actions—such as its attacks on Lebanon, its continued occupation of territory by force, its violations of the UN charter and the Fourth Geneva Convention—directly conflict with those of the United States. Yet despite these actions that disqualify Israel as a true ally, the Reagan administration went out of its way to pamper Israel with a series of extraordinary concessions even beyond designating the Jewish state a strategic ally.

In 1985, the Reagan administration established a unique free trade zone with Israel. The pact opened U.S. markets to Israeli goods, duty free, in direct competition with such American products as textiles and citrus. It was the first time the United States had ever granted such access to its markets to a foreign government.[14]

In 1986, Israel was granted the right to take part in sophisticated research for President Reagan's controversial Strategic

Defense Initiative, better known as Star Wars. Israel became the third country enlisted in the program, after Great Britain and West Germany.[15] So far Israel has received $126 million in funding for the development of its Arrow antimissile defense system under the SDI program, with another $60 million appropriated for the Arrow follow-on in fiscal year 1992 and, according to Senator Robert Byrd, the prospect of several hundred million dollars more in the future.[16]

In 1987, Israel was designated alongside such U.S. allies as Australia and Japan as a "non-NATO ally," meaning it could participate in coproduction of weapons, bid on servicing and maintenance contracts, utilize U.S. funds for research and development projects, and sell conventional weapons systems to the U.S. armed forces.[17]

Commented AIPAC Executive Director Thomas A. Dine in 1986: "We are in the midst of a revolution that is raising U.S.-Israel relations to new heights. . . . The old order in which Israel was regarded as a liability, a hindrance to America's relationship with the Arab world, a loud and naughty child—that order has crumbled. In its place, a new relationship is being built, one in which Israel is treated as—and acts as—an ally, not just a friend, an asset rather than a liability, a mature and capable partner, not some vassal state."[18]

FALLACY

"Over and above 'strategic cooperation,' as such, the U.S.-Israeli relationship has yielded our nation invaluable security intelligence for many years."
—*Hyman Bookbinder, former representative of the American Jewish Committee, 1987*[19]

FACT

According to former Director of Central Intelligence Stansfield Turner: "Israeli intelligence has failed. Ninety percent of the statements made about Israel's contributions to

America's security are public relations." Responding to an Israeli journalist during an interview, Turner added: "You have failed in your treatment of terror. You failed in preparatory reading of the data in Lebanon [before the 1982 invasion]. You thought that you would be able to establish a Christian government there. You thought you would be able to throw out the Syrians. You have even failed in dealing with terror inside Israel. Israeli intelligence is good, but not in all areas. Above all it is good at overselling its own capabilities."[20]

FALLACY

"Israel is a unique and impressive ally."
—*Professor Steven L. Spiegel, 1983*[21]

FACT

In the 1990–1991 war against Iraq's invasion of Kuwait, the greatest contribution Israel could make was to do nothing and stay out of the war while American troops did the fighting. U.S. officials quickly recognized that Israel, instead of being an asset, was an enormous handicap. The United States had to send high-ranking officials to Israel to make clear it was not welcomed as a member of the international effort led by the United States, because of wide suspicions that Israel might use the war to further its own expansionist interests and because its participation would endanger the alliance of Arab countries formed by Washington.[22]

The cost to the United States to buy Israel's noninvolvement was an additional $650 million supplement to Israel's annual $3 billion aid grant; the award of $700 million worth of used weapons being withdrawn from Europe; $117 million dollars worth of Patriot missiles; and a $400 million housing loan guarantee.[23]

Israel is now seeking new justifications to continue the alliance. The current, most popular rationale is the resurrection of an old idea, namely that Israel could serve U.S. interests by acting as its forward storage base. As one Israeli put it to *The Washington Post* in mid-1992, Israel can serve as the "biggest [aircraft] carrier in the Mediterranean."[24]

In this scenario, the port at Haifa becomes central. It already services and repairs about twenty-five U.S. warships from the Sixth Fleet each year as well as acting as a regular port of call for the fleet. Some 45,000 American sailors were scheduled to enjoy shore leave in Haifa in 1992. In addition, Israel Aircraft Industries now services all U.S. F-15 warplanes stationed in Europe, and the United States and Israel are jointly developing the Arrow antimissile missile.[25]

TWENTY-EIGHT

THE ILLUSION
OF
SHARED VALUES

One of the most widely held and harmful fallacies about the U.S.-Israeli relationship is that the two countries share ideals, democratic structure, and respect for human rights. This is a delusion that complicates our quest for peace. Israel is not a democracy. It does not have a constitution. It discriminates broadly on the basis of religion and is harsh and often brutal in its treatment of minorities. It is an exclusionary and expansionist state. For nearly a half century Israeli practices have been repeatedly condemned by the world community as violations of international law. Although these practices contradict American law, the United States, to its great discredit, has usually acted to protect Israel.

FALLACY

"[The United States has a] special relationship with Israel, based on shared values, a mutual commitment to democracy, and a strategic alliance."

—*Democratic party platform, 1992*[1]

Israel has neither a written constitution nor a bill of rights, and its government is in part actually a theocracy.[2] According to the Rabbinical Courts Jurisdiction Law of 1953, all Jewish residents came under the authority of rabbinical courts in the areas of domestic and social relations. Thus only kosher meat is allowed in Israel and proselytizing by Christians and others is a crime punishable by five years in prison.[3] A religious judge can order a husband to divorce his wife or deny a divorce to a wronged wife, and a brother-in-law can keep a childless widow from remarrying.[4] Christians or Muslims cannot marry Jews in Israel, and if they are married elsewhere their bond is not recognized by the rabbinical court in Israel.

In December 1990, the leaders of Christian churches in Jerusalem were so concerned by Jewish encroachments on traditional Christian institutions that they restricted Christmas celebrations to prayers "without any manifestation of jubilation." The Christians were worried about attempts by Jewish settlers to move into the Christian Quarter of the Old City and about an "erosion of the traditional rights and centuries-old privileges of the churches," including imposition by Israel of municipal and state taxes. Their statement said, in part: "We express our deep concern over new problems confronting the local church. They interfere with the proper functioning of our religious institutions, and we call upon the civil authorities in the country to safeguard our historic rights and status honored by all governments."[5]

To grasp the absurdity of the notion that Israel is like America, one need only contemplate what life would be like if America operated by the Israeli rule book. Under those rules, American Christians, the predominant religious community, would enjoy a highly privileged status. They alone could confiscate the property of non-Christians, carry firearms, buy or lease government property, secure subsidized housing, and enjoy other social benefits. Non-Christians could be shot on suspicion of carrying a gun or Molotov cocktail. Their bones could be broken by police as a means of disciplinary education. Their homes could be entered forcibly without a search warrant, dynamited, or sealed. They would be subject to arrest and incarceration for long periods without due process.

Under Israeli-style rules, non-Christians living in territory conquered by U.S. military forces years ago could never become citizens of the United States or have the right to determine their own political future free from U.S. authority. Nor could non-Christians who fled during these military conquests return to their homes.

FALLACY

"This is a relationship based on a shared commitment to democracy and to common values."
—*President George Bush, 1992*[6]

FACT

Israel practices as state policy a number of measures that are illegal in the United States and other Western countries. These include assassination, kidnapping, expulsion, detention without charges or trial, land confiscation, and collective punishment—not to mention Israel's long-standing practice of espionage against the United States, its principal benefactor. Moreover, Israel is the only country that officially sanctions torture.[7]

Prime Ministers Yitzhak Shamir and Menachem Begin, leaders of the two largest Jewish terrorist groups in Palestine before the formation of Israel, have never expressed any remorse about their bloody activities. In fact, Shamir went out of his way at the Madrid peace conference in 1991 to say in response to charges about his earlier terrorist days: "I have always said, I always say, I am proud of everything I have done in my past. I do not disown a single step. . . . I am proud of what I have done and I do not owe an accounting to anyone."[8]

Some years earlier Shamir had told an interviewer: "There are those who say that to kill [an individual] is terrorism, but an attack on an army camp is guerrilla warfare and to bomb civilians is professional warfare. But I think it is the same from the moral point of view. . . . It was more efficient and more moral to go for selected targets."[9]

Such an attitude has led to Israel's practice of assassinating its foes. Among the operations that are documented, in the early 1960s Israel carried on a campaign of terror against German scientists working for Egypt,[10] including at least five persons killed by a letter bomb. An Egyptian scientist was killed in 1979 while working for Iraq.[11] In 1990 Gerald Vincent Bull, a Canadian artillery expert, was shot to death outside his Brussels apartment after being publicly linked to Iraq's weapons program. Bull was reported to be the victim of Israeli assassins.[12]

Over the decades Israel has waged an unrelenting assassination campaign against Palestinians belonging to the Palestine Liberation Organization, including the mistaken killing of an Arab waiter in Lillehammer, Norway, in 1973,[13] and the 1991 assassination of the PLO's military chief Khalil Wazir, better known by the nom de guerre Abu Jihad (Father of Struggle), at his home in Tunis.[14]

FALLACY

"The basis of the relationship between Israel and the United States is the unshakable foundation of shared values and hopes. Our joint commitment to democracy and freedom stands on a permanent solid rock on which our very special relationship is built."
—*Yitzhak Rabin, Israeli prime minister, 1992*[15]

FACT

Israel's state policy condoning kidnapping has affected U.S. security and cost American lives. The best-known and most recent example of this practice was the 1989 abduction of Shiite Sheikh Abdul Karim Obeid from his home in southern Lebanon. In retaliation a U.S. hostage held in Lebanon, Marine Lieutenant Colonel William R. Higgins, was hanged by his Shiite Muslim captors.[16]

After Higgins's hanging, President Bush said publicly: "On Friday, I said that the taking of any hostages was not helpful to the Middle East peace process. The brutal and tragic events of today have underscored the validity of that statement. Tonight, I wish to go beyond that statement with an urgent call to all—all—parties who hold hostages in the Middle East, to release them forthwith as a humanitarian gesture, to begin to reverse the cycle of violence in that region."[17]

Israel refused to release Obeid and hundreds of other Palestinians held hostage. This provoked criticism from Senate Republican leader Bob Dole, who charged that Israeli actions "endangered American lives." He added that "a little more responsibility on the part of the Israelis one of these days would be refreshing."[18]

Israel also routinely imposes such barbaric measures as collective punishment, "administrative detention," torture, and expulsion in its attempt to suppress the Palestinian uprising.[19] Book burning is another mark of Israel's occupation. Israel Shahak, an Israeli scholar who survived a Nazi extermination camp and now campaigns for Palestinian rights, reports: "Israeli soldiers enter a Palestinian library, public or private, gather up all the books, put them in a pile outside and set them on fire. Because they cannot read Arabic, they say, they must burn all books, just to make sure the evil ones are destroyed."[20]

FALLACY

"Israel . . . has proved to be one of the few U.S. foreign aid recipients that has responded positively to U.S. overtures to make major reforms in its economy."

—*AIPAC, 1992*[21]

Israel is one of the few nations in the world that clings to an essentially socialist economy.[22] Despite major efforts by Washington to reform Israel's outmoded and inefficient system, massive government involvement dominates its economy. In late 1991 a study by the Export-Import Bank noted that Israel for two decades had "put off free-market reforms" and as a result was increasingly dependent on U.S. aid.[23]

Another report issued about the same time by the Congressional Research Service (CRS), an arm of Congress within the Library of Congress, concluded that "Israel is not economically self-sufficient, and relies upon foreign assistance and borrowing to maintain its economy." The CRS report added that Israel's economy was pushed into a near crisis by "growing debt servicing costs, mounting government social services expenditures, perennial high defense spending levels, and a stagnant domestic economy combined with worldwide inflation and declining foreign markets for Israeli goods." Its inflation rate has averaged 20 percent in recent years, a high figure for most nations but an improvement over 1984 when Israel's inflation hit a record 445 percent.[24]

Israel's wasteful economy is a major reason the Jewish state was unable to finance the cost of absorbing recent immigrants from the former Soviet Union and had to seek billions of dollars in loan guarantees from the United States. The situation was so bad that the Bank of Israel predicted in a report that as many as 200,000 of the new immigrants would leave in the next few years if jobs were not created. The 1991 report said inflation was in the double-digit range and unemployment was currently 11 percent and could hit 18 percent.[25]

In Israeli economist Steven Pault's opinion, "Economic policy in Israel consists of pork barrel politics run amok. . . . Whereas most countries have rigorous anti-trust policies and powerful enforcement agencies, economic policy in Israel is decidedly pro-trust. . . . Production, marketing, export quotas, and water and land allotments are distributed as patronage; they are never auctioned. . . . Israeli commercial policy is the most protectionist in the democratic world. . . . Any other country would be subject to international trade sanctions for even a handful of the import restrictions and export manipulations that Israel maintains." He adds, "Israel's own policy makers have shown themselves unwilling or unable to produce serious economic reforms." Yet, Pault concludes, the United States makes no effort to use its massive aid program to pressure Israel to make reforms, without which Israel will become even more dependent.[26]

FALLACY

"Israelis have long recognized the need to dramatically reform their economy."

—AIPAC, 1992[27]

FACT

Despite a major effort by the United States during the 1980s to reform Israel's socialism, more than 60 percent of Israel's economic activity in 1991 continued to be based on government subsidies and government-related spending. Concluded a study by the Jerusalem-based Institute for Advanced Strategic and Political Studies: "The Israeli vision of the future is to continue down the same failed, dismal path of more and bigger government."[28]

The Export-Import Bank in its 1991 study noted that Israel has resisted reforms and instead uses debt "to finance high defense expenditures, an extensive social welfare system, and a relatively high standard of living. . . . If new lending is sharply increased . . . it is likely that by the end of the decade the U.S. government will be in a position where the scheduled repayments exceed disbursements. Thus the U.S. government would become a net capital importer from Israel."[29]

A study by U.S. experts in 1989 had reported similar flaws depressing Israel's government-directed economy. These included government "mismanagement" and the absence of a long-term economic program; heavy dependence on government spending, which accounted for two-thirds of Israel's gross national product; liberal government bailouts of failed businesses; and a trend among Israelis to go on unemployment rather than accept low-paying jobs.[30]

In large part, this inefficiency resulted from the extraordinary influence of Histadrut, the massive Jewish General Federation of Workers, in Israel's economy.[31] Histadrut has dominated the Israeli economy since the beginning of the Jewish state. It has been Israel's largest employer and its enterprises have included the biggest Israeli building firms, banks, insurance companies, and marketing and consumer cooperatives.[32]

Historian Howard M. Sachar noted in the mid-1970s that Israel had suffered what he called a collapse of the work ethic in its work force, in part because of the power of Histadrut: "Surely the Histadrut leadership could not escape a major responsibility for this collapse of the work ethic. With employees' rights guaranteed and institutionalized to the last degree over the years, it had become all but impossible for employers to dismiss malingerers and sluggards. The tendency, rather, for workers in factories, shops, and offices alike, and not least of all in government, to perform at the lowest common denominator of exertion or conscientiousness unquestionably was infecting society at large."[33]

Nearly twenty years later, the dismal picture had not changed much. This is largely the fault of massive U.S. aid, which allows Israel to ignore its basic problems, among them not only bureaucratic sluggishness but rampant corruption.[34] Says Republican Senator Malcolm Wallop of Wyoming: "The world is marching away from socialism, yet we're propping up a basically socialist country, Israel, which is not willing to change. It has very little free enterprise and huge, distorting subsidies wandering through its economy. In many ways, our aid supports that."[35]

Or, in the words of Israeli economist Alvin Rabushka: "One can question the wisdom of the U.S. taxpayer subsidizing the

government of Israel, which in turn uses the money to subsi-
dize its own socialistic economy."[36]

FALLACY

"In large part due to the government's extraordinary defense
burden, Israelis have seen their standard of living slowly
decline."

—AIPAC, 1992[37]

FACT

Israelis these days are enjoying a far higher standard of living
than ever.[38] This results from massive U.S. aid as well as about
$1 billion annually in donations and bond purchases from
Jewish supporters abroad.[39] A major share of Israel's defense
expenditures is actually paid for by the United States. A study
by the U.S. General Accounting Office reported that by 1983
the United States was already paying for 37 percent of Israel's
military budget.[40]

Reported Jackson Diehl of *The Washington Post* in mid-
1992: "In the 25 years since winning the 1967 Arab-Israeli
war, Israel has changed from a Spartan, socialist, isolated and
highly militarized country into a modern consumer society
that is suffused by Western secular culture. In the last decade,
in particular, there has been a burst of affluence and consump-
tion."[41]

Yet Israel's basic socialist economy is going downhill. As
Martin Baral, a Holocaust survivor and now an American
industrialist, observes: "Israel has been committing economic
suicide from the very inception of the establishment of the
state."[42] He notes that David Ben-Gurion and all the early
Zionist settlers in Palestine were East European socialists and
Communists dedicated to a controlled economy. Baral's advice, like that of many economists who have studied Israel's
economic mess, is to sell to private ownership such government-owned enterprises as telephone, chemical, aircraft, de-

fense, and other industries; drastically reduce the excessive bureaucracy, which stifles free enterprise; and lower taxes.

One result of its state-directed system is that Israel proportionately has fewer small businesses than Western countries. Israel's persistent unemployment at rates above 10 percent could be greatly reduced if small businesses were allowed to flourish, Baral notes, because such businesses provide "the fastest route for rapid expansion of employment."

As Prime Minister Yitzhak Rabin said in his inaugural address in mid-1992: "There is too much paperwork and too little productivity."[43]

FALLACY

"America and Israel share a special bond. Our relationship is unique among all nations."
—*Bill Clinton, Democratic presidential candidate, 1992*[44]

FACT

Israeli leaders regularly and harshly criticize the United States in ways that British writer Eric Silver has described as "among the most vitriolic assaults ever directed by a junior partner at a rich and mighty patron."[45]

Silver was referring to Prime Minister Menachem Begin's assault on U.S. Ambassador Samuel Lewis, one of Israel's closest friends, after the United States temporarily suspended its new strategic alliance agreement with Israel in 1981. Begin summoned Lewis to his home and declared: "You have no moral right to preach to us about civilian casualties. We have read the history of World War Two and we know what happened to civilians when you took action against an enemy. We have also read the history of the Vietnam war and your phrase 'bodycount.' . . . Are we a vassal state? A banana republic? Are we fourteen-year-old boys, that if they don't behave they have their knuckles smacked? . . . The people of Israel has lived for 3,700 years without a memorandum of understanding with America—and it will continue to live without it for another 3,700 years."[46]

When Secretary of State Alexander Haig, who a number of critics believe secretly gave a green light to Israel to invade Lebanon in 1982, officially urged Begin not to carry out the invasion, the prime minister shot back:[47] "Mr. Secretary, my dear friend, the man has not yet been born who will ever obtain from me consent to let Jews be killed by a bloodthirsty enemy and allow those who are responsible for the shedding of the blood to enjoy immunity."[48]

Secretary of State George Shultz, regarded by Israelis as one of their best friends in Washington, warned Israel in late 1984 that it would not get an additional $800 million emergency grant—on top of its regular $2.6 billion aid grant that year—unless it imposed economic austerity measures. In return for that advice, Israeli Minister of Economic Coordination Gad Yaacovi replied: "Israel does not need moral preaching from the United States. The responsibility of the Jewish people is in the hands of the Jewish people alone."[49]

When the Carter administration urged Israel to withdraw from the West Bank, Foreign Minister Moshe Dayan haughtily declared in 1979: "I know you Americans think you're going to force us out of the West Bank. But we're here and you're in Washington. What will you do if we maintain settlements? Squawk? What will you do if we keep the army there? Send troops?"[50]

Nor have the insults stopped. A member of Shamir's cabinet, Science Minister Yuval Neeman, said of President George Bush in 1992: "We've never had in the United States an anti-Jewish and an anti-Israeli regime like the present one."[51]

EPILOGUE

This book, I believe, presents the most balanced and candid profile ever compiled on Israel. From it emerge these stark realities:

■ Israel is an embattled state largely because of its long history of aggressive territorial expansion at the expense of Arabs, especially the Palestinians.

■ In its zeal to control the Arabs whose land it seized, Israel engages in inhumane practices that violate international law and the idealistic vision that brought Israel itself into being.

■ Israel will remain an embattled state until it ends its occupation of Arab land, its subjugation of the inhabitants, and its discrimination against Arab citizens.

■ The United States provides the support without which Israel could not maintain its repression of human rights and territorial expansion. This collusive relationship severely damages U.S. influence worldwide. It has led our government into the disgraceful practice of turning a blind eye to Israeli violations of both international and U.S. law, a habit widely noted by foreign leaders.

■ Largely because of the powerful influence of pro-Israel activists over public perceptions of Israel and Middle East issues, most Americans are unaware of the collusion and the cost that it entails.

In citing these realities, I do not question Israel's legal standing as a nation. Like other peoples—including the Palestinians—Israelis have a right to decide their political future and choose their own government. I must add that I feel compassion for the pro-Israel activists who are devoted to an idealistic vision of Israel and ignore the truth. The influence they exercise in America is powerful and often injurious to U.S. interests, but it is not, in my opinion, conspiratorial in any sense. They simply want to believe only good things about Israel, but their pleadings, no matter how poignant, do not relieve either Israel or the United States of its obligation to law and justice.

The growing crisis in the Middle East demands inspired, courageous leadership by the United States and Israel, but neither government displays these qualities. Both keep putting off the decisions that common sense must recognize as inevitable and urgent.

Sooner or later, Israel must grant justice and equality to all Arabs under its authority or witness the further corruption of the nation that most Jews and many Christians hold dear. The beleaguered Palestinians in the occupied territories must be permitted to decide their own political future, and Israel must reform its domestic law and practice to extend full rights and benefits to all of its citizens without regard to religion or nationality.

Just as inevitably, the United States must end its complicity in Israeli violations and summon the leadership needed to break the Arab-Israeli impasse. So far its endeavors have been limited to providing encouragement for diplomatic negotiations, but commitment to procedure alone will not suffice. The U.S. government must take an unequivocal stand on principle. It must call for an end to Israel's human rights violations and announce firm, new conditions that must be met before the state is eligible for a continuation of U.S. aid.

In setting these conditions, the United States must, of course, recognize Israel's security needs. Even though Israel is the superpower of the region, its concern for the integrity of its borders is understandable. It has had a long history of conflict with the Palestinians and Arab states, and, except for Egypt, all of the adjacent states remain technically at war with Israel. Its land area is small and vulnerable. Given these circumstances, Israel will insist on extraordinary guarantees to its national integrity before agreeing to political self-determination for the inhabitants of the occupied territories.

To ease these anxieties, the United States should recommend that, once withdrawal has occurred, the occupied territories be maintained under United Nations supervision as a demilitarized region, no matter what type of political entity is created there.

In addition, the U.S. government should offer permanent on-site border security for the entire new perimeter of Israel. This would be an extension of the system that has long been successful on the border between Israel and Egypt where, since 1976, more than one thousand U.S. troops, the main element in a multinational force, have provided security for both nations.[1] The proposed extension would serve the same dual purpose, protecting both Israel and adjoining Arab states from cross-border violations. While it would constitute a major new U.S. obligation, including risk to our forces if violence should erupt, these costs would be minor when compared with the price America will pay if the Arab-Israeli conflict is not brought to an end.

The future of Jerusalem is a complicated political challenge but it is not unsolvable. The answer may be found in a concept called "joint and undivided sovereignty," a political arrangement that is unusual but not unprecedented. Under it, both Israel and the new Palestine would claim sovereignty over the Holy City but leave actual administration to a locally elected council. Jerusalem would be the capital of both Israel and the new Palestine. Several Arab officials have embraced the concept, but Israelis so far have not.[2]

Towering over these challenges, important as they are, is Israel's continued violation of Arab human rights and U.S. collusion in these practices. As Noam Chomsky counsels: "Either we provide the support for the establishment of a greater Israel with all that it entails and refrain from condemning the grim consequences of this decision, or we withdraw the means and the license for the pursuit of these programs and act to ensure that the valid demands of Israelis and Palestinians be satisfied."[3]

In America's own interest as well as that of all other parties, the United States must pressure Israel to end its violations without further delay. The U.S. government must put Israel firmly on notice that all U.S. aid will be suspended until Israel agrees to withdraw from the occupied territories and to extend equal rights to all its citizens.

In presenting this ultimatum, the U.S. government would end American complicity in Israeli violations. It would also be doing Israel a great favor: as former Under Secretary of State George W. Ball contended when he recommended a similar course of action in 1977, the withdrawal of U.S. aid could rescue Israel from a burden that threatens its own well-being.[4] Fifteen years later, Ball's wise counsel still receives no serious consideration.

The problem is a critical lack of willpower on the part of officials in both Congress and the executive branch. Most of them recognize the folly of present policy and the need for strong U.S. leadership in the Middle East, but they are so intimidated by the government of Israel and its U.S. supporters that they are afraid to pursue our nation's own best interests. This intimidation is harmful to the basic interests of Israel, not just the United States, and it must be ended without delay. There is, however, scant hope that our elected leaders will muster the necessary courage to act until they hear a powerful demand from the countryside. The American people can no longer afford to leave the resolution of the Arab-Israeli conflict in the hands of the powerful interests, in and out of government, that have maintained this costly and corrosive collusion for more than a quarter of a century. Reform must be undertaken and advanced by persevering people at the community level who insist that our government stand once more against repression and for human dignity.

APPENDIX

MAJOR ORGANIZATIONS FOCUSED ON MIDDLE EAST POLICY

American-Arab Anti-Discrimination Committee, 4201 Connecticut Ave. NW, Suite 500, Washington, DC 20008. Albert Mokhiber, executive director. (202) 244-2990.

American Educational Trust, 1902 18th St. NW, Washington, DC 20009. Publisher of the monthly *Washington Report on Middle East Affairs*, edited by Richard H. Curtiss. Ambassador Andrew I. Killgore, president. (202) 939-6050.

Americans for Middle East Understanding, 475 Riverside Dr., Suite 241, New York, NY 10115. Publisher of the monthly report *The Link*. John F. Mahoney, executive director. (212) 870-2053.

American Muslim Council, 1212 New York Ave. NW, Suite 525, Washington, DC 20005. Dr. Abdulrahman al-Amoudi, executive director. (202) 789-2262.

Arab-American Institute, 918 16th St. NW, Suite 501, Washington, DC 20006. Dr. James Zogby, executive director. (202) 429-9210.

Center for Policy Analysis on Palestine, 2435 Virginia Ave. NW, Washington, DC 20037. Dr. Muhammed Hallaj, director. (202) 338-1290.

Churches for Middle East Peace, 110 Maryland Ave. NE, Suite 308, Washington, DC 20002. Corinne Whitlatch, manager. (202) 546-8425.

Council for the National Interest, 1511 K St. NW, Suite 1043, Washington, DC 20005. Eugene Bird, president. (202) 628-6962.

Foundation for Middle East Peace, 555 13th St. NW, Suite 800, Washington, DC 20004. Merle Thorpe, Jr., president. (202) 637-6558.

Institute for Palestine Studies, 3501 M St. NW, Washington, DC 20007. Philip Mattar, executive director. (202) 342-3990.

Jewish Peace Lobby, 8604 2nd Ave., Suite 317, Silver Spring, MD 20910. Dr. Jerome M. Segal, president. (301) 589-8764.

Middle East Children's Alliance, 2140 Shattuck Ave., Suite 207, Berkeley, CA 94704. Barbara Lubin, director. (501) 548-0542.

Middle East Institute, 1761 N St. NW, Washington, DC 20036. Ambassador Robert Keeley, president. (202) 785-1141.

Middle East Justice Network, P.O. Box 558, Cambridge, MA 02238. Hady Amr, director. (617) 666-8061.

Middle East Policy Council, 1730 M St. NW, Suite 512, Washington, DC 20036. The Hon. George McGovern, president. (202) 296-6767.

Middle East Research and Information Project, 1500 Massachusetts Ave. NW, Suite 119, Washington, DC 20005. Joe Stork, director. (202) 223-3677.

Middle East Watch, 485 Fifth Ave., 3rd Fl., New York, NY 10017. Aryeh Neier, director. (212) 972-8400.

National Association of Arab Americans, 1212 New York Ave. NW, Suite 300, Washington, DC 20005. Khalil Jahshan, executive director. (202) 847-1840.

National Council on U.S.-Arab Relations, 1735 I St. NW, Suite 515, Washington, DC 20006. Dr. John Duke Anthony, president. (202) 293-0801.

North American Coordinating Committee for Non-Governmental Organizations on the Question of Palestine, 1747 Connecticut Ave. NW, 3rd Floor, Washington, DC 20009. Larry Ekin, chair. (202) 319-0757.

Palestine Aid Society, 2025 I St. NW, Washington, DC 20006. Dr. Anan Ameri, president. (202) 728-9425.

Palestine Human Rights Information Center, 4753 N. Broadway, Suite 930, Chicago, IL 60640. Louise Cainkar, director. (312) 271-4492.

Palestine Solidarity Committee, 11 John St., Room 806, New York, NY 10038. (212) 227-1435.

ACKNOWLEDGMENTS

My gratitude, first of all, must go to the hundreds of people who, after reading my book *They Dare to Speak Out: People and Institutions Confront Israel's Lobby*, urged me to keep writing and speaking out.

This remarkable response inspired the book you are reading and led also three years ago to the formation of the Council for the National Interest (CNI), a nonprofit Washington-based organization headed by Eugene Bird, a retired U.S. foreign service officer and Middle East expert. CNI advocates Middle East policies that are consistent with American principles and values. Its members, now numbering more than six thousand, work for these goals at the community level throughout the United States.

Two CNI members unacquainted with each other deserve special acknowledgment. Arthur J. Kobacker, a businessman and philanthropist who lives in Columbus, Ohio, and generously supported my last campaigns for reelection to Congress, and Frank F. Espey, a neurosurgeon in Greenville, South Carolina, wrote within days of each other last summer with the same urgent message: a book is needed that responds in detail to the propaganda misleading the American people about the Israeli record. They were not the first to cite the need, but their letters provided the spark that got the project under way.

Most of all, I salute Donald Neff for his assistance in assembling and verifying events and documents and for providing wise counsel. His database, a remarkable storehouse of historical information on the Arab-Israeli-Palestinian-U.S. relationship, proved to be invaluable. This highly respected historian and former Middle East correspondent for *Time* magazine is the author of three books, the *Warriors* trilogy, which have been deemed by reviewers to be the best available histories of the major Middle East crises in 1956, 1967, and 1973. The trilogy is indispensable to an understanding of the complex U.S.-Israeli relationship. Without the Neff database, my task would have been magnified enormously.

I also wish to thank Frank Collins, a veteran journalist who knows Israel from frequent and extended visits there, for his insight and evaluations. Laura Drake, a staff member at CNI, and Professor Francis A. Boyle, an expert on international law, examined the manuscript and offered valuable suggestions, as did my wife, Lucille, my favorite proofreader and critic, who has now survived the publication of four books. Each time her support has been the sine qua non.

I am grateful for the encouragement provided by the leaders of other organizations, especially former Senator James G. Abourezk, founder of the American-Arab Anti-Discrimination Committee, as well as the cooperation, excellent advice, and strong support of Shirley Cloyes, publisher of Lawrence Hill Books, and her colleague in editing Barbara G. Flanagan.

Paul Findley
1040 West College Avenue
Jacksonville, Illinois 62650

NOTES

PROLOGUE

1. *U.S.A. Today*, 19 January 1993, 4A.
2. Art Stevens, *The Persuasion Explosion* (Washington, D.C.: Acropolis, 1985), 104–5.
3. Findley, *They Dare to Speak Out*, rev. ed. (Brooklyn: Lawrence Hill, 1989).
4. George W. Ball, remarks to a conference of the American-Arab Anti-Discrimination Committee, Washington, D.C., 5 September 1985.
5. Donald McHenry, interview with author, 24 April 1985.
6. Steven M. Cohen, "Attitudes of American Jews toward Israel and Israelis," 1983 Survey of American Jews and Jewish Communal Leaders, American Jewish Committee, 3.
7. Arthur Hertzberg, "Israel and American Jewry," *Commentary*, August 1967.
8. Quoted in Urofsky, *We Are One!*, 435.
9. Ralph Nurnberger, interview with author, 2 August 1991.
10. Grace Halsell, *Prophecy and Politics*, 22–24.

ONE

1. See, for instance, Genesis 15:18: "On that day the Lord made a covenant with Abram, saying, 'To your descendants I give this land, from the river of Egypt to the great river, the river Euphrates.'"
2. Ben-Gurion, *Israel*, 80. The text of the declaration is reprinted on pp. 79–81.
3. Bright, *A History of Israel*, 17–18. Also see Nakhleh, *Encyclopedia of the Palestine Problem*, 953–70.
4. Epp, *Whose Land Is Palestine?*, 39–40. Also see *The New Oxford Annotated Bible*, 1549–50; Beatty, *Arab and Jew in the Land of Canaan*, 85.
5. Grose, *Israel in the Mind of America*, 88–89. Excerpts from the King-Crane Commission report are in Khalidi, *From Haven to Conquest*, 213–18, and Laqueur and Rubin, *The Israel-Arab Reader*, 34–42.
6. Nakhleh, *Encyclopedia of the Palestine Problem*, 4.
7. Bard and Himelfarb, *Myths and Facts*, 1.
8. Epp, *Whose Land Is Palestine?*, 38, 41.

9. Guillaume, *Zionists and the Bible*, 25–30, reprinted in Khalidi, *From Haven to Conquest*. Also see Nakhleh, *Encyclopedia of the Palestine Problem*, 953–70.

10. Dewey Beegle, interview with author, 12 January 1984.

11. Ben-Gurion, *Israel*, 80.

12. Sanders, *The High Walls of Jerusalem*, 612–13.

13. Sachar, *A History of Israel*, 222.

14. Quoted in Elon, *The Israelis*, 149.

15. *Palestine: Blue Book, 1937* (Jerusalem: Government Printer, 1937), cited in Epp, *Whose Land Is Palestine?*, 144. Also see Khalidi, *From Haven to Conquest*, Appendix I.

16. United Nations, subcommittee report to the Special Committee on Palestine, A/AC 14/32, reprinted in Khalidi, *From Haven to Conquest*, 675.

17. Sachar, *A History of Israel*, 163.

18. Said et al., "A Profile of the Palestinian People," in Said and Hitchens, *Blaming the Victims*, 235–37.

19. Quigley, *Palestine and Israel*, 73. Also see Khalidi, *Before Their Diaspora*; Nakhleh, *Encyclopedia of the Palestine Problem*, especially chaps. 1 and 2.

20. Ben-Gurion, *Israel*, 80.

21. Sheldon L. Richman, "'Ancient History': U.S. Conduct in the Middle East since World War II and the Folly of Intervention," Cato Institute pamphlet, 16 August 1991.

22. Welles, *We Need Not Fail*, quoted in ibid. Also see Muhammad Zafrulla Khan, "Thanksgiving Day at Lake Success, November 17, 1947"; Carlos P. Romulo, "The Philippines Changes Its Vote"; and Kermit Roosevelt, "The Partition of Palestine: A Lesson in Pressure Politics," all in Khalidi, *From Haven to Conquest*, 709–22, 723–26, 727–30, respectively.

23. The text of Resolution 181 (II) is in Tomeh, *United Nations Resolutions on Palestine and the Arab-Israeli Conflict*, 1:4–14.

24. Mallison and Mallison, *The Palestine Problem in International Law and World Order*, 171.

25. Quigley, *Palestine and Israel*, 47.

26. Cattan, *Palestine, the Arabs, and Israel*, 29; John Ruedy, "Dynamics of Land Alienation," in Abu-Lughod, *Transformation of Palestine*, 125, 134; Said, *The Question of Palestine*, 98.

27. David Ben-Gurion, *War Diaries*, quoted in Flapan, *The Birth of Israel*, 13.

28. Findley, *They Dare to Speak Out*, 273.

29. Sharon, *Warrior*, 246.

30. Ibrahim Abu-Lughod, "Territorially-based Nationalism and the Politics of Negation" in Said and Hitchens, *Blaming the Victims*, 195.

31. Klieman, *Foundations of British Policy in the Arab World*, 68.

32. Ibid., 234–35. Also see Fromkin, *A Peace to End All Peace*, 560.

TWO

1. Dupuy, *Elusive Victory*, 3–19; Flapan, *The Birth of Israel*, 192–93.
2. Meir, *My Life*, 211.
3. Quigley, *Palestine and Israel*, 39.
4. Palumbo, *The Palestinian Catastrophe*, 40.
5. Khalidi, *From Haven to Conquest*, lxxix. The text of the plan is in a special "1948 Palestine" issue of the *Journal of Palestine Studies*, Autumn 1988, 20–38.
6. *New York Times*, 20 December 1947. Also see Quigley, *Palestine and Israel*, 41. The official British military report is WO 275/64 (London: Public Record Office), cited in Nakhleh, *Encyclopedia of the Palestine Problem*, 153.
7. Sykes, *Crossroads to Israel*, 337. Also see Green, *Taking Sides*, 69.
8. Palumbo, *The Palestinian Catastrophe*, 40.
9. Quoted in Flapan, *The Birth of Israel*, 121.
10. Khalidi, *From Haven to Conquest*, lxxix.
11. Morris, *The Birth of the Palestinian Refugee Problem*, 63.
12. Ibid., 128; Quigley, *Palestine and Israel*, 62.
13. Flapan, *The Birth of Israel*, 132–33.
14. Cable 513 from Cairo, 13 May 1948, cited in Flapan, *The Birth of Israel*, 192.
15. Quoted in Flapan, *The Birth of Israel*, 192. Also see Shlaim, *Collusion across the Jordan*, 197.
16. Khalidi, *From Haven to Conquest*, lxxxii.
17. Allon, *Shield of David*, 187.
18. Khalidi, *Before Their Diaspora*, 316. Also see Cockburn, *Dangerous Liaison*, 20–21; Peres, *David's Sling*, 32–33. In return for such favors, Israel passed on some secret U.S. military equipment to Czechoslovakia, including a mobile early approach radar system; see Green, *Living by the Sword*, 217–18.
19. Khalidi, *From Haven to Conquest*, 861–66.
20. Grose, *Israel in the Mind of America*, 210–11.
21. Raviv and Melman, *Every Spy a Prince*, 326–30; Cockburn, *Dangerous Liaison*, 24–25.
22. Cockburn, *Dangerous Liaison*, 24–25, 158.
23. Ibid., 24–25.
24. In a letter to President Truman, quoted in Flapan, *The Birth of Israel*, 189.
25. Khalidi, *From Haven to Conquest*, 867–71.
26. Green, *Taking Sides*, 71.
27. Flapan, *The Birth of Israel*, 195. Emphasis is in the original. For a discussion of various reasonable estimates reflecting all sides see Flapan, 194–97.
28. Quoted in Flapan, *The Birth of Israel*, 189.
29. Secret telegram "INFOTEL from Secretary of State," 14 May 1948, cited in Green, *Taking Sides*, 70–71.

30. Cable 513 from Cairo, 13 May 1948, quoted in Flapan, *The Birth of Israel*, 192.
31. Glubb, *A Soldier with the Arabs*, 152.
32. Shlaim, *Collusion across the Jordan*, 271–72.
33. Flapan, *The Birth of Israel*, 123.
34. el-Edroos, *The Hashemite Arab Army*, 244.
35. Morris, *The Birth of the Palestinian Refugee Problem*, 7.
36. Fallaci, *Interview with History*, 100.
37. Ben-Gurion, *Israel*, 63.
38. Michael C. Hudson, "The Transformation of Jerusalem: 1917–1987 A.D.," in Asali, *Jerusalem in History*, 257.
39. Quigley, *Palestine and Israel*, 41. Also see Flapan, *The Birth of Israel*, 90–91.
40. Bethell, *The Palestine Triangle*, 263; Sachar, *A History of Israel*, 267. For details on the bombing and reaction of British officials, see Nakhleh, *Encyclopedia of the Palestine Problem*, 269–70.
41. Silver, *Begin*, 78–80.
42. CO 537/3855 (London: Public Record Office), cited in Nakhleh, *Encyclopedia of the Palestine Problem*, 270–71; Tannous, *The Palestinians*, 474. The British government publicly condemned the Semiramis bombing as a "dastardly and wholesale murder of innocent people." When the Jewish Agency complained that Great Britain did not condemn killings by Arabs, British officials rejoined that Arabs had not carried out organized attacks on buildings containing women and children; see Quigley, *Palestine and Israel*, 43.
43. Khalidi, *From Haven to Conquest*, 761–78, contains Jacques de Reynier's moving firsthand account, "Deir Yassin," as well as accounts of attacks on other Palestinian centers. Many writers have discussed the massacre, perhaps none better than Silver, *Begin*, 88–96. Also see details in Nakhleh, *Encyclopedia of the Palestine Problem*, 271–72.
44. Morris, *The Birth of the Palestinian Refugee Problem*, 222. Also see Palumbo, *The Palestinian Catastrophe*, xii–xiv; Quigley, *Palestine and Israel*, 85; Nakhleh, *Encyclopedia of the Palestine Problem*, 272.
45. Persson, *Mediation and Assassination*, 204. Also see Kurzman, *Genesis 1948*, 555–56; Avishai Margalit, "The Violent Life of Yitzhak Shamir," *New York Review of Books*, 14 May 1992; Palumbo, *The Palestinian Catastrophe*, 36.
46. Teveth, *Ben-Gurion and the Palestinian Arabs*, 27.
47. Segev, *1949*, 69–72.
48. Thomas J. Hamilton, *New York Times*, 19 November 1949; "Report of the Special Representative's Mission to the Occupied Territories, 15 Sept. 1967," UN report No. A/6797*.
49. Walid Khalidi, "The Palestine Problem: An Overview," *Journal of Palestine Studies*, Autumn 1991, 9.

50. Anne O'Hare McCormick, *New York Times*, 18 January 1949. Also see Morris, *The Birth of the Palestinian Refugee Problem*, 135–36; Cattan, *Jerusalem*, 61; Segev, *1949*, 95.

51. Israel Shahak, "Arab Villages Destroyed in Israel," in Davis and Mezvinsky, *Documents from Israel*, 43–54. Also see Morris, *The Birth of the Palestinian Refugee Problem*, xiv–xviii, who did a study similar to Shahak's in the 1980s and lists by name, date, and cause the abandonment of 369 Arab villages in 1948–1949. Nakhleh, *Encyclopedia of the Palestine Problem*, reproduces the list of all cities, towns, and villages in Palestine in 1945 as published in the *Palestine Gazette* (295–306) and also lists the fate of all those political units after 1948 (315–32).

52. A study completed in 1991 under scholar Walid Khalidi reported that 418 villages had been destroyed; see Khalidi, *All That Remains*.

53. Israel Shahak, "Arab Villages Destroyed in Israel," in Davis and Mezvinsky, *Documents from Israel*, 43.

54. Bard and Himelfarb, *Myths and Facts*, 84.

55. Shlaim, *Collusion across the Jordan*, 289. An abbreviated paperback version of Shlaim's important book was published in 1990 by Columbia University Press under the title *The Politics of Partition: King Abdullah, the Zionists, and Palestine*.

56. Sachar, *A History of Israel*, 350; Epp, *Whose Land Is Palestine?*, 195. For details of Israel's plans for occupying Palestinian territory, see Khalidi, *From Haven to Conquest*, lxxv–lxxxiii, 755–61. For an excellent study of Jewish land ownership, see Ruedy, "Dynamics of Land Alienation," in Abu-Lughod, *Transformation of Palestine*, 119–38. Also see Davis and Mezvinsky, *Documents from Israel*, 43–54; Morris, *The Birth of the Palestinian Refugee Problem*, 155, 179; Nakhleh, *Encyclopedia of the Palestine Problem*, 305–45; Nyrop, *Israel*, 52; Shipler, *Arab and Jew*, 32–36; Segev, *1949*, 69–71.

57. McDowall, *Palestine and Israel*, 193. The text of the declaration is in Ben-Gurion, *Israel*, 79–81.

58. Morris, *The Birth of the Palestinian Refugee Problem*, 155, 179.

59. Quoted in Nakhleh, *Encyclopedia of the Palestine Problem*, 310, from *Ha'aretz* (Tel Aviv), 4 April 1969.

60. Nakhleh, *Encyclopedia of the Palestine Problem*, 369.

61. Don Peretz, "The Arab Refugee Dilemma," *Foreign Affairs*, October 1954.

62. Palumbo, *The Palestinian Catastrophe*, 146.

63. Lustick, *Arabs in the Jewish State*, 59.

64. Nyrop, *Israel*, xix; Foundation for Middle East Peace, *Report on Israeli Settlement in the Occupied Territories*, Special Report, July 1991.

65. Ahmad Beydoun, "The South Lebanon Border Zone: A Local Perspective," *Journal of Palestine Studies*, Spring 1992, 44.

66. Thomas L. Friedman, *New York Times*, 22 September 1986.

67. Israel attempted to retain a 250-acre patch of Sinai shorefront south of Eilat called Taba. However, a group of five arbitrators ruled in 1988 that the land rightfully belonged to Egypt, and Israel was finally forced to give it up ten years after the treaty; Edward Cody, *Washington Post*, 30 September 1988.

THREE

1. "Repcrt of the Special Representative's Mission to the Occupied Territories, 15 Sept. 1967," UN report no. A/6797*.
2. Ben-Gurion, *Diaries*, 29 May 1959, quoted in Segev, *1949*, 35.
3. Glubb, *A Soldier with the Arabs*, 162.
4. U.S. Department of State, *A Decade of American Foreign Policy: 1940–1949*, 850–51. For a touching personal story of the plight of the refugees, see Turki, *The Disinherited*.
5. "The Special Representative of the United States in Israel (McDonald) to President Truman," 17 October 1948, 4 PM, *Foreign Relations of the United States 1948* (hereafter referred to as *FRUS*), 5:1486.
6. *New York Times*, 17 February 1949.
7. Ibid. Also see Beryl Cheal, "Refugees in the Gaza Strip, December 1948–May 1950," *Journal of Palestine Studies*, Autumn 1988, 138–57.
8. *FRUS 1949*, "Palestine Refugees" (secret), 15 March 1949, 6:828–42.
9. Ibid.
10. Davis, *Myths and Facts (1989)*, 114.
11. Thomas J. Hamilton, *New York Times*, 19 November 1949; "Report of the Special Representative's Mission to the Occupied Territories, 15 Sept. 1967," UN report no. A/6797*. Also see Janet L. Abu-Lughod, "The Demographic Transformation of Palestine," in Abu-Lughod, *Transformation of Palestine*, 139–64. The State Department estimate, which apparently was not made public at the time, was around 820,000; see *FRUS 1949*, "Editorial Note," 6:688.
12. Morris, *The Birth of the Palestinian Refugee Problem*, 297.
13. Ibid., 297.
14. "Report on the Mission of the Special Representative to the Occupied Territories," UN report no. A/6797*. Also see Davis, *The Evasive Peace*, 69; Neff, *Warriors for Jerusalem*, 320. Davis puts the second-time refugees at 145,000.
15. Aronson, *Creating Facts*, 19. For a poignant eyewitness account of the destruction of the Latrun villages, see the article by Israeli reporter Amos Kenen, "Report on the Razing of Villages and the Expulsion of Refugees," in Davis and Mezvinsky, *Documents from Israel*, 148–51. Also see Nakhleh, *Encyclopedia of the Palestine Problem*, 400–401.
16. Bard and Himelfarb, *Myths and Facts*, 121.

17. Israeli scholars have thoroughly documented the causes of the flight of the refugees; see in particular Flapan, *The Birth of Israel*, 84–87; Morris, *The Birth of the Palestinian Refugee Problem*, 58; Segev, *1949*, 25–29. Also see Ball, *The Passionate Attachment*, 29–30, 35–36. The issue also received close attention in a special fortieth anniversary edition called "Palestine 1948" published by the *Journal of Palestine Studies*, Autumn 1988: see especially Appendix D, "Maps: Arab Villages Emptied and Jewish Settlements Established in Palestine, 1948–49," 38–50; Donald Neff, "U.S. Policy and the Palestinian Refugees," 96–111; Nur-eldeen Masalha, "On Recent Hebrew and Israeli Sources for the Palestinian Exodus, 1947–49," 120–37.
18. Morris, *The Birth of the Palestinian Refugee Problem*, 292.
19. *FRUS 1949*, "Palestine Refugees" (secret), 15 March 1949, 6:831, 837.
20. Morris, *The Birth of the Palestinian Refugee Problem*, 281.
21. Ibid., 63.
22. Flapan, *The Birth of Israel*, 42.
23. Ibid., 89.
24. Palumbo, *The Palestinian Catastrophe*, 18, 115.
25. Morris, *The Birth of the Palestinian Refugee Problem*, 218. Also see Alexander Cockburn, "Beat the Devil," *The Nation*, 31 August–7 September 1992, 198.
26. Segev, *1949*, 28.
27. Flapan, *The Birth of Israel*, 90.
28. MacDonald, *My Mission in Israel*, 176.
29. Patai, *The Complete Diaries of Theodor Herzl*, 88.
30. Aronson, *Creating Facts*, 18.
31. McDowall, *Palestine and Israel*, 164–69.
32. Morris, *The Birth of the Palestinian Refugee Problem, 1947–1949*, 24–26.
33. McDowall, *Palestine and Israel*, 165.
34. Yossi Melman and Dan Raviv, "Expelling Palestinians," *Washington Post*, Outlook section, 7 February 1988. The writers are Israeli reporters who wrote the Hebrew-language book *A Hostile Partnership: Israelis, Jordanians and Palestinians*.
35. The figures do not include Jerusalem, which was to have a Jewish population of 100,000 alongside 105,000 Arabs; see Muhammad Zafrulla Khan, "Thanksgiving Day at Lake Success," in Khalidi, *From Haven to Conquest*, 714.
36. Epp, *Whose Land Is Palestine?*, 185.
37. Morris, *The Birth of the Palestinian Refugee Problem*, 136.
38. Ben-Gurion, *Israel*, 150.
39. Morris, *The Birth of the Palestinian Refugee Problem*, 135–36.
40. Ibid., 140.
41. Ben-Gurion, *Israel*, 361.
42. McDowall, *Palestine and Israel*, 165.
43. Ibid., 124, 221.

44. Quoted in Palumbo, *The Palestinian Catastrophe*, xv.
45. Erskine B. Childers, "The Other Exodus," in Khalidi, *From Haven to Conquest*.
46. Glubb, *A Soldier with the Arabs*, 251.
47. Flapan, *The Birth of Israel*, 84–87; Morris, *The Birth of the Palestinian Refugee Problem*, 58; Segev, *1949*, 25–29.
48. Flapan, *The Birth of Israel*, 85.
49. Morris, *The Birth of the Palestinian Refugee Problem*, 290.
50. Christopher Hitchens, "Broadcasts," in Said and Hitchens, *Blaming the Victims*.
51. Joel Himelfarb, "And You Thought Peter Jennings Was Bad," *Near East Report*, 27 May 1991.
52. Morris, *The Birth of the Palestinian Refugee Problem*, 290.
53. Speech in the United Nations, 19 November 1955; this text is in Medzini, *Israel's Foreign Relations*, 1:405.
54. Resolution 194(III). The text is in *New York Times*, 12 December 1948; U.S. State Department, *A Decade of American Foreign Policy 1940–1949*, 851–53; Tomeh, *United Nations Resolutions on Palestine and the Arab-Israeli Conflict*, 1:15–16; Medzini, *Israel's Foreign Relations*, 1:116–18. The General Assembly repeated the right of Palestinians to return or to receive compensation nineteen times in subsequent resolutions between 1950 and 1973: 394, 818, 916, 1018, 1191, 1215, 1465, 1604, 1725, 1865, 2052, 2154, 2341, 2452, 2535, 2672, 2792, 2963, and 3089. The State Department publicly reaffirmed U.S. support of the formula of return-or-compensate in a 1992 resolution, but spokesperson Margaret Tutwiler added that the issue must be negotiated directly between Israel and the Palestinians; see *Washington Times*, 14 May 1992.
55. See Medzini, "The Arab Refugees," in *Israel's Foreign Relations*, 1:365–467.
56. *FRUS, 1949*, "Editorial Note," 6:688.
57. Quigley, *Palestine and Israel*, 105.
58. *FRUS 1949*, "Palestinian Refugees," 6:836–37. The DP immigration figure is on p. 831.
59. Anne O'Hare McCormick, *New York Times*, 18 January 1949.
60. Bard and Himelfarb, *Myths and Facts*, 143.

FOUR

1. Neff, *Warriors at Suez*, 342–46. Also see Ben-Gurion's diary entries in S. I. Troen and M. Shemesh, eds., *The Suez-Sinai Crisis: Retrospective and Reappraisal* (London: Frank Cass, 1990), 305–15.
2. Neff, *Warriors at Suez*, 364.
3. Ibid.
4. Love, *Suez*, 503.
5. Eisenhower, *Waging Peace*, 74.
6. Ibid.
7. Eban, *An Autobiography*, 229.

8. Ibid.
9. Love, *Suez*, 639.
10. Neff, *Warriors at Suez*, 416.
11. Resolution 1002 (ES-I); the text is in Tomeh, *United Nations Resolutions on Palestine and the Arab-Israeli Conflict*, 1:34.
12. Resolution 1124 (XI); the text is in Tomeh, *United Nations Resolutions on Palestine and the Arab-Israeli Conflict*, 1:39.
13. Neff, *Warriors at Suez*, 416.
14. Love, *Suez*, 666.
15. Ibid.
16. Kissinger, *White House Years*, 347.
17. Ambrose, *Eisenhower*, 361.
18. Neff, *Warriors at Suez*, 417.

FIVE

1. Cockburn, *Dangerous Liaison*, 145.
2. Eban, "Statement to the General Assembly by Foreign Minister Eban, 19 June 1967," quoted in Medzini, *Israel's Foreign Relations*, 2:803.
3. William B. Quandt, "Lyndon Johnson and the June 1967 War: What Color Was the Light?" *The Middle East Journal*, Spring 1992.
4. John Law, "A New Improved Myth," *Middle East International*, 12 July 1991.
5. All the quotations in this paragraph are from Cockburn, *Dangerous Liaison*, 153–54. Also see Richard B. Parker, "The June War: Whose Conspiracy?," *Journal of Palestine Studies*, Summer 1992; Nakhleh, *Encyclopedia of the Palestine Problem*, 897.
6. Rabin, *The Rabin Memoirs*, 75. Also see Sheldon L. Richman, "'Ancient History': U.S. Conduct in the Middle East since World War II and the Folly of Intervention," Cato Institute pamphlet, 16 August 1991, 20.
7. Neff, *Warriors for Jerusalem*, 140.
8. Quigley, *Palestine and Israel*, 170.
9. Embassy Tel Aviv to Secretary of State, telegram 3928 (secret), 5 June 1967 (declassified 13 December 1982), quoted in Green, *Taking Sides*, 218–19.
10. Moskin, *Among Lions*, 308.
11. Neff, *Warriors for Jerusalem*, 233.
12. Nyrop, *Israel*, xix. Also see Epp, *Whose Land Is Palestine?*, 185; Foundation for Middle East Peace, *Report on Israeli Settlement in the Occupied Territories*, July 1991.
13. Halabi, *The West Bank Story*, 35–36. Also see Hirst, "Rush to Annexation: Israel in Jerusalem," *Journal of Palestine Studies*, Summer 1974; Neff, *Warriors for Jerusalem*, 289–90.
14. Neff, *Warriors for Jerusalem*, 213; Bar-Zohar, *Embassies in Crisis*, 220.

15. Neff, *Warriors for Jerusalem*, 213.
16. Roche to the President, "EYES ONLY memorandum," 6 June 1967, Johnson Library, quoted in Neff, *Warriors for Jerusalem*, 222.
17. Neff, *Warriors for Jerusalem*, 213. Also see Cockburn, *Dangerous Liaison*, 145–47; Green, *Taking Sides*, 204–11; Quandt, "Lyndon Johnson and the June 1967 War."
18. Rostow to the President, 5 June 1967 (secret).
19. Bundy to the President, memorandum, "The 6:30 Meeting," 6:15 PM, 9 June 1967, Johnson Library, quoted in Neff, *Warriors for Jerusalem*, 273.
20. Quandt, "Lyndon Johnson and the June 1967 War."
21. Moskin, *Among Lions*, 117–19.
22. Ibid., 119.
23. Ennes, *Assault on the* Liberty, 156–57.
24. Ibid., 52–53.
25. Johnson, *The Vantage Point*, 300.
26. James M. Ennes, Jr., "Victims of 1967 Attack Honored, Israeli Motives Still Uninvestigated," *Washington Report on Middle East Affairs*, May/June 1991.
27. Bill McAllister, *Washington Post*, 15 June 1991.
28. Rowland Evans and Robert Novak, *Washington Post*, 6 November 1991.

SIX

1. The text of the resolution is in Tomeh, *United Nations Resolutions*, 1:143. Also see Rafael, *Destination Peace*, 198; Brecher, *Decisions in Israel's Foreign Policy*, 487–90.
2. Medzini, *Israel's Foreign Relations*, 4:14. A U.S. State Department study said of Begin's comment: "In an Israeli television interview on June 23, [1977], Begin stated there was no contradiction between Israel's insistence on its right to retain the West Bank permanently and Resolution 242." Noring and Smith, "The Withdrawal Clause in UN Security Council Resolution 242 of 1967" (February 1978): 47. The Noring and Smith study remains classified secret/NODIS ("no distribution") but is widely quoted in Neff, *Warriors for Jerusalem*, Chapter 25, "Passage of U.N. Resolution 242." The text is in Medzini, *Israel's Foreign Relations*, 4:15–16.
3. Noring and Smith, "The Withdrawal Clause," 47.
4. Ibid., 53–54.
5. Lord Caradon et al., *UN Security Council Resolution 242* (Washington, D.C.: Georgetown University, 1981), 9.
6. The text is in U.S. Department of State, *American Foreign Policy 1977–1980*, 617–18, and *New York Times*, 28 June 1977. Also see Quandt, *Camp David*, 73.

7. Boudrealt et al., *U.S. Official Statements Regarding UN Resolution 242* (Washington, D.C.: The Institute for Palestine Studies, 1992), 129.
8. Bard and Himelfarb, *Myths and Facts*, 67.
9. See Mallison, *The Palestine Problem in International Law and World Order*, 220.
10. Noring and Smith, "The Withdrawal Clause," 12–13, quoted in Neff, *Warriors for Jerusalem*, 342.
11. Neff, *Warriors for Jerusalem*, 349.
12. *New York Times*, 25 February 1992.
13. Rabin, *The Rabin Memoirs*, 137.
14. See "Saunders to W. W. Rostow, secret memorandum, 'Eshkol's Knesset Speech Yesterday,' 31 October 1967," and other documents cited in Neff, *Warriors for Jerusalem*, 338–39.
15. Boudrealt et al., *U.S. Official Statements Regarding UN Resolution 242*, 122.
16. The text is in Tomeh, *United Nations Resolutions*, 1:151.

SEVEN

1. Ball, *The Passionate Attachment*, 68–72. The war raged from March 8, 1969, to August 7, 1970.
2. Medzini, *Israel's Foreign Relations*, 2: 869.
3. Ibid., 1: 799.
4. Eric Pace, *New York Times*, 10 July 1968; Nakhleh, *Encyclopedia of the Palestine Problem*, 438.
5. Neff, *Warriors against Israel*, 80; Bar-Siman-Tov, *The Israeli-Egyptian War of Attrition*, 44, 46.
6. Ibid., 44.
7. Heikal, *The Road to Ramadan*, 86; Ro'i, *From Encroachment to Involvement*, 528–29.
8. Bar-Siman-Tov, *The Israeli-Egyptian War of Attrition*, 171–72.
9. Medzini, *Israel's Foreign Relations*, 2: 884.
10. Bar-Siman-Tov, *The Israeli-Egyptian War of Attrition*, 92–97. Also see Neff, *Warriors against Israel*, 23.
11. Whetten, *The Canal War*, 60.
12. Rubinstein, *Red Star on the Nile*, 88.
13. O'Ballance, *The Electronic War in the Middle East*, 108.
14. Ibid., 113. Original reports said thirty were killed but many of the wounded later died.
15. The remark was in an article published in February 1970, quoted in Whetten, *The Canal War*, 89.
16. Bar-Siman-Tov, *The Israeli-Egyptian War of Attrition*, 200.
17. Dupuy, *Elusive Victory*, 369.

EIGHT

1. Statement to the Knesset, 26 July 1972; see Medzini, *Israel's Foreign Relations*, 998.
2. Quandt, *Decade of Decisions*, 133–34. Also see Rubinstein, *Red Star on the Nile*, 135.
3. Neff, *Warriors against Israel*, 42.
4. Quandt, *Decade of Decisions*, 136.
5. Kissinger, *White House Years*, 1296.
6. Kissinger, *Years of Upheaval*, 220.
7. Ibid., 221.
8. Kissinger, *White House Years*, 354.
9. Quandt, *Decade of Decision*, 147, 164.
10. Published on June 4, 1973; see Eban, *An Autobiography*, 489.
11. Dupuy, *Elusive Victory*, 406.
12. Eban, *An Autobiography*, 488.
13. *Facts on File 1973*, 654.
14. Neff, *Warriors against Israel*, 107.
15. *Facts on File 1973*, 267.
16. Ibid., 346.
17. *Newsweek*, 9 April 1973.
18. Meir, *My Life*, 420.
19. Neff, *Warriors Against Israel*, 116.
20. O'Brien, *The Siege*, 530–31.
21. See, for instance, Henry Kissinger, "The Path to Peaceful Coexistence in the Middle East," *Washington Post* Outlook section, 2 August 1992. Kissinger traces what he calls a half century of Israeli "procrastination" in the peace process.
22. Viorst, *Sands of Sorrow*, 170.
23. Rubinstein, *Red Star on the Nile*, 283.

NINE

1. Bookbinder and Abourezk, *Through Different Eyes*, 52.
2. Ball, *Error and Betrayal in Lebanon*, 35; Khouri, *The Arab-Israeli Dilemma*, 429; Schiff and Ya'ari, *Israel's Lebanon War*, 69–70.
3. Schiff and Ya'ari, *Israel's Lebanon War*, 98. Three Palestinians were sentenced in London on 5 March 1983, to sentences of thirty to thirty-five years for the attempt; the radical Abu Nidal group later admitted the men belonged to it.
4. *New York Times*, 5 June 1982. The Lebanese Information Ministry put the casualties at 60 killed and 270 wounded; see Nakhleh, *Encyclopedia of the Palestine Problem*, 795.
5. Benziman, *Sharon*, 269.
6. *New York Times*, 22 June 1982.

7. Thomas L. Friedman, *New York Times*, 22 September 1986; Ahmad Beydoun, "The South Lebanon Border Zone: A Local Perspective," *Journal of Palestine Studies*, Spring 1992, 48.
8. Augustus Richard Norton, *Washington Post*, 1 March 1988.
9. Paraphrase of Dayan's comments in Moshe Sharett's diary, quoted in Rokach, *Israel's Sacred Terrorism*, 28.
10. Schiff and Ya'ari, *Israel's Lebanon War*, 105.
11. Ball, *Error and Betrayal in Lebanon*, 25–29.
12. Claudia A. Wright, "The Israeli War Machine," *Journal of Palestine Studies*, Winter 1983, 39; also see Ball, *Error and Betrayal in Lebanon*, 56.
13. *New York Times*, 7 June 1985.
14. Schiff and Ya'ari, *Israel's Lebanon War*, 105.
15. Randal, *Going All the Way*, 249. Also see Cheryl Rubenberg, "Beirut under Fire," *Journal of Palestine Studies*, Summer/Fall 1982, 62–68.
16. Friedman, *From Beirut to Jerusalem*, 145; Edward Walsh, *Washington Post*, 5 June 1983.
17. MacBride, *Israel in Lebanon*, 209.
18. Green, *Living by the Sword*, 168.
19. *New York Times*, 2 October 1982.
20. Ball, *The Passionate Attachment*, 132–34.
21. Schiff and Ya'ari, *Israel's Lebanon War*, 259–60.
22. "Final Report of the Israeli Commission of Inquiry into the Events at the Refugee Camps in Beirut," *Journal of Palestine Studies*, Spring 1983, 97.
23. Silver, *Begin*, 236.
24. Ball, *Error and Betrayal in Lebanon*, 58.
25. The text of the letter is in *New York Times*, 2 October 1982.
26. *New York Times*, 6 March 1987.
27. Excerpts from the report are in *New York Times*, 9 February 1983, and in "Final Report of the Israeli Commission of Inquiry," *Journal of Palestine Studies*, Spring 1983, 89–116.
28. Schiff and Ya'ari, *Israel's Lebanon War*, 237.
29. Friedman, *From Beirut to Jerusalem*, 164.
30. "Final Report of the Israeli Commission of Inquiry," *Journal of Palestine Studies*, Spring 1983, 105.
31. Ball, *Error and Betrayal in Lebanon*, 57. Also see Jack Redden, United Press International, 13 October 1982; Carol Collins, "Chronology of the Israeli War in Lebanon," *Journal of Palestine Studies*, Winter 1983, 116.
32. MacBride, *Israel in Lebanon*, 57.
33. For a study of the question, see chap. 8, "Civilian Population," in MacBride, *Israel in Lebanon*, 49–65.
34. Carol Collins, "Chronology of the Israeli War in Lebanon," *Journal of Palestine Studies*, Winter 1983, 113.
35. Ibid., 113, 145.
36. Rubenberg, *Israel and the American National Interest*, 281.

37. Palumbo, *The Palestinian Catastrophe*, 69, reporting on 1948; Dayan, *Diary of the Sinai Campaign 1956*, 164; *Facts on File 1973*, 248, reporting on looting in 1967. There was no looting in the War of Attrition or the 1973 war since they were confined to barren territory.

38. *Washington Post*, 29 September 1982; Ihsan A. Hijazi, *New York Times*, 30 September 1982.

39. Friedman, *From Beirut to Jerusalem*, 159.

40. Resolution A/38/180. The text is in Simpson, *United Nations Resolutions on Palestine and the Arab-Israeli Conflict*, 3:73–80.

41. In all, the act has been invoked against Israel five times: by the Reagan administration in July 1982, on June 10, 1981, and on March 31, 1983; and by President Carter on April 5, 1978, and August 6, 1979. In none of the five cases did Congress take any action, which could have included a halt to military aid.

42. London *Sunday Times*, 8 August 1982.

43. Schiff and Ya'ari, *Israel's Lebanon War*, 195–229. Also see Fisk, *Pity the Nation*, 395; Chomsky, *The Fateful Triangle*, 267–68.

44. Ball, *Error and Betrayal in Lebanon*, 45.

45. Schiff and Ya'ari, *Israel's Lebanon War*, 225.

46. "Chronology of the Israeli Invasion of Lebanon," *Journal of Palestine Studies*, Summer/Fall 1982, 189.

47. Ball, *Error and Betrayal in Lebanon*, 46.

48. Schiff and Ya'ari, *Israel's Lebanon War*, 226.

49. The text of the statement is in "Documents and Source Material," *Journal of Palestine Studies*, Summer/Fall 1982, 339–40.

50. MacBride, *Israel in Lebanon*, 53–54.

51. Sharon, *Warrior*, 494.

52. Fisk, *Pity the Nation*, 391–93. Excerpts are in "Documents and Source Material," *Journal of Palestine Studies*, Summer/Fall 1982, 318–19.

53. Quoted in Chomsky, *The Fateful Triangle*, 281.

54. *Washington Post*, 16 June 1982.

55. *New York Times*, 15 August 1982. See Chomsky, *The Fateful Triangle*, 203, who calls these optimistic forecasts about the invasion "naiveté or cynicism."

56. Fisk, *Pity the Nation*, 395. Also see Chomsky, *The Fateful Triangle*, 267–68.

57. Fisk, *Pity the Nation*, 408–9, 421–22.

58. Morris B. Abrams, *New York Times*, 24 August 1982. Also see Chomsky, *The Fateful Triangle*, 264.

59. Norman Podhoretz, *New York Times*, 15 June 1982. Also see Chomsky, *The Fateful Triangle*, 269–71.

60. Rubenberg, *Israel and the American National Interest*, 339.

61. Fisk, *Pity the Nation*, 407.

TEN

1. Elfi Pallis, "The Likud Party: A Primer," *Journal of Palestine Studies*, Winter 1992, 42.
2. Silver, *Begin*, 16, 120; Bar-Zohar, *Ben-Gurion*, 303.
3. Pallis, "The Likud Party," 42–43.
4. Bethell, *The Palestine Triangle*, 294–95.
5. Silver, *Begin*, 113. For the genesis of the Irgun and its aims, see Bethell, *The Palestine Triangle*, 121, and Sachar, *A History of Israel*, 265–67. For some of Irgun's more dramatic and bloody deeds, see, among others, Hirst, *The Gun and the Olive Branch*; Bell, *Terror out of Zion*.
6. Silver, *Begin*, 145.
7. Pallis, "The Likud Party," 42–43.
8. Foundation for Middle East Understanding, *Report on Israeli Settlement in the Occupied Territories*, Special Report, July 1991.
9. Silver, *Begin*, 254.
10. David K. Shipler, *New York Times*, 16 September 1983.
11. Silver, *Begin*, 254–58.
12. Davis, *Myths and Facts 1989*, 241–42.
13. Quigley, *Palestine and Israel*, 176.
14. U.S. State Department, *Israeli Settlement in the Occupied Territories*, May 1991, cited in Foundation for Middle East Peace, *Report on Israeli Settlement in the Occupied Territories*, July 1992.
15. Jackson Diehl, *Washington Post*, 27 January 1992, 29 January 1992. See Peace Now, "Report Number Four of the Settlements Watch Committee" (Jerusalem and Washington, D.C.), 22 January 1992.
16. Jackson Diehl, *Washington Post*, 29 January 1992.
17. Jackson Diehl, *Washington Post*, 27 January 1992.
18. Clyde Haberman, *New York Times*, 27 June 1992.
19. Jackson Diehl, *Washington Post*, 21 January 1992.

ELEVEN

1. John Kifner, *New York Times*, 15 December 1987; Strum, *The Women Are Marching*, 17.
2. David B. Ottaway, *Washington Post*, 30 March 1988. The text of Schifter's remarks is in *American-Arab Affairs*, Spring 1988, 156–58, and *Journal of Palestine Studies*, Summer 1988, 197–200.
3. Cited in *Washington Report on Middle East Affairs* (American Educational Trust, Washington, D.C.), February 1992, 15.
4. See U.S. Department of State, *Country Reports on Human Rights Practices* (Washington, D.C.: Government Printing Office), for the years starting in 1988.

5. John Kifner, *New York Times*, 20 January 1988. Also see Jonathan C. Randal, *Washington Post*, 21 January 1988; Glenn Frankel, *Washington Post*, 23 January 1988.

6. *Time*, 8 February 1988, 39.

7. Robert D. McFadden, *New York Times*, 5 March 1988. Kissinger's remarks were contained in a three-page, single-spaced memorandum written by one of the leaders of the group, Julius Berman, former head of the Conference of Presidents of Major American Jewish Organizations. The American-Arab Anti-Discrimination Committee of Washington, D.C., obtained a copy of the memo and circulated it among its membership. The text of the memo is in *American-Arab Affairs*, Spring 1988, 158–61, and *Journal of Palestine Studies*, Summer 1988, 184–87. Kissinger later denied he made the remarks, saying they were a "gross distortion of the truth." See Barbara Vobejda, *Washington Post*, 6 March 1988.

8. John Kifner, *New York Times*, 23 January 1988.

9. Jackson Diehl, *Washington Post*, 17 May 1990. Excerpts from the thousand-page, three-volume report, "The Status of Palestinian Children during the Uprising in the Occupied Territories," appear in "Documents and Source Material," *Journal of Palestine Studies*, Summer 1990, 136–49.

10. Thomas L. Friedman, "The Week in Review," *New York Times*, 27 December 1987.

11. UN Document S/19443, 21 January 1988. The text is in "Special Document," *Journal for Palestine Studies*, Spring 1988, 66–79.

12. Davis, *Myths and Facts 1089*, 194.

13. Dani Rubinstein, *Ha'aretz* (Tel Aviv), 7 February 1992.

14. Jackson Diehl, *Washington Post*, 19 October 1990.

15. Ibid.

16. Amnesty International was particularly alert in reporting Israel's conduct; the *Journal for Palestine Studies*, starting in its Spring 1988 issue, reprinted the texts of many reports from various groups condemning Israel over the following years.

17. UN Document S/19443, 21 January 1988.

18. Karen DeYoung, *Washington Post*, 9 February 1988; Shadda Islam, "Weighing Their Words," *Middle East International*, 20 February 1988.

19. Excerpts from the report are in *American-Arab Affairs*, Summer 1988, 178–83. The members of the visiting team, all medical doctors, were H. Jack Geiger, City University of New York Medical School; Jennifer Leaning, Harvard Medical School; Leon A. Shapiro, Harvard Medical School; and Bennett Simon, Harvard Medical School.

20. Glenn Frankel, *Washington Post*, 31 May 1988. Also see Amnesty International, "Israel and the Occupied Territories: The Misuse of Tear-Gas by Israeli Army Personnel in the Israeli Occupied Territories," 1 June 1988. The text is in *American-Arab Affairs*, Summer

1988, 183–87, and *Journal of Palestine Studies*, Autumn 1988, 259–63.

21. The text is in *Journal of Palestine Studies*, Autumn 1988, 263–71.
22. Paul Lewis, *New York Times*, 4 November 1988.
23. Reuters, *New York Times*, 21 April 1989.
24. Martin Rubenberg, "Medical Care as a Political Weapon in Gaza," *Middle East International*, 2 March 1990.
25. Associated Press, 19 March 1990, 19:11 EST, V0368.
26. *New York Times*, 20 March 1990.
27. The report was titled "The Israeli Army and the Intifada: Policies That Contribute to the Killings." See Daoud Kuttab, *Middle East International*, 3 August 1990. For some sharp comment on Israel's human rights abuses, see Anthony Lewis, *New York Times*, 31 July 1990; Colman McCarthy, *Washington Post*, Style section, 15 July 1990.
28. Javier Perez de Cuellar, "Report Submitted to the Security Council by the Secretary-General in Accordance with Resolution 672 (1990)," UN Document S/21919, 31 October 1990. Also see Resolution 33/113 A. For a detailed discussion, see Mallison, *The Palestine Problem in International Law and World Order*, chap. 6.
29. Perez de Cuellar, "Report Submitted to the Security Council."
30. Associated Press, *Washington Post*, 5 November 1990.
31. Resolution 726; the text is in *New York Times*, 7 January 1992.
32. Trevor Rowe, *Washington Post*, 7 January 1992. The U.S. abstentions were on Resolutions 608 of 14 January 1988, 636 of 6 July 1989, and 641 of 30 August 1989.
33. John M. Goshko and Nora Boustany, *Washington Post*, 10 May 1990.
34. Ibid.
35. *ADC Times* (Washington, D.C.), March 1990. For a critique of the report, see George Moses, "What Does the Human Rights Report Say about Its Author?," *Washington Report on Middle East Affairs*, April 1990. A critique of earlier reports is in Rabbi Elmer Berger, "A Critique of the Department of State's 1981 Country Report on Human Rights Practices in the State of Israel," Americans for Middle East Understanding (New York, undated). Schifter retired in 1992 and became a senior foreign policy adviser for Bill Clinton's presidential campaign.
36. U.S. Department of State, *Country Reports on Human Rights Practices for 1988* (Washington, D.C.: Government Printing Office, February 1989): 1376–87. The text is reproduced in *Journal of Palestine Studies*, Spring 1989, 110–25.
37. U.S. Department of State, *Country Reports on Human Rights Practices for 1989* (Washington, D.C.: Government Printing Office, February 1990): 1432–45. The text is reproduced in *Journal of Palestine Studies*, Spring 1990, 76–88.

38. For details, see Palestine Human Rights Information Center, *Targeting to Kill: Israel's Undercover Units* (Jerusalem, May 1992).

39. U.S. Department of State, *Country Reports on Human Rights Practices for 1990* (Washington, D.C.: Government Printing Office, February 1991): 1477–96. The text is reproduced in *Journal of Palestine Studies*, Spring 1991, 98–111.

40. See Palestine Human Rights Information Center, *Targeting to Kill*.

41. U.S. Department of State, *Country Reports on Human Rights Practices for 1991* (Washington, D.C.: Government Printing Office, February 1992): 1440–55. The text is reproduced in *Journal of Palestine Studies*, Spring 1992, 114–24.

TWELVE

1. McDowall, *Palestine and Israel*, 124.

2. See, for instance, Ball, *The Passionate Attachment*, 163–67; Keller, *Terrible Days*, 89–111; McDowall, *Palestine and Israel*, 123–45; Quigley, *Palestine and Israel*, 97–150.

3. Testimony before the UN Special Committee on Palestine in 1947, quoted in Lustick, *Arabs in the Jewish State*, 38. The Jewish Agency acted as the Zionist quasi-government for the Jews in Palestine prior to the establishment of Israel.

4. McDowall, *Palestine and Israel*, 123–24, 145. Under Yitzhak Rabin's new government in 1992, two Palestinian Israelis became deputy ministers.

5. Lustick, *Arabs in the Jewish State*, 49.

6. Quigley, *Palestine and Israel*, 97.

7. Ibid., 145. For a review of Israel's use of town arrests, see Nakhleh, *Encyclopedia of the Palestine Problem*, 683–92.

8. James Feron, *New York Times*, 1 December 1966; Quigley, *Palestine and Israel*, 145. Also see Ze'ev Chafets, "Arab Rage inside Israel," *New York Times Magazine*, 3 April 1988.

9. Said, *The Question of Palestine*, 103. Also see Zogby, *Palestinians: The Invisible Victims*, American-Arab Anti-Discrimination Committee (Washington, DC, 1981): 32.

10. Bard and Himelfarb, *Myths and Facts*, 206.

11. U.S. Department of State, *Country Reports on Human Rights Practices for 1989* (Washington, D.C.: Government Printing Office, February 1990), 1428.

12. Said, *The Question of Palestine*, 105. Also see Lustick, *Arabs in the Jewish State*. A number of works have been written by Palestinians who suffered Israeli rule; see, for instance, El-Asmar, *To Be an Arab in Israel*; Jiryis, *The Arabs in Israel*. Also see *Journal of Palestine Studies*, Winter 1985, a special edition devoted to Palestinians in Israel.

13. Quigley, *Palestine and Israel*, 126.

14. The text of the law is in Davis and Mezvinsky, *Documents from Israel*, 80–87; critiques of the law follow on 88–101. Also see

Mallison, *The Palestine Problem in International Law and World Order*, 165; Quigley, *Palestine and Israel*, 126–30.

15. Said, *The Question of Palestine*, 48. Also see Nyrop, *Israel*, 53, 101; Ben-Gurion, *Israel*, 408–9. The text is in Mallison and Mallison, *The Palestine Problem in International Law and World Order*, 431–33; a discussion of the law is on 106–16.

16. Davis, *The Evasive Peace*, 74–75.

17. Dana Adams Schmidt, *New York Times*, 15 August 1953.

18. Lustick, *Arabs in the Jewish State*, 175–76. A dunam is roughly equal to one-quarter of an acre.

19. Quigley, *Palestine and Israel*, 124.

20. Lustick, *Arabs in the Jewish State*, 68.

21. The text is in Ben-Gurion, *Israel*, 79–81.

22. Quigley, *Palestine and Israel*, 116.

23. Ibid.

24. David Shipler, *New York Times*, 29 December 1983.

25. Allon, *A Curtain of Sand*, (Hebrew) 337, quoted in Lustick, *Arabs in the Jewish State*, 65.

26. McDowall, *Palestine and Israel*, 231–32. For the text of the report see "The Koenig Report: 'Memorandum Proposal—Handling the Arabs of Israel,'" *Journal of Palestine Studies*, Autumn 1976, 190–200. Also see Lustick, *Arabs in the Jewish State*, 68–69.

27. Nyrop, *Israel*, 102.

28. Lustick, *Arabs in the Jewish State*, 68.

29. The text of Rabin's 1992 inaugural address is in Foreign Broadcast Information Service, 14 July 1992, 23–27.

THIRTEEN

1. The lobby was first called the American Zionist Council for Public Affairs and changed its name in 1959. For the history of the American Zionist Council and its evolution into AIPAC, see Kenen, *Israel's Defense Line*, 106–7. In 1962–1963, the Senate Foreign Relations Committee under Chairman J. W. Fulbright investigated AIPAC and its various associated groups to see whether it should be required to register as a foreign agent; no action was taken. See Kenen, *Israel's Defense Line*, 109.

2. There are a number of excellent studies on the Israeli lobby, among them Ball, *The Passionate Attachment*; Bookbinder and Abourezk, *Through Different Eyes*; Curtiss, *A Changing Image* and *Stealth Pacs*; Feuerlicht, *The Fate of the Jews*; Halsell, *Prophecy and Politics*; Isaacs, *Jews and American Politics*; Lilienthal, *The Zionist Connection*; Neff, *Warriors for Jerusalem*; O'Brien, *American Jewish Organizations and Israel*; Rubenberg, *Israel and the American National Interest*; Saba, *The Armageddon Network*; Smith, *The Power Game*; Tillman, *The United States in the Middle East*; Tivnan, *The Lobby*.

3. Robert I. Friedman, Washington Post, Outlook section, 1 November 1992.
4. Washington Jewish Week, 18 July 1985.
5. David K. Shipler, New York Times, 6 July 1987.
6. Eric Alterman, "Pumping Iron," Regardie's, March 1988.
7. Kathleen Christison, "Blind Spots: Official U.S. Myths about the Middle East," Journal of Palestine Studies, Winter 1988.
8. Kenen, Israel's Defense Line, 2–3.
9. Smith, The Power Game, 216.
10. The text of Dine's speech, "The Revolution in U.S.-Israel Relations," is in "Special Document," Journal of Palestine Studies, Summer 1986, 134–43. Also see Robert G. Neumann, "1992: A Year of Stalemate in the Peace Process?," Middle East Policy, 1, no. 2 (1992).
11. Dine, "The Revolution in U.S.-Israel Relations."
12. Richard B. Straus, Washington Post, 27 April 1986.
13. Rubenberg, Israel and the American National Interest, 345–46; Smith, The Power Game, 221; New York Times, 24 March 1984; John M. Goshko and John E. Yang, Washington Post, 7 September 1991.
14. Rubenberg, Israel and the American National Interest, 346.
15. Bernard Gwertzman, New York Times, 22 March 1984.
16. John M. Goshko and John E. Yang, Washington Post, 7 September 1991.
17. Davis, Myths and Facts, 266.
18. Rubenberg, Israel and the American National Interest, 258; Smith, The Power Game, 220–24; Tivnan, The Lobby, 135–61.
19. Tillman, The United States in the Middle East, 121.
20. A. Craig Murphy, "Congressional Opposition to Arms Sales to Saudi Arabia," American-Arab Affairs, Spring 1988, 106. A good analysis of the incident is in Smith, The Power Game, 215–20.
21. Rubenberg, Israel and the American National Interest, 258; also see Smith, The Power Game, 220–24.
22. Findley, They Dare to Speak Out, 113.
23. Smith, The Power Game, 216.
24. Tivnan, The Lobby, 163.
25. From AIPAC promotional letter, 1982, quoted in O'Brien, American Jewish Organizations and Israel, 170.
26. Charles McC. Mathias, Jr., "Ethnic Groups and Foreign Policy," Foreign Affairs, Summer 1981.
27. Gregory D. Slabodkin, "The Secret Section in Israel's U.S. Lobby That Stifles American Debate," Washington Report on Middle East Affairs, July 1992.
28. Amy Kaufman Goott and Steven J. Rosen, The Campaign to Discredit Israel (Washington, D.C.: American Israel Public Affairs Committee, 1983). Another AIPAC publication was The AIPAC College Guide: Exposing the Anti-Israel Campaign on Campus, 1984.

29. Rubenberg, *Israel and the American National Interest*, 338.
30. Slabodkin, "The Secret Section in Israel's U.S. Lobby."
31. Robert I. Friedman, "The Israel Lobby's Blacklist," *Village Voice*, 4 August 1992.
32. Slabodkin, "The Secret Section in Israel's U.S. Lobby."
33. Bookbinder and Abourezk, *Through Different Eyes*, 81.
34. Transcript of David Steiner's remarks, 22 October 1992; available through the American-Arab Anti-Discrimination Committee (Washington, D.C.).
35. Nixon, *Memoirs*, 481.
36. Transcripts of Dulles telephone conversations, quoted in Neff, *Warriors at Suez*, 416.
37. *New York Times*, 31 October 1954.
38. Tivnan, *The Lobby*, 253.
39. Charles R. Babcock, *Washington Post*, 26 September 1991.
40. John J. Fialka, *Wall Street Journal*, 24 June 1987.
41. Edward Roeder, *News/Sun-Sentinel* (Fort Lauderdale, Florida): 28 June 1987.
42. Tivnan, *The Lobby*, 242.
43. John M. Goshko, *Washington Post*, 8 April 1992.
44. Findley, *They Dare to Speak Out*, 161.
45. Kalb, *Kissinger*, 475.
46. Quandt, *Camp David*, 129.
47. Brzezinski, *Power and Principle*, 108.
48. Rabin, *The Rabin Memoirs*, 232; Slater, *Rabin of Israel*, 186.
49. *Washington Post*, 11 June 1972.
50. Richard C. Gross, *Washington Times*, 8 April 1992. Excerpts are in *Near East Report*, 18 May 1992.
51. *The Economist*, 12 November 1992, 28.
52. *Village Voice*, 7 November 1992, 30.

FOURTEEN

1. The best single report on the U.S. aid program to Israel is in Robert Byrd, *Congressional Record*, 102d Cong., 2d sess., 1 April 1992, and "Special Document," *Journal of Palestine Studies*, Summer 1992, 130–39. Also see Ball, *The Passionate Attachment*, 255–61; Clyde Mark, "Israel: U.S. Foreign Assistance Facts," Foreign Affairs and National Defense Division, Congressional Research Service (Washington, D.C.), updated 5 July 1991; Rubenberg, *Israel and the American National Interest*, 330; U.S. General Accounting Office, "US Assistance to the State of Israel, Report by the Comptroller General of the United States," GAO/ID-83-51, 24 June 1983.
2. U.S. Senate and House of Representatives, *Legislation on Foreign Relations through 1991*, Joint Committee Print, Committee on Foreign Affairs and Committee on Foreign Relations (Government

Printing Office, Washington, D.C.), July 1992, 4:44–45, 160–61, 167.

3. Amy Kaufman Goott and Steven J. Rosen, eds., *The Campaign to Discredit Israel* (Washington, D.C.: AIPAC, 1983), 22.
4. *Congressional Record*, 1 April 1992. Also see Clyde Mark, "Israel: U.S. Foreign Assistance Fact," Foreign Affairs and National Defense Division, Congressional Research Service, updated 5 July 1991.
5. Rubenberg, *Israel and the American National Interest*, 330.
6. The text of Byrd's speech is in *Congressional Record*, 1 April 1992, and "Special Document," *Journal of Palestine Studies*, Summer 1992, 130–39.
7. Davis, *Myths and Facts 1989*, 226.
8. David R. Francis, *Christian Science Monitor*, 23 October 1984. Also see Chomsky, *The Fateful Triangle*, 10.
9. Quoted in "Documents and Source Material," *Journal of Palestine Studies*, Spring 1992, 178.
10. Davis, *Myths and Facts 1989*, 220.
11. U.S. Senate and U.S. House of Representatives, *Legislation on Foreign Relations through 1986*, 1032.
12. Jackson Diehl, *Washington Post*, 2 June 1990.

FIFTEEN

1. Keith Brasher, *New York Times*, 23 September 1991. Israel's credit rating is a low BBB minus—compared with AAA for top borrowers. It is thus forced to pay a 2 percent premium on loans and is restricted in the amount of money it can borrow.
2. *Near East Report*, 2 March 1992.
3. Title VI under the Foreign Aid Bill of 1 October 1992.
4. Rowland Evans and Robert Novak, *Washington Post*, 2 September 1991.
5. Keith Brasher, *New York Times*, 23 September 1991.
6. *Washington Times*, 28 February 1992.
7. Michael Lerner, quoted in Fox Butterfield, *New York Times*, 16 September 1991.
8. Nehama Duek and Gideon Eshet, *Yediot Aharonot* (Tel Aviv), 10 January 1992.
9. Jackson Diehl, *Washington Post*, 9 September 1991.
10. Ball, *The Passionate Attachment*, 298.
11. Joel Brinkley, *New York Times*, 19 June 1988; John M. Goshko, *Washington Post*, 24 October 1988.
12. Robert Pear, *New York Times*, 24 September 1989.
13. *Near East Report*, 13 January 1992.
14. Clyde Haberman, *New York Times*, 14 February 1992.
15. John Asfour, "Soviet Immigration to Israel Continues to Plummet," *Washington Report on Middle East Affairs*, July 1992. Also see Frank Collins, "If Soviet Jews Have Stopped Coming, Does Israel

Need Loan Guarantees?," *Washington Report on Middle East Affairs*, August/September 1992.

16. Sheldon L. Richman, *USA Today*, 11 August 1992.
17. *Hadashot* (Tel Aviv), 29 September 1991.
18. *Near East Report*, 2 March 1992.
19. U.S. General Accounting Office, "Israel: U.S. Loan Guaranties for Immigrant Absorption," GAO/NSIAD-92-119, 12 February 1992, 5.
20. Bard and Himelfarb, *Myths and Facts*, 244.
21. General Accounting Office, "Israel: U.S. Loan Guaranties," 4.
22. Ibid., 5.
23. John M. Goshko, *Washington Post*, 20 February 1992.
24. *Congressional Record*, 102d Cong., 2d sess., 1 April 1992.
25. Foundation for Middle East Peace, *Report on Israeli Settlement in the Occupied Territories*, Special Report, Winter 1991–1992.
26. Clyde Haberman, *New York Times*, 23 January 1992. Haberman rounded the figure off to 13,000 but Jackson Diehl reported the specific figure in *Washington Post*, 27 January 1992 and 29 January 1992. See Peace Now (Jerusalem and Washington, D.C.), "Report Number Four of the Settlements Watch Committee," 22 January 1992.
27. Jackson Diehl, *Washington Post*, 29 January 1992.
28. Jackson Diehl, *Washington Post*, 27 January 1992.
29. Jackson Diehl, *Washington Post*, 29 January 1992.
30. *Congressional Record*, 102d Cong., 2d sess., 1 April 1992.
31. Rabin's 1992 inaugural address, text in Foreign Broadcast Information Service, 14 July 1992, 23–27.

SIXTEEN

1. Scott Armstrong, *Washington Post*, 1 February 1982. For a survey of Israeli spying on the United States, see a three-part series in *The Wall Street Journal* by Edward T. Pound and David Rogers, 17 January, 20 January, 22 January 1992. Also see Jeff McConnell and Richard Higgins, "The Israeli Account," *Boston Globe Magazine*, 14 December 1986; Claudia Wright, *Spy, Steal and Smuggle: Israel's Special Relationship with the United States* (Belmont, Mass.: AAUG Press, 1986). For general stories on Israeli spying on the United States, see *Washington Post*, 5 January 1986; *Baltimore Sun*, 16 November 1986. Two stories detail efforts by the Reagan administration to play down the seriousness of Israeli espionage: *Los Angeles Times*, 11 June 1986; *New York Times*, 12 June 1986. Useful books include Cockburn, *Dangerous Liaison*; Hersh, *The Samson Option*; Ostrovsky and Hoy, *By Way of Deception*.
2. Bard and Himelfarb, *Myths and Facts*, 250.
3. Pound and Rogers, *Wall Street Journal*, 17 January 1992.
4. Ostrovsky and Hoy, *By Way of Deception*, 269; also see Roger Cohen, *New York Times*, 13 September 1990. Israel tried to smear

Ostrovsky as a liar and braggart, but some experts in a position to know tended to believe him; see, for instance, Black and Morris, *Israel's Secret Wars*, 493.

5. Wright, *Spy, Steal and Smuggle*.
6. Bard and Himelfarb, *Myths and Facts*, 250.
7. For background, see Cockburn, *Dangerous Liaison*, 203–9; Hersh, *The Samson Option*, 285–305; Raviv and Melman, *Every Spy a Prince*, 301–23. For early reaction see *New York Times*, 2 December 1985. The text of the government's case against Pollard is in "Documents and Source Material," *Journal of Palestine Studies*, Autumn 1986, 229–34.
8. Hersh, *The Samson Option*, 285, 297.
9. Ibid., 285, claims Pollard actually began spying for Israel three years earlier than he admitted, and that the total number of pages of classified documents he passed on to Israel was about 500,000; see 286.
10. "Government's Memorandum in Aid of Sentencing," U.S. District Court for the District of Columbia, Criminal No. 86-0207, 6 January 1987.
11. Hersh, *The Samson Option*, 295.
12. Specifics of the government's claims of the harm done by the Pollards are spelled out in documents filed with the U.S. District Court for the District of Columbia: "Government's Memorandum in Aid of Sentencing," Criminal Nos. 86-0207 and 86-0208, 6 January 1987, in the case of *USA v. Jonathan Jay Pollard and Anne Henderson Pollard*. The text of the lengthy sentencing memo on Jonathan Pollard can be found in *American-Arab Affairs*, Fall 1987, 123–46.
13. Robert I. Friedman, "The Secret Agent," *New York Review of Books*, 26 October 1989. Friedman reviews *Territory of Lies* (New York: Harper and Row, 1989), a book-length treatment of the case by *Jerusalem Post* reporter Wolf Blitzer. Friedman calls the book "sometimes apologetic."
14. Bard and Himelfarb, *Myths and Facts*, 251.
15. Ostrovsky and Hoy, *By Way of Deception*, 268.
16. He should not be confused with another Israeli by the same name who was chief of staff during Israel's 1982 invasion of Lebanon and later became head of the right-wing political faction called Tsomet.
17. Dan Raviv and Yossi Melman, *Washington Post*, Outlook section, 3 September 1989; *New York Times*, 9 January 1986.
18. David B. Ottaway, *Washington Post*, 30 October 1985. Also see Raviv and Melman, *Every Spy a Prince*, 321–22.
19. Jack Anderson and Dale Van Atta, *Washington Post*, 9 May 1988.
20. Robert I. Friedman, *Washington Post*, Outlook section, 19 June 1988.
21. *Jerusalem Post International Edition*, 9 September 1989.
22. Associated Press, *Washington Times*, 2 August 1990.

23. Howard Kurtz, *Washington Post*, 19 July 1990.
24. Neil A. Lewis, *New York Times*, 21 March 1992.
25. Linda Greenhouse, *New York Times*, 14 October 1992.
26. "The Week in Review," *New York Times*, 18 October 1992.
27. "An Open Letter to President George Bush Concerning Jonathan Pollard," *New York Times*, 23 October 1992.
28. Raviv and Melman, *Every Spy a Prince*, 321–22.
29. *New York Times*, 10 June, 11 June 1986.

SEVENTEEN

1. For background on Israel's nuclear program see, among others, Geoffrey Aronson, "Hidden Agenda: US-Israeli Relations and the Nuclear Question," *Middle East Journal*, Autumn 1992; Frank Barnaby, "The Nuclear Arsenal in the Middle East," *Journal of Palestine Studies*, Autumn 1987; Beit-Hallahmi, *The Israeli Connection*; Cockburn, *Dangerous Liaison*; Gaffney, *Dimona: The Third Temple?*; Green, *Taking Sides*; Hersh, *The Samson Option*; Jabber, *Israel and Nuclear Weapons*; Raviv and Melman, *Every Spy a Prince*; Rogers and Cervenka, *The Nuclear Axis*; Spector, *Nuclear Proliferation Today*; Weissman and Krosney, *The Islamic Bomb*. Hersh's is the latest work, appearing in mid-1991, and is devoted entirely to Israel's nuclear program.
2. Dana Adams Schmidt, *New York Times*, 22 December 1960; U.S. Department of State, "Statement Issued by the Department of State, December 19, 1960," *American Foreign Policy: Current Documents, 1960*, 501.
3. Bar-Zohar, *Ben-Gurion*, 270–71.
4. *New York Times*, 22 December 1960.
5. Schmidt, *New York Times*, 22 December 1960.
6. Spector, *Nuclear Proliferation Today*, 121.
7. Hersh, *The Samson Option*, 111.
8. James Feron, *New York Times*, 19 May 1966. Also see Aronson, *Conflict and Bargaining in the Middle East*, 50–51.
9. Spector, *Nuclear Proliferation Today*, 117.
10. *New York Times*, 25 June 1981. The document was released in 1978 under a Freedom of Information Act request; the CIA later said the release had been a "mistake."
11. Ali A. Mazrui et al., *Study on Israeli Nuclear Armament* (United Nations, 1982), 16; Beit-Hallahmi, *The Israeli Connection*, 136.
12. Glenn Frankel, *Washington Post*, 20 September 1988; Thomas L. Friedman, *New York Times*, 24 March 1989.
13. Hersh, *The Samson Option*, 319.
14. Ibid.
15. Quoted in Israel Shahak, "Israel's Nuclear Weapons Strategy: Not for Discussion in English," *Washington Report on Middle East Affairs*, July 1992.
16. Cockburn, *Dangerous Liaison*, 323–24.

17. Tillman, *The United States in the Middle East*, 38. Also see Green, *Living by the Sword*, 135–52; Hersh, *The Samson Option*, 8–10; Raviv and Melman, *Every Spy a Prince*, 250–52; Woodward, *Veil*, 160.

18. Seale, *Asad of Syria*, 359–62; Donald Neff, "The U.S., Iraq, Israel and Iran: Backdrop to War," *Journal of Palestine Studies*, Summer 1991.

19. *New York Times*, 9 June 1981.

20. Abu Nidal's May 15 group became especially active in 1982–1983, hitting Israeli, Jewish, and U.S. targets around the world; see Steven Emerson, "Capture of a Terrorist," *New York Times Magazine*, 21 April 1991.

21. Jeffrey Smith, *Washington Post*, 22–23 July 1992.

22. Ostrovsky and Hoy, *By Way of Deception*, 1–28; Raviv and Melman, *Every Spy a Prince*, 250–52.

23. In addition to Ostrovsky and Hoy, *By Way of Deception*, and Raviv and Melman, *Every Spy a Prince*, see Weissman and Krosney, *The Islamic Bomb*.

24. Spector, *Nuclear Proliferation Today*, 176–77.

25. Ostrovsky and Hoy, *By Way of Deception*, 23.

26. Judith Miller, *New York Times*, 9 December 1981.

27. Bard and Himelfarb, *Myths and Facts*, 292.

28. *Washington Post*, 2 March 1978; David Burnham, *New York Times*, 2 March 1978.

29. For instance, on July 31, 1975, *The Boston Globe* reported that Israel was believed by "senior American analysts in the American security community" to have more than ten nuclear bombs; on April 12, 1976, *Time* reported that Israel had thirteen bombs and for a time had considered using them in the 1973 war; in 1980 the former head of France's Atomic Energy Commission, Francis Perrin, said: "We are sure the Israelis have nuclear bombs. . . . They have sufficient facilities to produce one or two bombs a year." See Spector, *Nuclear Proliferation Today*, 132.

EIGHTEEN

1. Adams, *The Unnatural Alliance*, 3–15; Ball, *The Passionate Attachment*, 290–92; Beit-Hallahmi, *The Israeli Connection*, 117; Cockburn, *Dangerous Liaison*, 280–312; Hersh, *The Samson Option*, 263.

2. Bookbinder and Abourezk, *Through Different Eyes*, 214.

3. Beit-Hallahmi, *The Israeli Connection*, 116.

4. Hersh, *The Samson Option*, 263; Beit-Hallahmi, *The Israeli Connection*, 117.

5. C. L. Sulzberger, *New York Times*, 30 April 1971.

6. Resolution 3411 G (XXX). The text is in Sherif, *United Nations Resolutions on Palestine and the Arab-Israeli Conflict*, 2:8–10.

7. Beit-Hallahmi, *The Israeli Connection*, 109.

8. Cockburn, *Dangerous Liaison*, 281.
9. Terence Smith, *New York Times*, 18 April 1976.
10. Rogers and Cervenka, *The Nuclear Axis*, 326.
11. William E. Farrell, *New York Times*, 18 August 1976.
12. Cockburn, *Dangerous Liaison*, 291.
13. Ibid.
14. Jane Hunter, "Burying Armscorp?," *Middle East International*, 22 November 1991; "Did de Klerk Discuss Transfer of Arms Firm to Israel?," *Israeli Foreign Affairs* (special double issue), 16 December 1991.
15. Bard and Himelfarb, *Myths and Facts*, 292.
16. *Washington Post*, 2 March 1978; David Burnham, *New York Times*, 2 March 1978; Spector, *Nuclear Proliferation Today*, 304.
17. Beit-Hallahmi, *The Israeli Connection*, 133.
18. Hersh, *The Samson Option*, 264.
19. Cockburn, *Dangerous Liaison*, 283–88; Green, *Living by the Sword*, 111–34; Hersh, *The Samson Option*, 271–83.
20. Interagency Intelligence Memorandum, "The 22 September 1979 Event," December 1979, quoted in Cockburn, *Dangerous Liaison*, 285.
21. Cockburn, *Dangerous Liaison*, 287.
22. Beit-Hallahmi, *The Israeli Connection*, 133; Cockburn, *Dangerous Liaison*, 282–83.
23. NBC-TV News with Tom Brokaw, 25–26 October 1989. For a summary of the two main reports, see "NBC Reports Israeli–South African Nuclear Missile Partnership," *Israeli Foreign Affairs*, November 1989.
24. David B. Ottaway and R. Jeffrey Smith, *Washington Post*, 27 October 1989.
25. David Hoffman and R. Jeffrey Smith, *Washington Post*, 27 October 1991. Also see "New Light on Israeli–South African Arms Trade," *Israeli Foreign Affairs*, 5 November 1991; Edward T. Pound, *Wall Street Journal*, 13 March 1992.

NINETEEN

1. Viorst, *Sands of Sorrow*, 275.
2. Beit-Hallahmi, *The Israeli Connection*, 13.
3. Walter Pincus, *Washington Post*, 9 December 1991. Also see Seale, *Asad of Syria*, 360–61.
4. Seymour M. Hersh, *New York Times*, 8 December 1991.
5. Gary Sick, *New York Times*, 15 April 1991, and his book *October Surprise*. Also see Jane Hunter, "Covert Operations: The Human Factor," *The Link*, August 1992.
6. Ball, *The Passionate Attachment*, 292–94; Beit-Hallahmi, *The Israeli Connection*, 8; Cockburn, *Dangerous Liaison*, 99; Seale, *Asad of Syria*, 265–66, 359–60; Tamir, *A Soldier in Search of Peace*, 241. An unofficial updated version of the strategy for the

1980s was written by former Israeli Foreign Ministry official Oded Yinon in 1982 under the English title "A Strategy for Israel in the Nineteen Eighties." The essay was widely commented on, since in the words of Israeli antiestablishment scholar Israeli Shahak it "represents, in my opinion, the accurate and detailed plan of the present Zionist regime (of Sharon and Eitan) for the Middle East which is based on the division of the whole area into small states, and the dissolution of all the existing Arab states"; quoted in Nakhleh, *Encyclopedia of the Palestine Problem*, 892–95. Prime Minister David Ben-Gurion explained it thus in a 1958 letter to President Eisenhower: "With the purpose of erecting a high dam against the Nasserist-Soviet tidal wave, we have begun tightening our links with several states on the outside perimeter of the Middle East.... Our goal is to organize a group of countries, not necessarily an official alliance, that will be able to stand strong against Soviet expansion by proxy through Nasser"; quoted in Segev, *The Iranian Triangle*, 35.

7.   Donald Neff, "The U.S., Iraq, Israel and Iran: Backdrop to War," *Journal of Palestine Studies*, Summer 1991.
8.   Quoted in Beit-Hallahmi, *The Israeli Connection*, 15.
9.   Bard and Himelfarb, *Myths and Facts*, 265.
10.   Tamir, *A Soldier in Search of Peace*, 209.
11.   Beit-Hallahmi, *The Israeli Connection*, 14; Cockburn, *Dangerous Liaison*, 344.
12.   Glenn Frankel, *Washington Post*, 28 October 1987.
13.   Seale, *Asad of Syria*, 360, 362; Neff, "The U.S., Iraq, Israel and Iran."
14.   Bard and Himelfarb, *Myths and Facts*, 218.
15.   Beit-Hallahmi, *The Israeli Connection*, 40–41; Cockburn, *Dangerous Liaison*, 109–10.
16.   Beit-Hallahmi, *The Israeli Connection*, 41.
17.   Ali A. Mazrui, "Black Africa and the Arabs," *Foreign Affairs*, July 1975.
18.   Neff, *Warriors against Israel*, 131–32.
19.   Terence Smith, *New York Times*, 12 January 1973.
20.   Beit-Hallahmi, *The Israeli Connection*, 43–44.
21.   Chomsky, *The Fateful Triangle*, 21. Also see Ball, *The Passionate Attachment*, 284–94.
22.   Bard and Himelfarb, *Myths and Facts*, 218.
23.   Beit-Hallahmi, *The Israeli Connection*, 11; Chomsky, *The Fateful Triangle*, 23–26.
24.   David K. Shipler, *New York Times*, 19 May 1982.
25.   Cockburn, *Dangerous Liaison*, 327–28.
26.   Beit-Hallahmi, *The Israeli Connection*, 58.
27.   Chomsky, *The Fateful Triangle*, 23.
28.   Jack Anderson and Dale Van Atta, *Washington Post*, 20 October 1991.

29. Ibid. Also see Sachar, *A History of Israel*, 516, which reports a sudden surge in Jewish emigration from Romania starting in 1958.
30. *Al Hamishmar*, 29 December 1981, quoted in Chomsky, *The Fateful Triangle*, 23.
31. Beit-Hallahmi, *The Israeli Connection*, xii.
32. Ibid., 11; Chomsky, *The Fateful Triangle*, 23–26; Cockburn, *Dangerous Liaison*, 218.
33. Woodward, *Veil*, 355–57; Beit-Hallahmi, *The Israeli Connection*, 78.
34. Cockburn, *Dangerous Liaison*, 218.
35. Edward Cody, *Washington Post*, 17 August 1983.
36. Cockburn, *Dangerous Liaison*, 230.
37. *Washington Post*, 26 November 1986.
38. John Tower, "Report of the President's Special Review Board," 26 February 1987, IV-12.
39. Klieman, *Israel's Global Reach*, 133–34. Also see Ball, *The Passionate Attachment*, 285–89.
40. David Halevy and Neil C. Livingstone, *Washington Post* Outlook section, 7 January 1990. Also see Raviv and Melman, *Every Spy a Prince*, 350–54. There are various negative references to Harari in Ostrovsky, *By Way of Deception*.
41. Douglas Farah, *Washington Post*, 17 July 1990. Also see Cockburn, *Dangerous Liaison*, 212–13; Raviv and Melman, *Every Spy a Prince*, 355.
42. Associated Press, *New York Times*, 30 November 1990.
43. *Israeli Foreign Affairs*, January 1991. Also see Cockburn, *Dangerous Liaison*, 290.
44. Beit-Hallahmi, *The Israeli Connection*, 78.

TWENTY

1. From Rabin's 1992 inaugural address. The text is in Foreign Broadcast Information Service, 14 July 1992, 23–27, while major excerpts are in "Documents and Source Material," *Journal of Palestine Studies*, Autumn 1992, 146–49.
2. Glenn Frankel, *Washington Post*, 20 January 1988.
3. John Kifner, *New York Times*, 20 January 1988. For an excellent report on the effects of the curfew, see Glenn Frankel, *Washington Post*, 20 January 1988.
4. Kifner, *New York Times*, 20 January 1988. Also see Jonathan C. Randal, *Washington Post*, 21 January 1988; Glenn Frankel, 23 January 1988.
5. John Kifner, *New York Times*, 23 January 1988.
6. John Kifner, *New York Times*, 23 March 1988.
7. Glenn Frankel, *Washington Post*, 13 May 1988.
8. Joel Brinkley, *New York Times*, 21 January 1989.
9. Joel Brinkley, *New York Times*, 8 May 1989.
10. Glenn Frankel, *Washington Post*, 29 March 1988.

11. Avishai Margalit, "Israel: The Rise of the Ultra-Orthodox," *New York Review of Books*, 9 November 1989.
12. Joel Brinkley, *New York Times*, 14 May 1988.
13. Joel Brinkley, *New York Times*, 20 June 1988.
14. Glenn Frankel, *Washington Post*, 28 September 1988.
15. Rabin candidly wrote about the incident in his memoirs in the late 1970s but the passage was censored by Israel. It was later published by both *The New York Times* (23 October 1979) and *Newsweek* (9 November 1979) and by Rabin's English translator, Peretz Kidron. See Kidron, "Truth Whereby Nations Live," in Said and Hitchens, *Blaming the Victims*. Also see Palumbo, *The Palestinian Catastrophe*, 127.
16. "Report on the Mission of the Special Representative to the Occupied Territories, 15 September 1967," UN Report no. A/6797*. Also see Davis, *The Evasive Peace*, 69; Neff, *Warriors for Jerusalem*, 320. Davis puts the second-time refugees at 145,000.
17. Terence Smith, *New York Times*, 21 June 1974; James F. Clarity, *New York Times*, 20 June 1974. Also see Nakhleh, *Encyclopedia of the Palestine Problem*, 791, 824.
18. Quandt, *Decade of Decisions*, 267; Sheehan, *The Arabs, Israelis, and Kissinger*, 165–68.
19. The text of the agreement and of the MOU and its secret addenda are in Medzini, *Israel's Foreign Relations*, 3:281–90. Also see Sheehan, *The Arabs, Israelis, and Kissinger*, Appendix Eight.
20. Over the next five years the State Department reported that total aid to Israel equaled $1.742 billion in 1977, $1.792 billion in 1978, $4.790 billion in 1979 (reflecting the costs to move Israel out of the Sinai), $1.786 billion in 1980, and $2.164 billion in 1981; see *New York Times*, 8 August 1982.
21. The text is in Yodfat and Arnon-Ohanna, *PLO*, 191, and Sheehan, *The Arabs, Israelis, and Kissinger*, 256–57.
22. Ibid.
23. Quandt, *Decade of Decisions*, 201.
24. The text is in *Journal of Palestine Studies*, Autumn 1991, 183–84.
25. Neff, *Warriors against Israel*, 302–3; Sheehan, *The Arabs, Israelis, and Kissinger*, 190.
26. Kissinger, *White House Years*, 568.
27. From Rabin's 1992 inaugural address.
28. Elfi Pallis, "The Likud Party: A Primer," *Journal of Palestine Studies*, Winter 1992, 45–46.
29. Quoted in Aronson, *Creating Facts*, 111. Also see Peter Edelman, cochair for Americans for Peace Now, testimony before the House Subcommittee on Foreign Operations, 21 February 1992.
30. Foundation for Middle East Peace, *Report on Israeli Settlement in the Occupied Territories*, July 1992.
31. Weizman, *The Battle for Peace*, 226.
32. From Rabin's 1992 inaugural address.
33. Ibid.

34. Sicherman, *Palestinian Self-Government (Autonomy)*, 8–9. Also see Carter, *Keeping Faith*, 300; Quandt, *Camp David*, 156; Rubenberg, *Israel and the American National Interest*, 218–19; U.S. State Department, *American Foreign Policy 1977–1980*, 641–44.
35. Weizman, *The Battle for Peace*, 119.
36. *Ha'aretz* (Tel Aviv), 2 March 1992.
37. The text of the letter is in Aronson, *Creating Facts*, 132–37, and Thorpe, *Prescription for Conflict*, 167–82. It was published in *Dissent* in Fall 1980.
38. From Rabin's 1992 inaugural address.
39. News conference, broadcast by CNN, 11 August 1992.
40. Gary Milhollin and Gerard White, *Washington Post*, Outlook section, 16 August 1992.

TWENTY-ONE

1. Bard and Himelfarb, *Myths and Facts*, 150.
2. Morris, *The Birth of the Palestinian Refugee Problem*, 155, 179; Don Peretz, "The Arab Refugee Dilemma," *Foreign Affairs*, October 1954. Also see Cattan, *Jerusalem*; Segev, *1949*; Khalidi, *All That Remains*.
3. Walid Khalidi, "The Palestine Problem: An Overview," *Journal of Palestine Studies*, Autumn 1991, 5–6.
4. Shlaim, *Collusion across the Jordan*, 16.
5. Medzini, *Israel's Foreign Relations*, 3:133–34.
6. Resolution 2535B (XXIV). The text is in Tomeh, *United Nations Resolutions on Palestine and the Arab-Israeli Conflict*, 1:74–75.
7. Mallison and Mallison, *The Palestine Problem in International Law and World Order*, 190.
8. McDowall, *Palestine and Israel*, 189.
9. Resolution 2672C (XXV). The text is in Tomeh, *United Nations Resolutions on Palestine and the Arab-Israeli Conflict*, 1:80–81.
10. Resolution 2649 (XXV). The text is in ibid., 78–79. For a discussion of the right to self-defense, see Quigley, *Palestine and Israel*, 189–97.
11. Resolution 3089D (XXVIII). The text is in Tomeh, *United Nations Resolutions on Palestine and the Arab-Israeli Conflict*, 1:102. Also see Hirst, *The Gun and the Olive Branch*, 332.
12. Ghayth Armanazi, "The Rights of the Palestinians: The International Definition," *Journal of Palestine Studies*, Spring 1974, 94–95.
13. Resolution 194 (III). The text is in *New York Times*, 12 December 1948; U.S. State Department, *A Decade of American Foreign Policy 1940–1949*, 851–53; Tomeh, *United Nations Resolutions on Palestine and the Arab-Israeli Conflict*, 1:15–16; Medzini, *Israel's Foreign Relations*, 1:116–18. The General Assembly repeated the formula for Palestinians to return or be compensated nineteen times

in subsequent resolutions between 1950 and 1973, usually using the language "permit the return of displaced Palestinians"; see Resolutions 394, 818, 916, 1018, 1191, 1215, 1465, 1604, 1725, 1865, 2052, 2154, 2341, 2452, 2535, 2672, 2792, 2963, 3089.

14. *Washington Times*, 14 May 1992.
15. Resolution No. 3210 (XXIX). The text is in Tomeh, *United Nations Resolutions on Palestine and the Arab-Israeli Conflict*, 1:109.
16. Paul Hofmann, *New York Times*, 15 October 1974. Also see Cobban, *The Palestinian Liberation Organization*, 62–63; Hart, *Arafat*, 408–13; Hirst, *The Gun and the Olive Branch*, 335; Sheehan, *The Arabs, Israelis, and Kissinger*, 151–53.
17. Abu Iyad, *My Home, My Land*, 146. The text of their statement is in "Arab Documents on Palestine and the Arab-Israeli Conflict," *Journal of Palestine Studies*, Winter 1975, 177–78; Yodfat and Arnon-Ohanna, *PLO*, 180.
18. Sheehan, *The Arabs, Israelis, and Kissinger*, 213; Quandt, *Decade of Decisions*, 279. Also see Marwan R. Bubeiry, "The Saunders Document," *Journal of Palestine Studies*, Autumn 1978, 28–40. The text is in Lukacs, *The Israeli-Palestinian Conflict*, 61–65, and Yodfat and Arnon-Ohanna, *PLO*, 192–95.
19. Yodfat and Arnon-Ohanna, *PLO*, 109.
20. *New York Times*, 17 November 1975.
21. Sheehan, *The Arabs, Israelis, and Kissinger*, 213; Quandt, *Decade of Decisions*, 278.
22. Quandt, *Decade of Decisions*, 279.
23. Bookbinder and Abourezk, *Through Different Eyes*, 203.
24. Jansen, *The Battle of Beirut*, 126; Schiff and Ya'ari, *Israel's Lebanon War*, 218.
25. Glenn Frankel, *Washington Post*, 29 March 1988.
26. Reuters, *New York Times*, 1 April 1988.
27. Associated Press, 6 February 1989.
28. David K. Shipler, *New York Times*, 14 April 1983; David K. Shipler, *Arab and Jew*, 235.
29. Peretz Kidron, "Rabin's Balancing Act Threatens His Commitment to Peace," *Middle East International*, 10 July 1992.
30. *Newsweek*, 17 February 1969, quoted in Said and Hitchens, *Blaming the Victims*, 241.
31. Hirst, *The Gun and the Olive Branch*, 264, quoting the *Sunday Times* (London), 15 June 1969. For an exegesis of Meir's position, see Aronson, *Conflict and Bargaining in the Middle East*, 108–9. Also see Cooley, *Green March, Black September*, chap. 9; Ibrahim Abu-Lughod, "Territorially-Based Nationalism and the Politics of Negation," in Said and Hitchens, *Blaming the Victims*.
32. Peres, *David's Sling*, 249.
33. Meir Kahane, "No Jewish Guilt!," *New York Times*, 2 February 1988.
34. See Tillman, *The United States in the Middle East*, chap. 5, for an insightful discussion of Israel's official attitude toward Palestinians.

TWENTY-TWO

1. *New York Times*, 31 July 1980.
2. Benvenisti, *Jerusalem*, 11–12. The text of Ben-Gurion's speech is in Medzini, *Israel's Foreign Relations*, 1:223–24.
3. George Barrett, *New York Times*, 30 April 1949; Bailey, *Four Arab-Israeli Wars*, 64.
4. Israeli forces had failed in their campaign to capture the Old City of Jerusalem during the 1948 war, and the Old City had remained under the control of Jordan's Arab Legion. Thus when Israelis mentioned Jerusalem between 1949 and 1967, when they finally captured the Old City, they were referring to Jewish West Jerusalem, the new part of the city.
5. Benvenisti, *Jerusalem*, 11–12. The text is in Medzini, *Israel's Foreign Relations*, 1:223–24.
6. Brecher, *Decisions in Israel's Foreign Policy*, 12. Also see Mallison, *The Palestine Problem in International Law and World Order*, 210–14.
7. *New York Times*, 21 December 1949; Benvenisti, *Jerusalem*, 12; Feintuch, *U.S. Policy on Jerusalem*, 88. Also see Cattan, *Jerusalem*, 55–65; Mallison and Mallison, *The Palestine Problem in International Law and World Order*, 214.
8. Resolution 114 (S-2). The text is in Tomeh, *United Nations Resolutions on Palestine and the Arab-Israeli Conflict*, 1:176.
9. *New York Times*, 1 January 1950.
10. Abba Eban letter to the United Nations, 10 July 1967, in Medzini, *Israel's Foreign Relations*, 1:249.
11. Benvenisti, *Jerusalem*, 117; Brecher, *Decisions in Israel's Foreign Policy*, 39–40. Also see Henry Cattan, "The Status of Jerusalem under International Law and United Nations Resolutions," *Journal of Palestine Studies*, Spring 1981, 3–15, as well as Cattan's book *Jerusalem*; Ibrahim Dakkak, "The Transformation of Jerusalem: Juridical Status and Physical Change," in Aruri, *Occupation*, 67–96; Hirst, "Rush to Annexation: Israel in Jerusalem," *Journal of Palestine Studies*, Summer 1974, 3–31; Mallison, *The Palestine Problem in International Law and World Order*, 207–39; Ghada Talhami, "Between Development and Preservation: Jerusalem under Three Regimes," *American-Arab Affairs*, Spring 1986, 93–107.
12. Halabi, *The West Bank Story*, 35–36. Also see Hirst, "Rush to Annexation: Israel in Jerusalem," *Journal of Palestine Studies*, Summer 1974; Neff, *Warriors for Jerusalem*, 289–90. The text of East Jerusalem Mayor Rouhi Khatib's statement before the U.N. Security Council meeting of 3 May 1968, about Israel's actions in Jerusalem during the first two weeks of occupation, is in Nakhleh, *Encyclopedia of the Palestine Problem*, 374–77. Nakhleh also carries extensive quotations from other witnesses about Israel's actions in Jerusalem as stated in UN Document S/13450 and

Addendum 1 of 12 July 1979. The commission was established by Security Council Resolution 446 on 22 March 1979 "to examine the situation relating to settlements in the Arab territories occupied since 1967 including Jerusalem."

13. Ann Lesch, "Israeli Settlements in the Occupied Territories," *Journal of Palestine Studies*, Autumn 1978. Also see Dayan, *Story of My Life*, 372.

14. Brecher, *Decisions in Israel's Foreign Policy*, 39–40. Also see Feintuch, *U.S. Policy on Jerusalem*, 127–29.

15. Cattan, *Jerusalem*, 72. Also see Joseph Judge, "This Year in Jerusalem," *National Geographic*, April 1983, 479–514. Jordan's East Jerusalem at the time had measured only six square kilometers; see Foundation for Middle East Peace, *Report on Israeli Settlement in the Occupied Territories*, Winter 1991–1992.

16. Benvenisti, *Jerusalem*, 251.

17. Ibrahim Mattar, "From Palestinian to Israeli: Jerusalem 1948–1982," *Journal of Palestine Studies*, Summer 1983, 57–63. Also see Neff, *Warriors for Jerusalem*, 312.

18. Benvenisti, *Jerusalem*, 251.

19. Michael C. Hudson, "The Transformation of Jerusalem: 1917–1987 AD," in Asali, *Jerusalem in History*, 259, 269.

20. Resolution 2254 (ES-V). The text is in Tomeh, *United Nations Resolutions on Palestine and the Arab-Israeli Conflict*, 1:68. Also see Mallison and Mallison, *The Palestine Problem in International Law and World Order*, 215–16.

21. UN A/6793. Excerpts in "Documents Concerning the Status of Jerusalem," *Journal of Palestine Studies*, Autumn 1971, 178–82, and Medzini, *Israel's Foreign Relations*, 1:251–53.

22. Aronson, *Creating Facts*, 137–39. The text is in *New York Times*, 31 July 1980. Also see Mallison, *The Palestine Problem in International Law and World Order*, 443; Quigley, *Palestine and Israel*, 172.

23. Khouri, *The Arab-Israeli Dilemma*, 418–19.

24. The background on Jerusalem is by David Shipler, *New York Times Magazine*, 14 December 1980. Also see Cattan, *Jerusalem*, 223. Lengthy excerpts of a letter from Egypt's Anwar Sadat to Israel's Menachem Begin protesting the annexation are in "Documents and Source Material," *Journal of Palestine Studies*, Autumn 1980, 202–4.

25. Feintuch, *U.S. Policy on Jerusalem*, xi.

26. Dana Adams Schmidt, *New York Times*, 11 July 1953; *New York Times*, 16 July 1953; the Israeli decision was announced on 10 July 1953. The U.S. position on the matter was spelled out in two State Department statements on July 28, 1953, and November 3, 1954; see U.S. State Department, *American Foreign Policy 1950–1955*, 2254–55. Also see Brecher, *Decisions in Israel's Foreign Policy*, 34; Feintuch, *U.S. Policy on Jerusalem*, 116; Neff, *Warriors at Suez*, 43. A valuable collection of historical documents touching on

Jerusalem, particularly after 1967, can be found in "Documents concerning the Status of Jerusalem," *Journal of Palestine Studies*, Autumn 1971, 171–94.

27. Feintuch, *U.S. Policy on Jerusalem*, 116.
28. Ibid., 117.
29. James Feron, *New York Times*, 31 August 1966. The Feron story noted the attendance of a large number of international guests, but it made no mention of the fact that the United States officially boycotted the opening.
30. Feintuch, *U.S. Policy on Jerusalem*, 72.
31. Sheehan, *The Arabs, Israelis, and Kissinger*, Appendix 2. Also see Brecher, *Decisions in Israel's Foreign Policy*, 479–80.
32. Feintuch, *U.S. Policy on Jerusalem*, 137. Also see Yodfat and Arnon-Ohanna, *PLO*, 136–37.
33. Transcript, president's remarks in Palm Springs, California, *New York Times*, 5 March 1990. The text is in "Documents and Source Material," *Journal of Palestine Studies*, Summer 1990, 179. Also see John M. Goshko, *Washington Post*, 7 March 1990.
34. Concurrent resolution S.106 and H.290, 1990. The text is in "Documents and Source Material," *Journal of Palestine Studies*, Summer 1990, 182–83.
35. See Francis A. Boyle memorandum to Representative Lee Hamilton, 21 July 1989, *Arab-American Affairs*, Fall 1989, 126. The text of Helms's remarks about his amendment is in *Congressional Record*, SS9919, 26 July 1988.
36. Helen Dewar, *Washington Post*, 20 April 1990; Donald Neff, *Middle East International*, 27 April 1990. The text of Dole's remarks is in *Congressional Record*, 20 April 1990.
37. The text is in *New York Times*, 18 July 1984.
38. Bernard Gwertzman, *New York Times*, 3 October 1984.
39. See, for instance, excerpts of AIPAC's policy statement in "Documents and Source Material," *Journal of Palestine Studies*, Summer 1985, 220–24.
40. Bernard Gwertzman, *New York Times*, 19 February 1984, 27 March 1984.

TWENTY-THREE

1. Ball, *The Passionate Attachment*, 178–91; Mallison and Mallison, *The Palestine Problem in International Law and World Order*, 240–75; Quigley, *Palestine and Israel*, 216–17.
2. Medzini, *Israel's Foreign Relations*, 3:58.
3. Bernard Gwertzman, *New York Times*, 13 March 1980; Yodfat and Arnon-Ohanna, *PLO*, 136–37.
4. See Bernard Gwertzman, *New York Times*, 13 March 1980, for a list of U.S. statements over the years of its position on Jerusalem. Also see Khouri, *The Arab-Israeli Dilemma*, 384; Lilienthal, *The Zionist Connection*, 646–49; Foundation for Middle East, *Report*

on Israeli Settlement in the Occupied Territories, Special Report, July 1991.

5. The text is in Lukacs, *The Israeli-Palestinian Conflict*, 67–69; excerpts are in *New York Times*, 25 March 1976.

6. *New York Times*, 25 March 1976.

7. See, for instance, *New York Times*, 29 July 1977; U.S. Department of State, *American Foreign Policy 1977–80*, 618, 650.

8. Office of the Legal Adviser, U.S. Department of State, *Digest of United States Practice in International Law 1978*, 1575–83. The text is in House Committee on International Relations, *Israeli Settlements in the Occupied Territories: Hearings before the Subcommittee on International Organizations and on Europe and the Middle East of the Committee on International Relations*, 95th Cong., 1st sess., 1978, 167–72, and in Thorpe, *Prescription for Conflict*, 153–58. Major excerpts are in Foundation for Middle East, *Report on Israeli Settlement in the Occupied Territories*, Special Report, July 1991. For a detailed discussion, see Mallison, *The Palestine Problem in International Law and World Order*, chap. 6.

9. *New York Times*, 3 February 1981; Tillman, *The United States in the Middle East*, 170. Unconfirmed rumors say Reagan made the statement to redeem a pledge given to Israel's supporters during the 1980 presidential campaign. The statement caused consternation and confusion within the State Department since it directly contradicted thirteen years of policy that considered settlements illegal.

10. See, for instance, *New York Times*, 28 August 1983, and David A. Korn, letter, *New York Times*, 10 October 1991. Excerpts on Reagan's remarks about settlements being an obstacle to peace are in Lukacs, *The Israeli-Palestinian Conflict*, 80–81.

11. The text of the EC statement is in "Documents and Source Material," *Journal of Palestine Studies*, Autumn 1990, 147–88.

12. David Hoffman and Jackson Diehl, *Washington Post*, 18 September 1991.

13. Asher Wallfish and Dan Izenberg, *Jerusalem Post International Edition*, 25 July 1992.

14. Quigley, *Palestine and Israel*, 175.

15. Aronson, *Creating Facts*, 16. Also see Israel Shahak, "Memory of 1967 'Ethnic Cleansing' Fuels Ideology of Golan Settlers," *Washington Report on Middle East Affairs*, November 1992.

16. Terence Smith, *New York Times*, 25 September 1967.

17. Hedrick Smith, *New York Times*, 27 September 1967.

18. Anne Lesch, "Israeli Settlements in the Occupied Territories," *Journal of Palestine Studies*, Autumn 1978. Israeli Housing Minister Zeev Sharef revealed details of the Jerusalem settlements on 18 February 1971. See *Facts on File 1971*, 123.

19. There are a number of good studies on Israel's settlements, which in the early years after 1967 were often established surreptitiously as a way of avoiding world censure. This changed with the coming

to power of Menachem Begin, who openly encouraged settlements. See, for instance, Aronson, *Creating Facts*, which has an excellent chronology since 1967 as well as maps and a list of Jewish settlements on the West Bank as of 1982; at the time they numbered 110. Also see the following in the *Journal of Palestine Studies*: Michael Adams, "Israel's Treatment of the Arabs in the Occupied Territories," Winter 1972, 19–40; Anne Mosley Lesch, "Israeli Settlements in the Occupied Territories, 1967–1977," Autumn 1977, 26–47; Ibrahim Matar, "Israeli Settlements in the West Bank and Gaza Strip," Autumn 1981, 93–110; Abu-Lughod, "Israeli Settlements in Occupied Arab Lands: Conquest to Colony," Winter 1982, 16–54.

20. Walid Khalidi, "The Palestine Problem: An Overview," *Journal of Palestine Studies*, Autumn 1991, 9–10.

21. U.S. Department of State, *Israeli Settlement in the Occupied Territories*, May 1991, cited in Foundation for Middle East Peace, *Report on Israeli Settlement in the Occupied Territories*, July 1992.

22. Khalidi, "The Palestine Problem."

23. Foundation for Middle East Peace, *Report on Israeli Settlement in the Occupied Territories*, July 1992.

24. Robert I. Friedman, *Washington Post*, 10 January 1988. Also see Michael C. Hudson, "The Transformation of Jerusalem: 1917–1987 AD," in Asali, *Jerusalem in History*, 257; Stephen J. Sosebee, "Seeds of a Massacre: Israeli Violations at Haram al-Sharif," *American-Arab Affairs*, Spring 1991, 109.

25. Foundation for Middle East Peace, *Report on Israeli Settlement in the Occupied Territories*, July 1992.

TWENTY-FOUR

1. U.S. Senate and U.S. House of Representatives, *Legislation on Foreign Relations through 1986*, 1032.

2. Kenen, *Israel's Defense Line*, 331.

3. Resolution 2649 (XXV). The text is in Tomeh, *United Nations Resolutions on Palestine and the Arab-Israeli Conflict*, 1:78–79. Also see Mallison, *The Palestine Problem in International Law and World Order*, 198; Ghayth Armanazi, "The Rights of the Palestinians: The International Definition," *Journal of Palestine Studies*, Spring 1974, 93–94. For a discussion of the right to self-defense, see Quigley, *Palestine and Israel*, 189–97.

4. Bard and Himelfarb, *Myths and Facts*, 113.

5. Resolution ES-9/1. The text is in *New York Times*, 6 February 1982, and Simpson, *United Nations Resolutions on Palestine and the Arab-Israeli Conflict*, 3:3–4.

6. *New York Times*, 31 March 1983, cited in Bard and Himelfarb, *Myths and Facts*, 113.

7. Resolution No. 59. The text is in Tomeh, *United Nations Resolutions on Palestine and the Arab-Israeli Conflict*, 1:129.

8. Resolution 93. The text is in ibid., 133–34. For a history of the zone and Israeli-Syrian clashes over it, see Burns, *Between Arab and Israeli*, 108–15. Bull, *War and Peace in the Middle East*, 49, has the best description of the zone and its three sectors. Also see Laura Drake, "The Golan Belongs to Syria," *Middle East International*, 11 September 1992.

9. The first time the United States had ever invoked its veto came in 1970 when it blocked a resolution involving Southern Rhodesia. The second time the United States used its veto was two years later, when it began employing the veto to shield Israel. See Ball, *The Passionate Attachment*, 307.

TWENTY-FIVE

1. Segev, *1949*, 6. Also see Ball, *The Passionate Attachment*, 298.
2. Begin press conference, 1 March 1979, quoted in Medzini, *Israel's Foreign Relations*, 5:644.
3. Henry Kissinger, "The Path to Peaceful Coexistence in the Middle East," *Washington Post* Outlook section, 2 August 1992.
4. Fred J. Khouri, "Major Obstacles to Peace: Ignorance, Myths and Misconceptions," *American-Arab Affairs*, Spring 1986, 60.
5. Meir, *My Life*, 383.
6. For reports on Israel's intransigence during this period, see such reports in U.S. Department of State, *Foreign Relations of the United States (FRUS) 1949*, "The Minister in Lebanon (Pinkerton) to the Secretary of State" (from Ethridge), 28 March 1949, 6:878; *FRUS 1949*, "The Minister in Lebanon (Pinkerton) to the Secretary of State" (from Ethridge), 28 March 1949, 6:876–77; *FRUS 1949*, "The Consul at Jerusalem (Burdett) to the Secretary of State," 28 February 1949, 9 AM, 6:775; *FRUS 1949*, "The Consul at Jerusalem (Burdett) to the Secretary of State," 20 April 1949, 4 PM, 6:928–30.
7. *FRUS 1949*, "The Acting Secretary of State to the Embassy in Israel," 28 May 1949, 11 AM, 6:1072–74. Also see Ball, *The Passionate Attachment*, 33–41.
8. Eisenhower diary, 13 March 1956, Eisenhower Library.
9. Eisenhower diary, 8 March 1956, Eisenhower Library, quoted in Neff, *Warriors at Suez*, 50–51.
10. Neff, *Warriors at Suez*, 44. Also see *New York Times*, 10 April 1954.
11. Kissinger, *Years of Upheaval*, 212.
12. Ibid., 550–51.
13. Sheehan, *The Arabs, Israelis, and Kissinger*, 159.
14. Ford, *A Time to Heal*, 245.
15. Sheehan, *The Arabs, Israelis, and Kissinger*, 199.
16. Ball, *The Passionate Attachment*, 84–107.
17. Carter, *Keeping Faith*, 312–13.
18. Khouri, "Major Obstacles to Peace," 60.

19. Ball, *The Passionate Attachment*, 108–30.
20. Thomas L. Friedman, *New York Times*, 13 May 1987.
21. Linda Gradstein, *Washington Post*, 3 July 1991. Excerpts in "Documents and Source Material," *Journal of Palestine Studies*, Autumn 1991, 185–86.
22. Thomas L. Friedman, *New York Times*, 25 July 1991.
23. Davis, *Myths and Facts, 1989*, 69.
24. Quandt, *Decade of Decisions*, 136. Also see Kissinger, *White House Years*, 1278–79; Neff, *Warriors against Israel*, 46; Whetten, *The Canal War*, 201.
25. The text of Roger's statement is in Lukacs, *The Israeli-Palestinian Conflict*, 55–60.
26. Brecher, *Decisions in Israel's Foreign Policy*, 479–83. The text of the cabinet statement is in Lukacs, *The Israeli-Palestinian Conflict*, 182–83.
27. The text is in U.S. Department of State, *American Foreign Policy 1977–1980*, 617–18, and *New York Times*, 28 June 1977.
28. Quandt, *Camp David*, 73.
29. Carter first publicly mentioned a homeland on 16 March 1977; see the text in Lukacs, *The Israeli-Palestinian Conflict*, 69–70. Reaction among Israel's supporters to Carter's homeland statement was so fierce that the White House quickly qualified the remarks, saying, "The exact definition of what that homeland might be, the degree of independence of the Palestinian entity, its relations with Jordan, or perhaps Syria and others, the geographical boundaries of it, all have to be worked out by the parties involved." See Rubenberg, *Israel and the American National Interest*, 210–11. The homeland issue was eventually dropped by Carter because of opposition by Israel's supporters, reported analyst William Quandt: "Before long, however, Carter was beginning to feel the political heat, and his statements on the Palestinians became more circumspect, first stressing his preference for a link between a Palestinian homeland and Jordan, then dropping all reference to a homeland, and eventually conveying his opposition to an independent Palestinian state"; see Quandt, *Camp David*, 60.
30. Quandt, *Camp David*, 84.
31. Ibid., 81.
32. Quandt, *Camp David*, is the best account of the negotiations and the meaning of the accords. Quandt was a member of the U.S. team and brings an insider's insight to the event.
33. As early as August 1967 Israel had secretly offered Egypt the return of the Sinai in exchange for demilitarization of the desert region, free navigation in the Suez Canal, internationalization of the Straits of Tiran, and a formal peace treaty; see Aronson, *Conflict and Bargaining in the Middle East*, 86. This Israeli offer was seen as a ploy to split its most powerful enemy from other Arab countries— and was brusquely rejected by Egypt's Gamal Abdel Nasser. Also see O'Brien, *The Siege*, 489, and texts of statements issued by the

PLO, Saudi Arabia, Jordan, Lebanon, Syria, Kuwait, Tunisia, Morocco, Palestinians, and so on, in "Documents and Source Material," *Journal of Palestine Studies*, Winter 1979, 177–204.

34. U.S. State Department, *American Foreign Policy 1977–1980*, 667.

35. The text is in "Documents and Source Material," *Journal of Palestine Studies*, Autumn 1981, 241–43. See Khouri, *The Arab-Israeli Dilemma*, 425.

36. Rubenberg, *Israel and the American National Interest*, 259. Also see O'Brien, *The Siege*, 617–18, for speculation on how the peace plan worried Israel about warming relations between the United States and Saudi Arabia and contributed to its decision to invade Lebanon in 1982.

37. Rubenberg, *Israel and the American National Interest*, 259.

38. The text is in *New York Times*, 2 September 1982, and "Documents and Source Material," *Journal of Palestine Studies*, Summer/Fall 1982, 340–43. Also see Khouri, *The Arab-Israeli Dilemma*, 436–41; Peck, *The Reagan Administration and the Palestinian Question*, 83–99.

39. Ball, *Error and Betrayal in Lebanon*, 53, and Tom Wicker, *New York Times*, 24 September 1982.

40. Khouri, *The Arab-Israeli Dilemma*, 438. The text of Begin's letter to Reagan explaining Israel's position is in *New York Times*, 5 September 1982, and "Documents and Source Material," *Journal of Palestine Studies*, Winter 1983, 211–18.

41. Rubenberg, *Israel and the American National Interest*, 309.

42. The text is in *New York Times*, 10 September 1982, and "Documents and Source Material," *Journal of Palestine Studies*, Winter 1983, 202–3. Also see Cobban, *The Palestine Liberation Organization*, 127.

43. Peck, *The Reagan Administration and the Palestinian Question*, 83–99.

44. Rubenberg, *Israel and the American National Interest*, 313.

45. The text of the "Political Communiqué" is in Lukacs, *The Israeli-Palestinian Conflict*, 411–15. A study of the council meeting and U.S. policy is in Rashid Khalidi, "The 19th PNC Resolutions and American Policy," *Journal of Palestine Studies*, Winter 1990. Also see Muhammad Muslih, "Towards Coexistence: An Analysis of the Resolutions of the Palestine National Council," *Journal of Palestine Studies*, Summer 1990, 3–29.

46. Joel Brinkley, *New York Times*, 16 November 1988. Text of Israel's statement is in Lukacs, *The Israeli-Palestinian Conflict*, 216–18.

47. Robert Pear, *New York Times*, 16 November 1988.

48. Thomas L. Friedman, *New York Times*, 21 June 1990. Texts of official PLO statements on the issue in *Journal of Palestine Studies*, "Documents and Source Material," Autumn 1990, 159–63. Text of President Bush's comments in same journal, 186–90.

49. Thomas L. Friedman, *New York Times*, 23 May 1989. The partial text of Baker's remarks is in the same issue. Full text is in *Department of State Bulletin*, July 1989, and "Documents and Source Material," *Journal of Palestine Studies*, Summer 1989, 172–76. Also see Ellen Fleischmann, "Image and Issues and the AIPAC Conference, 21–23 May 1989," *Journal of Palestine Studies*, Summer 1989, 84–90.

50. David S. Broder, *Washington Post*, 24 May 1989; Thomas L. Friedman, *New York Times*, 24 May 1989. Also see James Morrison and Martin Sieff, *Washington Times*, 24 May 1989.

51. Thomas L. Friedman, *New York Times*, 14 June 1990.

52. Thomas L. Friedman, *New York Times*, 23 May 1991. The text is in Sicherman, *Palestinian Self-Government (Autonomy)*, Appendix XVI.

53. The text of Syria's understanding of U.S. commitments on the conference is in "Documents and Source Material," *Journal of Palestine Studies*, Autumn 1991, 169.

54. Thomas L. Friedman, *New York Times*, 23 July 1991. The text of the statement presented to Baker by Palestinians is in "Documents and Source Material," *Journal of Palestine Studies*, Autumn 1991, 168–69.

55. Thomas L. Friedman, *New York Times*, 25 July 1991.

56. Jackson Diehl, *Washington Post*, 19 October 1991. Also see Thomas R. Mattair, "The Arab-Israeli Conflict: The Madrid Conference, and Beyond," *American-Arab Affairs*, Summer 1991.

57. Clyde Haberman, *New York Times*, 27 June 1992.

58. Muhammad Hallaj, "The Seventh Round of the Bilateral Peace Talks," *Middle East International*, 6 November 1992.

TWENTY-SIX

1. Bookbinder and Abourezk, *Through Different Eyes*, 7.

2. United Press International, *New York Times*, 26 September 1980.

3. *New York Times*, 12 October 1985. Also see Robert I. Friedman, "Who Killed Alex Odeh?," *Village Voice*, 24 November 1987; U.S. Department of Energy, *Terrorism in the United States and the Potential Threat to Nuclear Facilities*, R-3351-DOE, January 1986, 11F–16, quoted in Nakhleh, *Encyclopedia of the Palestine Problem*, 863.

4. Frank, *U.S. Marines in Lebanon*, 140, Appendix F.

5. Neff, *Warriors at Suez*, 56–62.

6. Ennes, *Assault on the Liberty*, Appendix O.

7. *New York Times*, 18 March 1983. For a detailed review of these clashes, see Green, *Living by the Sword*, 177–92. Aside from Barrow's letter, see Clyde Mark, "The Multinational Force in Lebanon," Congressional Research Service, 19 May 1983, which contains many examples of IDF harassment of U.S. troops. Also

see Frank, *U.S. Marines in Lebanon*, who tends to minimize the situation.

8. AIPAC, *Near East Report*, 13 July 1992.
9. See Jeff Gerth, *New York Times*, 2 August 1985; Mary Thornton, *Washington Post*, 23 April 1986; William Claiborne, *Washington Post*, 16 May 1986; Robert F. Howe, *Washington Post*, 15 June 1991, 19 October 1991; Edward T. Pound and David Rogers, *Wall Street Journal*, 20 January 1992.
10. Steven Pearlstein, *Washington Post*, 23 July 1992.
11. Opening statement by Chairman John D. Dingell (D-Mich.) of the House oversight committee of the House Committee on Energy and Commerce hearings on the Dotan case, 29 July 1992; printed in *Washington Report on Middle East Affairs*, August/September 1992.
12. Frank Collins, "House Subcommittee Protests Stonewalling of U.S. Investigation," *The Washington Report on the Middle East*, August/September 1992.
13. Allison Kaplan, *Jerusalem Post International Edition*, 8 August 1992.
14. Ostrovsky and Hoy, *By Way of Deception*, 270.
15. Robert F. Howe, *Washington Post*, 15 June 1991, 19 October 1991.
16. It was clear that by "someone else" he meant Israel; see *New York Times*, 7 January 1987. Although congressional investigating committees tended to ignore Israel's involvement in the affair, Israeli officials played a pivotal role in the Reagan administration's relations with Iran from before the 1980 election. For an interesting examination of Israel's role in influencing U.S. relations with Iran, see Jane Hunter, "The Shadow Government," *The Link*, October–November 1987. Along the same lines, also see Christopher Hitchens, "Minority Report," *The Nation*, 24 October 1987, 21 November 1987.
17. Bard and Himelfarb, *Myths and Facts*, 246–47.
18. Robert Byrd, *Congressional Record*, 1 April 1992.
19. John Newhouse, "Politics and Weapon Sales," *The New Yorker*, 9 June 1986, 41–61. Also see Briget Bloom and Richard Johns, *Financial Times* (London), 19 February 1986; Molly Moore and David B. Ottaway, *Washington Post*, 22 October 1988; A. Craig Murphy, "Congressional Opposition to Arms Sales to Saudi Arabia," *American-Arab Affairs*, Spring 1988, 108.
20. Molly Moore and David B. Ottaway, *Washington Post*, 22 October 1988. The text is in Office of Assistant Secretary of Defense (Public Affairs), No. 525–88, 21 October 1988. Also see Donald Neff, "The Backlash against Israel's Washington Lobby," *Middle East International*, 18 November 1988.
21. A. Craig Murphy, "Congressional Opposition to Arms Sales to Saudi Arabia," *American-Arab Affairs*, Spring 1988, 111.
22. Rubenberg, *Israel and the American National Interest*, 350–51.

23. Davis, *Myths and Facts 1989*, 229.

24. Ibid., 234.

25. Charles R. Babcock, *Washington Post*, 6 August 1986.

26. *New York Times*, 3 September 1987. Also see Ball, *The Passionate Attachment*, 264–68; Cockburn, *Dangerous Liaison*, 191; Clyde Mark, "Israel: U.S. Foreign Assistance Facts," Foreign Affairs and National Defense Division, Congressional Research Service, updated 5 July 1991; U.S. General Accounting Office, "Foreign Assistance: Analysis of Cost Estimates for Israel's Lavi Aircraft," January 1987.

27. Joshua Brilliant, *Jerusalem Post International Edition*, 11 July 1987.

28. Charles R. Babcock, *Washington Post*, 11 September 1987.

29. Cockburn, *Dangerous Liaison*, 191.

30. Ibid.

31. Thomas L. Friedman, *New York Times*, 15 March 1992.

32. Edward T. Pound, *Wall Street Journal*, 13 March 1992. Also see David Hoffman and R. Jeffrey Smith, *Washington Post*, 14 March 1992.

33. David Hoffman, *Washington Post*, 2 April 1992.

34. Bill Gertz and Rowan Scarborough, *Washington Times*, 12–13 March 1992. For a survey of U.S. support of Israel's arms industry, see Bishara A. Bahbah, "The US Role in Israel's Arms Industry," *The Link*, December 1987.

35. David Hoffman, *Washington Post*, 3 April 1992.

36. Bill Gertz, *Washington Times*, 9 April 1992. Also see Richard H. Curtiss, *Washington Report on Middle East Affairs*, April/May 1992.

37. Cockburn, *Dangerous Liaison*, 7.

38. United Press International, #0543, 13 June 1990. Also see David B. Ottaway, *Washington Post*, 23 May 1988, 19 December 1988; C. L. Sulzberger, *New York Times*, 30 April 1971; Beit-Hallahmi, *The Israeli Connection*, 108–74; Robert D. Shuey, et al., "Missile Proliferation: Survey of Emerging Missile Forces," Congressional Research Center, 3 October 1988.

39. See U.S. Accounting Office, "US Assistance to the State of Israel, Report by the Comptroller General of the United States," GAO/ID-83-51, 24 June 1983, 43. The report was at the time the most comprehensive survey ever made of the extraordinary special arrangements provided for Israel's profit. When it was released, the report was heavily censored, but uncensored versions quickly leaked to such organizations as the American-Arab Anti-Discrimination Committee. An uncensored early draft of the report can be found in El-Khawas and Abed-Rabbo, *American Aid to Israel*, 114–91.

40. Drew Middleton, *New York Times*, 15 March 1981. For a report on the state of Israel's arms industry in 1986, see Thomas L. Friedman, *New York Times*, 7 December 1986.

41. Klieman, *Israel's Global Reach*, 175.
42. Davis, *Myths and Facts 1989*, 248.
43. Sheehan, *The Arabs, Israelis, and Kissinger*, 69.
44. Ball, *The Passionate Attachment*, 269–72; Kelly, *Arabia, the Gulf, and the West*, 396.
45. Kissinger, *Years of Upheaval*, 515; Nixon, *Memoirs*, 927.
46. Kelly, *Arabia, the Gulf, and the West*, 39.
47. Neff, *Warriors against Israel*, 112–14; Sheehan, *The Arabs, Israelis, and Kissinger*, 67.
48. Lacey, *The Kingdom*, 413; Nixon, *Memoirs*, 932.
49. Lacey, *The Kingdom*, 413; State Department Middle East Task Force, Situation Report #51, 21 October 1973 (secret, declassified 31 December 1981). Also see Neff, *Warriors against Israel*, 260.

TWENTY-SEVEN

1. Text in "Special Document," *Journal of Palestine Studies*, Summer 1985, 122–28.
2. Titles of the monographs include *The Strategic Value of Israel; Israel and the US Air Force; Israel and the US Navy; Israeli Medical Support for the US Armed Forces; US Procurement of Israeli Defense Goods and Services*. For a review of the monographs, see Muhammed Hallaj, "Israel's Plans for Knotting Its US Ties," *Middle East International*, 26 October 1984. AIPAC's lobbying as one of the most effective in Washington is described in *New York Times*, 24 March 1984; David K. Shipler, *New York Times*, 6 July 1987.
3. Eban, *An Autobiography*, 184. Privately, Dulles had mentioned to President Eisenhower on 19 August 1955, that Israel wants "first of all a security treaty with the United States"; see *Foreign Relations of the United States 1955*, Letter from the Secretary of State to the President, 19 August 1955, 368–69. Dulles later indicated that he feared that Israel actually was interested in having the United States support Israel totally against the Arabs; see *Foreign Relations of the United States 1955*, Telegram from the Secretary of State to the Department of State, 8 November 1955, noon, 717.
4. Hersh, *The Samson Option*, 270.
5. Khouri, *The Arab-Israeli Dilemma*, 426–27. The text of the memorandum is in *New York Times*, 1 December 1981, and Institute for Palestine Studies, *International Documents on Palestine 1981*, 405–6. Also see Ball, *The Passionate Attachment*; Chomsky, *The Fateful Triangle;* McGovern, "The Future Role of the United States in the Middle East," *Middle East Policy*, 1, no. 3 (1992); Rubenberg, *Israel and the American National Interest;* Tivnan, *The Lobby*.
6. Resolution 36/266 A. The text is in Sherif, *United Nations Resolutions on Palestine and the Arab-Israeli Conflict*, 2:175–77.

7. Resolution 497. The text is in Sherif, *United Nations Resolutions on Palestine and the Arab-Israeli Conflict*, 2:200, and Mallison, *The Palestine Problem in International Law and World Order*, 476–77.
8. *New York Times*, 19 December 1981.
9. *New York Times*, 30 November 1983. Also see Bernard Gwertzman, "Reagan Turns to Israel," *New York Times Magazine*, 27 November 1983; Rubenberg, *Israel and the American National Interest*, 353; John M. Goshko, *Washington Post*, 22 November 1983; Charles R. Babcock, *Washington Post*, 5 August 1986; "Free Trade Area for Israel Proposed," *Mideast Observer*, 15 March 1984.
10. Smith, *The Power Game*, 619; Fred J. Khouri, "Major Obstacles to Peace: Ignorance, Myths, and Misconceptions," *American-Arab Affairs*, Spring 1986, 47. Also see Ball, *The Passionate Attachment*, 297–99.
11. *Near East Report*, 20 July 1992.
12. Rubenberg, *Israel and the American National Interest*, 330–31.
13. George W. Ball, "What Is an Ally?," *American-Arab Affairs*, Fall 1983.
14. Joseph C. Harsh, *Christian Science Monitor*, 30 October 1984. Also see Middle East Policy and Research Center, *Executive Report*, April 1985; "US, Israel Move toward Free Trade Pact," *Congressional Quarterly*, 29 December 1984. The text of the agreement is in *Journal of Palestine Studies*, Winter 1986, 119–31.
15. Fred Hiatt, *Washington Post*, 7 May 1986.
16. *Congressional Record*, 1 April 1992.
17. Middle East Policy and Research Center, February 1987.
18. From Dine's speech at the 27th Annual AIPAC Policy Conference, 6 April 1986. The text is in "Special Document," *Journal of Palestine Studies*, Summer 1986, 134–43.
19. Bookbinder and Abourezk, *Through Different Eyes*, 67.
20. Cheryl A. Rubenberg, "The Misguided Alliance," *The Link*, October/November 1986; Alexander Cockburn, "Beat the Devil," *The Nation*, 3 March 1986.
21. Steven L. Spiegel, "Israel as a Strategic Asset," *Commentary*, June 1983.
22. Michael R. Gordon, *New York Times*, 12 January 1991.
23. Thomas L. Friedman, *New York Times*, 6 March 1991; John E. Yang, *Washington Post*, 6 March 1991. Also see Clyde Mark, "Israel: U.S. Foreign Assistance Facts," Foreign Affairs and National Defense Division, Congressional Research Service, updated 5 July 1991.
24. David Hoffman, *Washington Post*, 28 July 1992.
25. Ibid.

TWENTY-EIGHT

1. The text is in *Near East Report*, 13 July 1992.
2. Ball, *The Passionate Attachment*, 153–54; Keller, *Terrible Days*, 78–86.
3. Nyrop, *Israel: A Country Study*, 105.
4. Sachar, *A History of Israel*, 379.
5. The text is in *Journal of Palestine Studies*, Spring 1991, 139.
6. News conference, broadcast by CNN, 11 August 1992.
7. Glenn Frankel, *Washington Post*, 31 October 1987. Also see Thomas L. Friedman, *New York Times*, 8 November 1987; Amnesty International, *Amnesty Report: 1988*, 239; Stanley Cohen, "Talking about Torture in Israel," *Tikkun*, November/December 1992.
8. Jack Redden, *Washington Times*, 5 November 1991.
9. Bethell, *The Palestine Triangle*, 277–78.
10. Steven, *The Spymasters of Israel*, 145–47. Also see Ball, *The Passionate Attachment*, 251–52; Bar-Zohar, *Ben-Gurion*, 301–2; Nakhleh, *Encyclopedia of the Palestine Problem*, 832; Neff, *Warriors for Jerusalem*, 101–2; Raviv and Melman, *Every Spy a Prince*, 122–25.
11. Ostrovsky and Hoy, *By Way of Deception*, 23.
12. William Scott Malone, David Halevy and Sam Hemingway, *Washington Post* Outlook section, 10 February 1991. Also see Glenn Frankel, *Washington Post*, 16 January 1992; Kevin Toolis, "The Man Behind Iraq's Supergun," *New York Times Magazine*, 26 August 1990; Cockburn, *Dangerous Liaison*, 301–6.
13. David Halevy and Neil C. Livingstone, "The Killing of Abu Jihad," *Washingtonian*, June 1988; Peter Kerr, *New York Times*, 17 April 1988.
14. Livingstone and Halevy, *Inside the PLO*, 43–58; Raviv and Melman, *Every Spy a Prince*, 397.
15. News conference, broadcast by CNN, 11 August 1992.
16. Nora Boustany, *Washington Post*, 1 August 1989. Also see Jackson Diehl, *Washington Post*, 29 July 1989; Ball, *The Passionate Attachment*, 251–52; Cooley, *Payback*, 155–56, 169.
17. David Hoffman and Ann Devroy, *Washington Post*, 1 August 1989.
18. Donald Lamboro, *Washington Times*, 7 August 1989.
19. U.S. Department of State, *Country Reports on Human Rights Practices for 1991*, February 1992, 1440–55; the text is reproduced in *Journal of Palestine Studies*, Spring 1992, 114–24. Also see the report for the preceding years, 1990, 1989, and 1988.
20. Capitol Hill luncheon address, Rayburn Building, 14 June 1989.
21. Bard and Himelfarb, *Myths and Facts*, 249.
22. Israeli economist Steven Pault, a senior lecturer at the University of Haifa, argues that Israel's economy is not socialist in the traditional sense but rather is "politicalist." By that he means "resources [are]

allocated and prices determined through an extremely complex political process. . . . The process involves the political interplay of competing special interest groups and competing agencies within the government sector." One result, says Pault, is that "the number of markets and economic decisions that is subordinated to pork barrel politics in Israel is without precedent in the democratic world." See Steven Pault, "Pork in Israel," *National Interest,* Summer 1992.

23. Jim McGee, *Washington Post,* 3 October 1991.
24. Clyde Mark, "Israel: U.S. Foreign Assistance Facts," Foreign Affairs and National Defense Division, Congressional Research Service, updated 5 July 1991.
25. Joel Brinkley, *New York Times,* 4 May 1991.
26. Steven Pault, "Pork in Israel," *National Interest,* Summer 1992.
27. Bard and Himelfarb, *Myths and Facts,* 248.
28. Joel Brinkley, *New York Times,* 4 May 1991.
29. Jim McGee, *Washington Post,* 3 October 1991.
30. Joel Brinkley, *New York Times,* 5 November 1989.
31. Keller, *Terrible Days,* 17–19.
32. Sachar, *A History of Israel,* 412. Also see Alvin Rabushka, *Scoreboard on the Israeli Economy: A Review of 1989,* Institute for Advance Strategic and Political Studies (Jerusalem), February 1990.
33. Sachar, *A History of Israel,* 833.
34. Ball, *The Passionate Attachment,* 302.
35. Ralph Z. Hallow, *Washington Times,* 15 February 1990.
36. Quoted in ibid.
37. Bard and Himelfarb, *Myths and Facts,* 249.
38. 1991 Export-Import Bank study, reported in Jim McGee, *Washington Post,* 3 October 1991.
39. Ball, *The Passionate Attachment,* 168.
40. U.S. General Accounting Office, "US Assistance to the State of Israel, Report by the Comptroller General of the United States," GAO/ID-83-51, 24 June 1983, 43. An uncensored early draft of the report can be found in El-Khawas and Abed-Rabbo, *American Aid to Israel,* 114–91. Also see Fred Hiatt, *Washington Post,* 25 June 1983. *The New York Times* printed a story on the study, 26 June 1983, as did Claudia Wright, "US Assistance to the State of Israel: US General Accounting Office Report," *Journal of Palestine Studies,* Fall 1983, 123–36.
41. Jackson Diehl, *Washington Post,* 8 June 1992.
42. Interview with the author, 22 March 1992.
43. From Rabin's 1992 inaugural address, text in Foreign Broadcast Information Service, 14 July 1992, 23–27.
44. From Clinton's remarks to the 1992 convention of B'nai B'rith, Washington, D.C., 9 September 1992.
45. Silver, *Begin,* 145.

46. The quotations are in *New York Times*, 21 December 1981, and Institute for Palestine Studies, *International Documents on Palestine 1981*, 429–31. Also see Silver, *Begin*, 45–46.
47. See, for instance, Schiff and Ya'ari, *Israel's Lebanon War*, 74, and Cockburn, *Dangerous Liaison*, 328.
48. Ball, *Error and Betrayal in Lebanon*, 35.
49. Editorial, *Washington Post*, 3 January 1985.
50. Tillman, *The United States in the Middle East*, 166.
51. Jackson Diehl, *Washington Post*, 20 January 1992.

EPILOGUE

1. The idea that both Arab nations and Israel would be protected from attack was proposed in 1970 in a major speech by Senator J. William Fulbright entitled "Old Myths and New Realities—the Middle East." See Tad Szulc, *New York Times*, 23 August 1970; major excerpts from the speech are in the same edition.
2. John Whitbeck, *Chicago Tribune*, 21 July 1992. A fuller version appears in the English-language edition of *Al-Fajr*, 13 July 1992.
3. Chomsky, *The Fateful Triangle*, 6.
4. George W. Ball, "How to Save Israel in Spite of Herself," *Foreign Affairs*, April 1977.

BIBLIOGRAPHY
AND
SELECTED READING

Abourezk, James G. *Advise and Dissent: Memoirs of South Dakota and the U.S. Senate*. Brooklyn: Lawrence Hill, 1989.

Abu Iyad, with Eric Rouleau. *My Home, My Land: A Narrative of the Palestinian Struggle*. New York: Times Books, 1978.

Abu-Lughod, Ibrahim, ed. *Transformation of Palestine*. 2nd ed. Evanston: Northwestern University Press, 1987.

Adams, James. *The Unnatural Alliance*. New York: Quartet, 1984.

Aldouby, Zwy, and Jerrold Ballinger. *The Shattered Silence*. New York: Lancer, 1971.

Allon, Yigal. *The Shield of David: The Story of Israel's Armed Forces*. London: Weidenfeld and Nicolson, 1970.

Ambrose, Stephen E. *Eisenhower: The President*. New York: Simon & Schuster, 1984.

American Friends Service Committee. *A Compassionate Peace: A Future for the Middle East*. New York: Hill & Wang, 1982.

Arkadie, Brian Van. *Benefits and Burdens: A Report on the West Bank and Gaza Strip Economies since 1967*. New York: Carnegie Endowment for International Peace, 1977.

Aronson, Geoffrey. *Creating Facts: Israel, Palestinians, and the West Bank*. Washington, D.C.: Institute for Palestine Studies, 1987.

Aronson, Shlomo. *Conflict and Bargaining in the Middle East: An Israeli Perspective*. Baltimore: Johns Hopkins University Press, 1978.

Aruri, Naseer H., ed. *Occupation: Israel over Palestine*. Belmont, Mass: Association of Arab-American University Graduates, 1983.

Asali, K. J., ed. *Jerusalem in History*. New York: Olive Branch Press, 1990.

Avner [pseud]. *Memoirs of an Assassin*. London: Anthony Blond, 1959.

Azcarate, Pablo de. *Mission in Palestine, 1948–1952*. Washington, D.C.: Middle East Institute, 1966.

Bailey, Sydney D. *Four Arab-Israeli Wars and the Peace Process*. London: Macmillan, 1990.

Balabkins, Nicholas. *West German Reparations to Israel*. New Brunswick: Rutgers University Press, 1971.

Ball, George W. *Error and Betrayal in Lebanon*. Washington, D.C.: Foundation for Middle East Peace, 1984.

———, and Douglas B. Ball. *The Passionate Attachment: America's Involvement with Israel, 1947 to the Present*. New York: Norton, 1992.

Bard, Mitchell G., and Joel Himelfarb. *Myths and Facts: A Concise Record of the Arab-Israeli Conflict*. Washington, D.C.: Near East Report, 1992.

Bar-Siman-Tov, Yaacov. *The Israeli-Egyptian War of Attrition, 1969–1970: A Case Study of Limited Local War*. New York: Columbia University Press, 1980.

Bar-Zohar, Michael. *Embassies in Crisis: Diplomats and Demagogues behind the Six-Day War*. Englewood Cliffs: Prentice-Hall, 1970.

———. *Ben-Gurion: A Biography*. New York: Delacorte, 1978.

Beatty, Ilene. *Arab and Jew in the Land of Canaan*. Chicago: Regnery, 1957.

Begin, Menachem. *The Revolt*. Los Angeles: Nash, 1972.

Beit-Hallahmi, Benjamin. *The Israeli Connection*. New York: Pantheon, 1987.

Bell, J. Bowyer. *Terror out of Zion*. New York: St. Martin's, 1977.

Ben-Gurion, David. *Israel: A Personal History*. New York: Funk & Wagnalls, 1971.

Benvenisti, Meron. *Jerusalem: The Torn City*. Jerusalem: Isratypeset, 1976.

———. *The West Bank Data Project: A Survey of Israel's Policies*. Washington, D.C.: American Enterprise Institute for Public Policy Research, 1984.

———, with Ziad Abu-Zayed and Danny Rubinstein. *The West Bank Handbook: A Political Lexicon*. Boulder: Westview, 1986.

Benziman, Uzi. *Sharon: An Israeli Caesar*. New York: Adama, 1985.

Bethell, Nicholas. *The Palestine Triangle: The Struggle for the Holy Land, 1935–48*. New York: Putnam, 1979.

Bialer, Uri. *Between East and West*. New York: Cambridge University Press, 1990.

Black, Ian, and Benny Morris. *Israel's Secret Wars: A History of Israel's Intelligence Service*. New York: Grove Weidenfeld, 1991.

Bober, Arie, ed. *The Other Israel: The Radical Case against Zionism*. New York: Anchor, 1972.

Bookbinder, Hyman, and James Abourezk. *Through Different Eyes: Two Leading Americans—a Jew and an Arab—Debate U.S. Policy in the Middle East*. Bethesda: Adler & Adler, 1987.

Boyle, Francis A. *World Politics and International Law*. Durham: Duke University Press, 1985.

———. *The Future of International Law and American Foreign Policy*. Ardsley-on-Hudson, N.Y.: Transnational Publishers, 1989.

Brecher, Michael. *Decisions in Israel's Foreign Policy*. London: Oxford University Press, 1974.

Brenner, Lenni. *Zionism in the Age of the Dictators*. Brooklyn: Lawrence Hill, 1983.

———. *The Iron Wall: Zionist Revisionism from Jabotinsky to Shamir*. London: Zed, 1984.

Bright, John. *A History of Israel*. Philadelphia: Westminster, 1959.

Brzezinski, Zbigniew. *Power and Principle: Memoirs of the National Security Adviser*. New York: Farrar, Straus & Giroux, 1983.

Bull, Odd. *War and Peace in the Middle East: The Experiences and Views of a U.N. Observer*. London: Leo Cooper, 1976.

Burns, Lt. Gen. E. L. M. *Between Arab and Israeli*. New York: Ivan Obolensky, 1962.

Carter, Jimmy. *Keeping Faith: Memoirs of a President*. New York: Bantam, 1982.

———. *The Blood of Abraham*. Boston: Houghton Mifflin, 1985.

Cattan, Henry. *Palestine, the Arabs, and Israel: The Search for Justice*. London: Longman, 1969.

———. *Jerusalem*. New York: St. Martin's, 1981.

Cervenka, Zdenek, and Barbara Rogers. *The Nuclear Axis: Secret Collaboration between West Germany and South Africa*. New York: Times Books, 1978.

Chomsky, Noam. *The Fateful Triangle: The United States, Israel, and the Palestinians*. Boston: South End Press, 1983.

———. *Pirates and Emperors: International Terrorism in the Real World*. Brattleboro, Vt.: Amana, 1986.

Cobban, Helena. *The Palestinian Liberation Organization*. New York: Cambridge University Press, 1984.

Cockburn, Andrew and Leslie. *Dangerous Liaison: The Inside Story of the U.S.-Israeli Covert Relationship*. New York: HarperCollins, 1991.

Cooley, John K. *Green March, Black September: The Story of the Palestinian Arabs*. London: Frank Cass, 1973.

———. *Payback: America's Long War in the Middle East*. New York: Brassey's, 1991.

Curtiss, Richard. *A Changing Image: American Perceptions of the Arab-Israeli Dispute*. 2nd ed. Washington, D.C.: American Educational Trust, 1986.

———. *Stealth PACs: How Israel's American Lobby Seeks to Control U.S. Middle East Policy*. Washington, D.C.: American Educational Trust, 1990.

Davenport, Elaine, et al. *The Plumbat Affair.* New York: Lippincott, 1978.

Davis, John H. *The Evasive Peace.* London: John Murray, 1970.

Davis, Leonard J. *Myths and Facts 1989: A Concise Record of the Arab-Israeli Conflict.* Washington, D.C.: Near East Report, 1988.

Davis, M. Thomas. *40 km into Lebanon: Israel's 1982 Invasion.* Washington, D.C.: National Defense University Press, 1987.

Davis, Uri, and Norton Mezvinsky. *Documents from Israel 1967–73: Readings for a Critique of Zionism.* London: Ithaca, 1975.

Dayan, Moshe. *Diary of the Sinai Campaign 1956.* London: Sphere, 1965.

———. *Story of My Life.* New York: Morrow, 1976.

———. *Breakthrough.* New York: Knopf, 1981.

Dupuy, Colonel Trevor N. *Elusive Victory: The Arab-Israeli Wars, 1947–74.* New York: Harper & Row, 1978.

Eban, Abba. *An Autobiography.* Tel Aviv: Steimatzky's Agency, 1977.

Eisenhower, Dwight D. *Waging Peace: 1956–61.* Garden City: Doubleday, 1965.

El-Asmar, Fouzi. *To Be an Arab in Israel.* Beirut: Institute for Palestine Studies, 1978.

El-Edroos, Brigadier S. A. *The Hashemite Arab Army 1908–1979.* Amman: The Publishing Committee, 1980.

El-Khawas, Mohammed, and Samir Abed-Rabbo. *American Aid to Israel: Nature and Impact.* Brattleboro, Vt.: Amana, 1984.

Elon, Amos. *The Israelis: Founders and Sons.* New York: Holt, Rinehart and Winston, 1971.

Ennes, James M., Jr. *Assault on the* Liberty. New York: Random House, 1979.

Epp, Frank H. *Whose Land Is Palestine?* Grand Rapids: Eerdmans, 1974.

Eveland, Wilbur Crane. *Ropes of Sand: America's Failure in the Middle East.* New York: Norton, 1980.

Fahmy, Ismail. *Negotiating for Peace in the Middle East.* Baltimore: Johns Hopkins University Press, 1983.

Fallaci, Oriana. *Interview with History.* Boston: Houghton Mifflin, 1976.

Feintuch, Yossi. *U.S. Policy on Jerusalem.* New York: Greenwood, 1987.

Feuerlicht, Roberta Strauss. *The Fate of the Jews: A People Torn between Israeli Power and Jewish Ethics.* New York: Times Books, 1983.

Findley, Paul. *They Dare to Speak Out: People and Institutions Confront Israel's Lobby.* Rev. ed. Brooklyn: Lawrence Hill, 1989.

Fisk, Robert. *Pity the Nation: The Abduction of Lebanon.* New York: Atheneum, 1990.

Flapan, Simha. *The Birth of Israel: Myths and Realities.* New York: Pantheon, 1987.

Ford, Gerald R. *A Time to Heal: The Autobiography of Gerald R. Ford.* New York: Harper & Row, 1979.

Forrest, A. C. *The Unholy Land.* Old Greenwich, Conn: Devin-Adair, 1974.

Frank, Benis M. *U.S. Marines in Lebanon: 1982–1984.* Washington, D.C.: History and Museums Division, Headquarters, U.S. Marine Corps, 1987.

Friedman, Robert I. *The False Prophet: Rabbi Meir Kahane—From FBI Informant to Knesset Member.* Brooklyn: Lawrence Hill, 1990.

———. *Zealots for Zion: Inside Israel's West Bank Settlement Movement.* New York: Random House, 1992.

Friedman, Thomas L. *From Beirut to Jerusalem.* New York: Farrar, Straus & Giroux, 1989.

Fromkin, David. *A Peace to End All Peace.* New York: Holt, 1989.

Gaffney, Mark. *Dimona: The Third Temple?* Brattleboro, Vt.: Amana, 1989.

Ghareeb, Edmund. *Split Vision: The Portrayal of Arabs in the American Media.* Washington, D.C.: American-Arab Affairs Council, 1983.

Ghilan, Maxim. *How Israel Lost Its Soul*. Middlesex, Eng.: Penguin, 1974.

Glubb, Pasha [Sir John Bagot Glubb]. *A Soldier with the Arabs*. London: Hodder and Stoughton, 1957.

Golan, Matti. *The Secret Conversations of Henry Kissinger*. New York: Quadrangle/New York Times Book Co., 1976.

Green, Stephen. *Taking Sides: America's Secret Relations with a Militant Israel*. New York: Morrow, 1984.

———. *Living by the Sword: America and Israel in the Middle East, 1968–1987*. Brattleboro, Vt.: Amana, 1988.

Grose, Peter. *Israel in the Mind of America*. New York: Knopf, 1983.

Grossman, David. *Sleeping on a Wire: Conversations with Palestinians in Israel*. New York: Farrar, Straus & Giroux, 1992.

Hadar, Leon T. *Quagmire: America in the Middle East*. Washington, D.C.: Cato Institute, 1992.

Hadawi, Sami. *Bitter Harvest*. New York: New World Press, 1967.

Halabi, Rafik. *The West Bank Story*. New York: Harcourt Brace Jovanovich, 1981.

Halsell, Grace. *Journey to Jerusalem*. New York: Macmillan, 1981.

———. *Prophecy and Politics: The Secret Alliance between Israel and the U.S. Christian Right*. Brooklyn: Lawrence Hill, 1989.

Harkabi, Y. *Israel's Fateful Hour*. New York: Harper & Row, 1988.

Harris, William Wilson. *Taking Root: Israeli Settlement in the West Bank, the Golan, and Gaza-Sinai, 1967–1980*. New York: Research Studies Press, 1980.

Hart, Alan. *Arafat: Terrorist or Peacemaker?* London: Sidgwick & Jackson, 1985.

Heikal, Mohamed. *Nasser: The Cairo Documents*. London: New English Library, 1973.

———. *The Road to Ramadan: The Inside Story of How the Arabs Prepared for and Almost Won the October War of 1973.* London: Collins, 1975.

———. *The Sphinx and the Commissar: The Rise and Fall of Soviet Influence in the Middle East.* New York: Harper & Row, 1978.

———. *Autumn of Fury: The Assassination of Sadat.* New York: Random House, 1983.

Hersh, Seymour M. *The Price of Power: Kissinger in the Nixon White House.* New York: Summit, 1983.

———. *The Samson Option: Israel's Nuclear Arsenal and American Foreign Policy.* New York: Random House, 1991.

Herzog, Chaim. *The Arab-Israeli Wars: War and Peace in the Middle East.* New York: Random House, 1982.

Hirst, David. *The Gun and the Olive Branch: The Roots of Violence in the Middle East.* New York: Harcourt Brace Jovanovich, 1977.

———, and Irene Beeson. *Sadat.* London: Faber & Faber, 1981.

Hoopes, Townsend. *The Devil and John Foster Dulles.* London: Andre Deutsch, 1974.

Howard, Harry N. *The King-Crane Commission.* Beirut: Khayats, 1963.

Hutchison, Commander E. H. *Violent Truce.* New York: Bevin-Adair, 1956.

Institute for Palestine Studies. *International Documents on Palestine, for the Years from 1967 through 1981.* Kuwait and Washington, D.C.: Kuwait University and Institute for Palestine Studies, last volume published in 1983.

———. *The Arabs under Israeli Occupation, for the Years from 1972 through 1980.* Beirut: Institute for Palestine Studies, last volume published in 1983.

Irani, George E. *The Papacy and the Middle East: The Role of the Holy See in the Arab-Israeli Conflict, 1962–1984.* Notre Dame: University of Notre Dame Press, 1986.

Isaac, Rael Jean. *Israel Divided: Ideological Politics in the Jewish State*. Baltimore: Johns Hopkins University Press, 1976.

Isaacs, Stephen D. *Jews and American Politics*. Garden City: Doubleday, 1974.

Jabber, Fuad. *Israel and Nuclear Weapons*. London: Chatto and Windus, 1971.

Jackson, Elmore. *Middle East Mission: The Story of a Major Bid for Peace in the Time of Nasser and Ben-Gurion*. New York: Norton, 1983.

Jansen, Michael. *The Battle of Beirut: Why Israel Invaded Lebanon*. London: Zed, 1982.

———. *Dissonance in Zion*. London: Zed, 1987.

Jiryis, Sabri. *The Arabs in Israel*. New York: Monthly Review Press, 1976.

Johnson, Lyndon B. *The Vantage Point: Perspectives of the Presidency, 1963–1969*. New York: Holt, Rinehart and Winston, 1971.

Kahane, Rabbi Meir. *They Must Go*. New York: Grosset & Dunlap, 1981.

Kalb, Marvin, and Bernard Kalb. *Kissinger*. Boston: Little, Brown, 1974.

Karp, Yehudit. *The Karp Report: Investigation of Suspicions against Israelis in Judea and Samaria*. Jerusalem: Israeli Government, 1984.

Katz, Doris. *The Lady Was a Terrorist: During Israel's War of Liberation*. New York: Futuro Press, 1953.

Keller, Adam. *Terrible Days: Social Divisions and Political Paradoxes in Israel*. Amsterdam: Cypres, 1987.

Kelly, J. B. *Arabia, the Gulf, and the West*. New York: Basic Books, 1980.

Kenen, I. L. *Israel's Defense Line: Her Friends and Foes in Washington*. Buffalo: Prometheus, 1981.

Kerr, Malcolm H. *The Arab Cold War: Gamal 'Abd Al-Nasir and His Rivals 1958–1970*. 3rd ed. New York: Oxford University Press, 1971.

———. *America's Middle East Policy: Kissinger, Carter, and the Future*. Beirut: Institute for Palestine Studies, 1980.

Khalidi, Walid, ed. *Before Their Diaspora: A Photographic History of the Palestinians 1948–1984.* Washington, D.C.: Institute for Palestine Studies, 1984.

———. *From Haven to Conquest: Readings in Zionism and the Palestine Problem until 1948.* Washington, D.C.: Institute for Palestine Studies, 1987.

———. *All That Remains: The Palestinian Villages Occupied and Depopulated by Israel in 1948.* Washington, D.C.: Institute for Palestine Studies, 1991.

Khouri, Fred J. *The Arab-Israeli Dilemma.* 3rd ed. Syracuse: Syracuse University Press, 1985.

Kissinger, Henry A. *White House Years.* Boston: Little, Brown, 1979.

———. *Years of Upheaval.* Boston: Little, Brown, 1982.

Klieman, Aaron S. *Foundations of British Policy in the Arab World: The Cairo Conference of 1921.* Baltimore: Johns Hopkins University Press, 1970.

———. *Israel's Global Reach: Arms Sales and Diplomacy.* Washington, D.C.: Pergamon-Brassey's, 1985.

Kurzman, Dan. *Genesis 1948: The First Arab-Israeli War.* New York: World Publishing Company, 1970.

———. *Ben-Gurion: Prophet of Fire.* New York: Simon & Schuster, 1983.

Lacey, Robert. *The Kingdom.* London: Hutchinson, 1981.

Langer, Felicia, *These Are My Brothers: Israel and the Occupied Territories.* London: Ithaca, 1979.

Laqueur, Walter, and Barry Rubin, eds. *The Israel-Arab Reader.* New York: Penguin, 1987.

Lebanese Center for Documentation and Research. *Political Violence in the World: 1967–1987.* Limassol, Cyprus: Publishing and Marketing House, 1988.

Lilienthal, Alfred M. *What Price Israel?* Chicago: Regnery, 1953.

———. *The Zionist Connection: What Price Peace?* New York: Dodd, Mead, 1978.

Livingstone, Neil C., and David Halevy. *Inside the PLO: Secret Units, Secret Funds, and the War against Israel and the United States.* New York: Morrow, 1990.

Locke, Richard, and Anthony Stewart. *Bantustan Gaza.* London: Zed, 1985.

Love, Kennett. *Suez: The Twice-Fought War.* New York: McGraw-Hill, 1969.

Lukacs, Yehuda, ed. *The Israeli-Palestinian Conflict: A Documentary Record.* New York: Cambridge University Press, 1992.

Lustick, Ian. *Arabs in the Jewish State: Israel's Control of a National Minority.* Austin: University of Texas Press, 1980.

MacBride, Sean, chair. *Israel in Lebanon: The Report of the International Commission to Enquire into Reported Violations of International Law by Israel during Its Invasion of Lebanon.* London: Ithaca, 1983.

MacDonald, Robert W. *The League of Arab States: A Study in the Dynamics of Regional Organization.* Princeton: Princeton University Press, 1965.

Mallison, Thomas, and Sally V. Mallison. *Armed Conflict in Lebanon, 1982: Humanitarian Law in a Real World Setting.* Washington, D.C.: American Educational Trust, 1985.

————. *The Palestine Problem in International Law and World Order.* London: Longman, 1986.

Masalha, Nur. *Expulsion of the Palestinians: The Concept of "Transfer" in Zionist Political Thought.* Washington, D.C.: Institute of Palestine Studies, 1992.

Mayhew, Christopher, and Michael Adams. *Publish It Not ... The Middle East Cover-Up.* London: Longman, 1975.

McDonald, John J. *My Mission to Israel.* New York: Simon & Schuster, 1951.

McDowall, David. *Palestine and Israel: The Uprising and Beyond.* Berkeley: University of California Press, 1989.

McGhee, George. *Envoy to the Middle World: Adventures in Diplomacy.* New York: Harper & Row, 1983.

Medzini, Meron, ed. *Israel's Foreign Relations: Selected Documents, 1947–1974.* Vols. 1 and 2. Jerusalem: Ministry of Foreign Affairs, 1976.

———. *Israel's Foreign Relations: Selected Documents, 1974–1977.* Vol. 3. Jerusalem: Ministry of Foreign Affairs, 1982.

———. *Israel's Foreign Relations: Selected Documents, 1977–1979.* Vols. 4 and 5. Jerusalem: Ministry of Foreign Affairs, 1981.

Meir, Golda. *My Life.* New York: Putnam, 1975.

Metzger, Jan, Martin Orth, and Christian Sterzing. *This Land Is Our Land: The West Bank under Israeli Occupation.* Translated by Dan and Judy Bryant, Janet Goodwin, and Stefan Schaaf. London: Zed, 1983.

Moore, John Norton, ed. *The Arab-Israeli Conflict.* Vols. 1–4. Princeton: Princeton University Press, 1974, 1991.

Morris, Benny. *The Birth of the Palestinian Refugee Problem, 1947–1949.* New York: Cambridge University Press, 1987.

Moskin, J. Robert. *Among Lions: The Battle for Jerusalem, June 5–7, 1967.* New York: Arbor House, 1982.

Nakhleh, Issa. *Encyclopedia of the Palestine Problem.* 2 vols. New York: Intercontinental Books, 1991.

National Lawyers Guild. *Treatment of Palestinians in Israeli-Occupied West Bank and Gaza: Report of the National Lawyers Guild, 1977 Middle East Delegation.* New York: National Lawyers Guild, 1978.

Nazzal, Nafez. *The Palestinian Exodus from Galilee 1948.* Beirut: Institute for Palestine Studies, 1978.

Neff, Donald. *Warriors at Suez: Eisenhower Takes America into the Middle East.* New York: Linden Press/Simon & Schuster, 1981; Brattleboro, Vt.: Amana, 1988.

———. *Warriors for Jerusalem: The Six Days That Changed the Middle East.* New York: Linden Press/Simon & Schuster, 1984; Brattleboro, Vt.: Amana, 1988.

———. *Warriors against Israel: How Israel Won the Battle to Become America's Ally, 1973.* Brattleboro, Vt.: Amana, 1988.

Nixon, Richard M. *The Memoirs of Richard Nixon.* New York: Grosset & Dunlap, 1978.

Norton, Augustus Richard. *Amal and the Shia: Struggle for the Soul of Lebanon.* Austin: University of Texas Press, 1987.

Nutting, Anthony. *No End of a Lesson: The Story of Suez.* New York: Clarkson N. Potter, 1967.

———. *Nasser.* London: Constable, 1972.

Nyrop, Richard F., ed. *Israel: A Country Study.* Washington, D.C.: U.S. Government Printing Office, 1979.

O'Ballance, Edgar. *The Electronic War in the Middle East: 1968–70.* London: Faber & Faber, 1974.

———. *No Victor, No Vanquished: The Yom Kippur War.* San Rafael, Calif.: Presidio, 1978.

O'Brien, Conor Cruise. *The Siege: The Saga of Israel and Zionism.* New York: Simon & Schuster, 1986.

O'Brien, Lee. *American Jewish Organizations and Israel.* Washington, D.C.: Institute for Palestine Studies, 1986.

Ostrovsky, Victor, and Claire Hoy. *By Way of Deception.* New York: St. Martin's, 1990.

Oz, Amos. *In the Land of Israel.* New York: A Helen & Kurt Wolff Book, Harcourt Brace Jovanovich, 1983.

Palumbo, Michael. *The Palestinian Catastrophe: The 1948 Expulsion of a People from Their Homeland.* Boston: Faber & Faber, 1987.

Patai, Raphael, ed. *The Complete Diaries of Theodor Herzl.* Translated by Harry Zohn. New York: Herzl Press and Thomas Yoseloff, 1960.

Peck, Juliana S. *The Reagan Administration and the Palestinian Question: The First Thousand Days.* Washington, D.C.: Institute for Palestine Studies, 1984.

Peres, Shimon. *David's Sling: The Arming of Israel.* London: Weidenfeld and Nicolson, 1970.

Persson, Sune O. *Mediation and Assassination: Count Bernadotte's Mission to Palestine in 1948.* London: Ithaca, 1979.

Petran, Tabitha. *Syria.* New York: Praeger, 1972.

Pollock, David. *The Politics of Pressure: American Arms and Israeli Policy since the Six Day War.* London: Greenwood, 1982.

Quandt, William B. *Decade of Decisions: American Policy toward the Arab-Israeli Conflict, 1967–1976.* Berkeley: University of California Press, 1977.

———. *Saudi Arabia in the 1980s.* Washington, D.C.: Brookings Institution, 1981.

———. *Camp David: Peacemaking and Politics.* Washington, D.C.: Brookings Institution, 1986.

Quigley, John. *Palestine and Israel: A Challenge to Justice.* Durham: Duke University Press, 1990.

Rabin, Yitzhak. *The Rabin Memoirs.* Boston: Little, Brown, 1979.

Rafael, Gideon. *Destination Peace: Three Decades of Israeli Foreign Policy, a Personal Memoir.* London: Weidenfeld and Nicolson, 1981.

Randal, Jonathan. *Going All the Way.* New York: Viking, 1983.

Raviv, Dan, and Yossi Melman. *Every Spy a Prince: The Complete History of Israel's Intelligence Community.* Boston: Houghton Mifflin, 1990.

Riad, Mahmoud. *The Struggle for Peace in the Middle East.* New York: Quartet, 1981.

Rodinson, Maxime. *Israel and the Arabs.* New York: Pantheon, 1968.

———. *Israel: A Colonial-Settler State?* New York: Monad, 1973.

Rogers, Barbara, and Zdenek Cervenka. *The Nuclear Axis: Secret Collaboration between West Germany and South Africa.* New York: Times Books, 1978.

Rokach, Livia. *Israel's Sacred Terrorism: A Study Based on Moshe Sharett's Personal Diary and Other Documents.* Belmont, Mass.: Association of Arab-American University Graduates, 1980.

Roosevelt, Archie. *For Lust of Knowing: Memoirs of an Intelligence Officer.* Boston: Little, Brown, 1988.

Roy, Sara. *The Gaza Strip Survey.* Boulder: Westview, 1986.

Rubenberg, Cheryl A. *Israel and the American National Interest: A Critical Examination.* Chicago: University of Illinois Press, 1986.

Rubinstein, Alvin Z. *Red Star on the Nile: The Soviet-Egyptian Influence Relationship since the June War*. Princeton: Princeton University Press, 1977.

Rubinstein, Ammon. *The Zionist Dream Revisited*. New York: Schocken, 1984.

Saba, Michael. *The Armageddon Network*. Brattleboro, Vt.: Amana, 1984.

Sachar, Howard M. *A History of Israel: From the Rise of Zionism to Our Time*. Tel Aviv: Steimatzky's Agency, 1976.

Sadat, Anwar. *In Search of Identity*. New York: Harper & Row, 1978.

Said, Edward W. *The Question of Palestine*. New York: Times Books, 1980.

———, and Christopher Hitchens, eds. *Blaming the Victims*. New York: Verso, 1988.

Sanders, Ronald. *The High Walls of Jerusalem: A History of the Balfour Declaration and the Birth of the British Mandate for Palestine*. New York: Holt, Rinehart and Winston, 1983.

Schechla, Joseph. *The Iron Fist: Israel's Occupation of South Lebanon, 1982–1985*. Issue Paper No. 17, Washington, D.C.: ADC Research Institute, 1985.

Schiff, Zeev, and Ehud Ya'ari. *Israel's Lebanon War*. New York: Simon & Schuster, 1984.

Schleifer, Abdullah. *The Fall of Jerusalem*. New York: Monthly Review Press, 1972.

Schweitzer, Avram. *Israel: The Changing National Agenda*. Dover, N.H.: Croom Helm, 1986.

Seale, Patrick. *Asad of Syria: The Struggle for the Middle East*. Berkeley: University of California Press, 1988.

Segev, S. *The Iranian Triangle*. Tel Aviv: Ma'ariv, 1981.

Segev, Tom. *1949: The First Israelis*. New York: Free Press, 1986.

Sharon, Ariel, with David Chanoff. *Warrior: The Autobiography of Ariel Sharon*. New York: Simon & Schuster, 1989.

Sheehan, Edward R. E. *The Arabs, Israelis, and Kissinger: A Secret History of American Diplomacy in the Middle East*. New York: Reader's Digest, 1976.

Shehadeh, Raja, assisted by Jonathan Kuttab. *The West Bank and the Rule of Law*. Geneva: International Commission of Jurists and Law in the Service of Man, 1980.

Sherif, Regina S. *United Nations Resolutions on Palestine and the Arab-Israeli Conflict*. Vol. 2, 1975–1981. Washington, D.C.: Institute for Palestine Studies, 1988.

Shipler, David K. *Arab and Jew: Wounded Spirits in the Promised Land*. New York: Times Books, 1986.

Shlaim, Avi. *Collusion across the Jordan: King Abdullah, the Zionist Movement, and the Partition of Palestine*. New York: Columbia University Press, 1988.

Shorris, Earl. *Jews without Mercy: A Lament*. Garden City: Anchor/Doubleday, 1982.

Sicherman, Harvey. *Palestinian Self-Government (Autonomy): Its Past and Its Future*. Washington, D.C.: Washington Institute for Near East Policy, 1991.

Sifry, Micah L., and Christopher Cerf, eds. *The Gulf War Reader*. New York: Times Books, 1991.

Silver, Eric. *Begin: The Haunted Prophet*. New York: Random House, 1984.

Simpson, Michael. *United Nations Resolutions on Palestine and the Arab-Israeli Conflict*. Vol. 3, 1982–1986. Washington, D.C.: Institute for Palestine Studies, 1988.

Slater, Robert. *Rabin of Israel: A Biography*. London: Robson, 1977.

Smith, Hedrick. *The Power Game*. New York: Ballantine, 1989.

Snow, Peter. *Hussein*. London: Barrie & Jenkins, 1972.

Spector, Leonard S. *Nuclear Proliferation Today*. New York: Vintage, 1984.

Stevens, Stewart. *The Spymasters of Israel*. New York: Macmillan, 1980.

Stone, Michael J. *Truman and Israel*. Berkeley: University of California Press, 1990.

Storrs, Ronald. *Orientations*. London: Nicholson & Watson, 1945.

Strum, Philippa. *The Women Are Marching: The Second Sex and the Palestinian Revolution*. Brooklyn: Lawrence Hill, 1992.

Sykes, Christopher. *Crossroads to Israel*. Bloomington: Indiana University Press, 1973.

Tamir, Avraham. *A Soldier in Search of Peace: An Inside Look at Israel's Strategy*. New York: Harper & Row, 1988.

Tannous, Izzat. *The Palestinians: A Detailed Documented Eyewitness History of Palestine under British Mandate*. New York: I.G.T. Company, 1988.

Tawil, Raymonda Hawa. *My Home, My Prison*. New York: Holt, Rinehart and Winston, 1979.

Teveth, Shabtai. *Ben-Gurion and the Palestinian Arabs*. New York: Oxford University Press, 1985.

Thorpe, Merle, Jr. *Prescription for Conflict: Israel's West Bank Settlement Policy*. Washington, D.C.: Foundation for Middle East Peace, 1984.

Tillman, Seth. *The United States in the Middle East: Interests and Obstacles*. Bloomington: Indiana University Press, 1982.

Timerman, Jacobo. *The Longest War: Israel in Lebanon*. Translated by Miquel Acoca. New York: Vintage, 1982.

Tivnan, Edward. *The Lobby: Jewish Political Power and American Foreign Policy*. New York: Simon & Schuster, 1987.

Tomeh, George J., ed. *United Nations Resolutions on Palestine and the Arab-Israeli Conflict*. Vol. 1, 1947–1974. Washington, D.C.: Institute for Palestine Studies, 1975.

Toscano, Louis. *Triple Cross: Israel, the Atomic Bomb, and the Man Who Spilled the Secrets*. New York: Birch Lane Press, 1990.

Truman, Harry S. *Memoirs by Harry S. Truman*. 2 vols. Garden City: Doubleday, 1955, 1956.

Turki, Fawaz. *The Disinherited*. New York: Monthly Review Press, 1972.

Urofsky, Melvin. *We Are One! American Jewry and Israel.* New York: Anchor/Doubleday, 1978.

U.S. Department of State. *American Foreign Policy: Current Documents, 1960.* Washington, D.C.: U.S. Government Printing Office, 1964.

———. *American Foreign Policy: Basic Documents, 1977–1980.* Washington, D.C.: U.S. Government Printing Office, 1983.

———. *A Decade of American Foreign Policy: Basic Documents, 1941–1949.* Washington, D.C.: U.S. Government Printing Office, 1950.

———. *Foreign Relations of the United States 1947.* Vol. 5, *The Near East and Africa.* Washington, D.C.: U.S. Government Printing Office, 1971.

———. *Foreign Relations of the United States 1948.* Vol. 5, *The Near East, South Asia, and Africa.* Washington, D.C.: U.S. Government Printing Office, 1975.

———. *Foreign Relations of the United States 1949.* Vol. 6, *The Near East, South Asia, and Africa.* Washington, D.C.: U.S. Government Printing Office, 1977.

Viorst, Milton. *Sands of Sorrow.* New York: Harper & Row, 1987.

Vocke, Harald. *The Lebanese War: Its Origins and Political Dimensions.* New York: St. Martin's, 1978.

Weissman, Steve, and Herbert Krosney. *The Islamic Bomb: The Nuclear Threat to Israel and the Middle East.* New York: Times Books, 1981.

Weizman, Ezer. *On Eagles' Wings: The Personal Story of the Leading Commander of the Israeli Air Force.* Tel Aviv: Steimatzky's Agency, 1976.

———. *The Battle for Peace.* New York: Bantam, 1981.

Whetten, Lawrence L. *The Canal War: Four-Power Conflict in the Middle East.* Cambridge: MIT Press, 1974.

Wilson, Evan M. *Decision on Palestine: How the U.S. Came to Recognize Israel.* Stanford: Hoover Institution Press, 1979.

Woodward, Bob. *Veil: The Secret Wars of the CIA, 1981–1987.* New York: Simon & Schuster, 1987.

Wright, Clifford. *Facts and Fables: The Arab-Israeli Conflict.* New York: Kegan Paul International, 1989.

Yodfat, Aryeh Y., and Yuval Arnon-Ohanna. *PLO: Strategy and Tactics.* London: Croom Helm, 1981.

Young, Ronald J. *Missed Opportunities for Peace: U.S. Middle East Policy, 1981–1986.* Philadelphia: American Friends Service Committee, 1987.

INDEX

Abdullah, King, 14
Abrams, Morris B., 67
Absentee's Property Law, 92
Activities (American Israel Public Affairs Committee (AIPAC)), 103–4
ADC. *See* Anti-Discrimination Committee (ADC)
Africa, 145–47
Agricultural Settlement Law, 92
AHC. *See* Arab Higher Committee (AHC)
AI. *See* Amnesty International (AI)
AIPAC. *See* American Israel Public Affairs Committee (AIPAC)
AIPAC Papers on US-Israeli Relations (American Israel Public Affairs Committee (AIPAC)), 219
airborne warning and control system (AWACS), 99–100
Al, 125
Aldoraty, Zvi, 94
Allen, Woody, 103
Allison, 211
Allon, Yigal, 11, 23, 45, 93, 165
Alterman, Eric, 96
Ambrose, Stephen E., 33
American Friends Service Committee's Advisory Committee on Human Rights, 63
American Israel Public Affairs Committee (AIPAC), 4, 16, 80, 164, 177, 219; on African-Israeli relations, 145, 147; on American military assistance, 212; on the economy of Israel, 229, 231; on espionage activities, 126, 127; on the Lavi project, 214; on loan guarantees, 121; on Palestinian citizens of Israel, 91; on Palestinian refugees, 21, 22, 27, 29; on peace, 201; on the standard of living in Israel, 233; on South African-Israeli relations, 139; on the United Nations, 186; and the United States, influence on, 95–109; on United States aid to Israel, 110, 113, 114

American Jewish Committee, 102, 104, 168
American Medical Association, 106
American Red Cross, 20
American Schools and Hospitals Grant Program, 112
Americans for a Safe Israel, 67
American Zionist Committee for Public Affairs, 105
Amin, Idi, 146
Amnesty International (AI), 82–83
Anderson, Terry, 104
Angola, 146
an-Nahar, 65
Anti-Defamation League of B'Nai B'rith, 103
Anti-Discrimination Committee (ADC), 86, 209
Appropriations Act, 176
Arab Higher Committee (AHC), 27
Arab-Israeli conflict, 35, 168; basic nature of, 164–65, 167; and Iraq, 144; Palestinian refugees created by, 19; requirements for resolution of, 236–39; and the Saunders Document, 167–68; underlying questions in, 55–56; and United Nations Resolution 242, 42; United Nations role in resolving, 186–87. *See also* Israel and Israelis; Palestine and Palestinians
Arab Propaganda in America: Vehicles and Voices (Anti-Defamation League of B'Nai B'rith), 103
Arad, Moshe, 72
Arafat, Yasser, 58
Arens, Moshe, 215
Argov, Shlomo, 57, 58
Armanazi, Ghayth, 166
Arms Export Control Act, 64
Arrow antimissile defense system, 222, 224
Ashkelon, 90
Assyrians, 4
Ateret Kohanim, 182
Australia, 222

AWACS. *See* airborne warning and control system (AWACS)

Babylonians, 4
Baker, James A. III, 98, 114, 143, 181, 195, 200; on peace negotiations, 205, 206
Balfour, Arthur James, 5
Balfour Declaration, 3, 5–6, 8
Ball, George W., 102, 221, 239
Bank of Israel, 230
Baral, Martin, 233–34
Barbour, Walworth, 36, 37
Bar-Lev, Haim, 159
Bar-Lev Line, 49, 50
Barrow, R.H., 209–10
Beegle, Dewey, 5
Begin, Binyamin Ze'ev, 159
Begin, Menachem, 15, 36, 153, 168, 227; autonomy plan offered by, 161–62; and the Carter peace plan, 202; and the Egyptian-Israeli peace treaty, 199–200, 202; on the invasion of Lebanon, 58, 60, 61, 62, 63, 64, 65–66; on Jewish settlements, 181; and Lewis, assault on, 234–35; Likud government under, 69, 71–72; on peace, 196; and the Reagan peace plan, 200, 203–4; on the Sabra and Shatila massacre, 62; and United Nations Resolution 242, 42, 43
Beirut, 67, 68, 188, 191, 193; and Israel's invasion of Lebanon, 60, 61, 63, 64. *See* also West Beirut
Beit-Hallahmi, Benjamin, 137, 148
Beit Nalu, Latrun Salient, 22
Ben-Gurion, David, 10, 15, 27, 59, 71, 156, 165; on the demographic problem, 24, 25; on the Dimona facility, 131; on Jerusalem, 171; Labor party affiliation of, 69, 70; on the 1967 war, 36; on Palestinian refugees, 19, 22, 23; on peace, 195; as a socialist, 233; and the Suez crisis, 32, 33; and the United Nations Partition Plan, 9–10
Bentov, Mordecai, 36
Benvenisti, Meron, 173
Bernadotte, Count Folke, 15, 20, 187
Bingham, Jonathan B., 134
Birth of the Palestinian Refugee Problem, The (Morris), 27

Black Thursday, 64
Bokassa regime, 146
Bonior, David, 104
Bookbinder, Hyman, 57, 104, 136, 168, 208, 222
Boyle, Francis A., 123
British Zionist Federation, 5
Brown, Harold, 219
Brown, William, 128
Buckley, James L., 134
Bulgaria, 29
Bull, Gerald Vincent, 228
Bundy, McGeorge, 38
Bush, Barbara, 128
Bush, George, 116, 119, 141, 180, 200, 227; and the American Israel Public Affairs Committee (AIPAC), 108, 109; on hostages, 229; Neeman on, 235; on the proliferation of nuclear weapons, 162–63
Bush administration, 45, 86, 98; on loan guarantees for Israel, 116, 118, 120, 121; peace plan offered by, 205, 207
Buy America Act, 212
Byrd, Robert, 111–13, 123, 222

Cable News Network (CNN), 103
Cairo, 50, 51
CAMERA. *See* Committee for Accuracy in Middle East Reporting (CAMERA)
Campaign to Discredit Israel, The (American Israel Public Affairs Committee (AIPAC)), 102–3
Canaanites, 3, 4
Caradon, Lord, 43
Carlucci, Frank C., 104, 213
Carmeli, Eliahu, 22
Carter, Jimmy, 39, 104, 143, 180, 202, 219; and Dayan, 107–8; and the Egyptian-Israeli peace treaty, 199–200, 202; on the intifada, 83–84
Carter administration, 43, 53, 235; on Jewish settlements, 180; peace plan offered by, 202–4
Ceausescu, Nicolae, 147
Center for Responsive Politics, 106
Central African Republic, 146
Central America, 148–49

Central Intelligence Agency (CIA), 125, 137, 146; on Israel's nuclear weapons, 131, 135, 139
Chafee, John, 104
Cheetah-E warplane, 215
Cheney, Dick, 215
Childers, Erskine, 26
Chile, 150
China, 213, 215
Chomsky, Noam, 238
Christison, Kathleen, 96–97
Christopher, Warren, 207
Church, Frank, 101
CIA. *See* Central Intelligence Agency (CIA)
Cizling, Aharon, 16
Clinton, Bill, 109, 128, 177, 207, 210, 234
CNN. *See* Cable News Network (CNN)
Cockburn, Alexander, 103
Cockburn, Andrew, 215
Cockburn, Leslie, 215
Cody, Edward, 149
Cohen, Geula, 128
Columbia, 150
Committee for Accuracy in Middle East Reporting (CAMERA), 67
Congress, 125, 157, 176; and loan guarantees for Israel, 116, 117, 120; and Romania, relations with, 147–48
Congressional Black Caucus, 138
Congressional Research Service (CRS), 230
Constructions Navales et Industrielles de la Méditerranée, 134
Contras, 148, 149, 211
Conyers, John, 104
Correa, Luis Fernando Jaramillo, 150
Costa Rica, 149
Country Reports on Human Rights Practices (United States State Department), 86–88
Cranston, Alan, 62, 114
Cranston amendment, 114
CRS. *See* Congressional Research Service (CRS)
Czechoslovakia, 12

Dangerous Liaison (Andrew and Leslie Cockburn), 215
D'Aubuisson, Roberto, 150

Davar, 92
Dawayima, 15
Dayan, Moshe, 17, 22, 37, 59, 107–8, 196; on the 1973 war, 54, 55; on the West Bank, 235
Dayan, Shmuel, 22
Debayle, Anastasio Somoza, 150
Defense Appropriations Act, 112
Defense (Emergency) Regulations, 90
Deir Yassin, 15
Democratic party, 176, 177, 225
Dershowitz, Alan, 128
Diehl, Jackson, 81, 122–23, 233
Dimona nuclear facility, 130, 131, 132, 135, 139
Dine, Thomas A., 97, 98, 100, 102, 106, 108–9, 222
Dineen, B., 13
Dingell, John D., 104, 211
Dinitz, Simcha, 107
Dole, Robert, 104, 176, 229
Dotan, Rami, 210, 211
Double Exodus, The (Prittie and Dineen), 13
Dow, Sir Hugh, 17
Draper, Morris, 61
Dreyfuss, Richard, 103
Drori, Amir, 62
Druze, the, 144
Dukakis, Michael, 177
Dulles, John Foster, 31, 105, 175, 219
Durenberger, David F., 212
Duvalier, Jean-Claude, 150
Dymally, Mervyn, 104

East Jerusalem, 120, 160, 175, 193, 203; annexation of, 172, 174, 181; Bush on, 176; Jewish settlements in, 71, 72, 73, 122, 123, 178, 182, 183; and the 1967 war, 35; in United Nations Resolution 242, 43, 44. *See also* Jerusalem; Old City of Jerusalem; West Jerusalem
Eban, Abba, 31, 172, 174; on the 1967 war, 35; on peace prospects, 196–97
EC. *See* European Community (EC)
Economic Support Fund, 112
Eden, Anthony, 196
Egypt and Egyptians, 17, 18, 156, 163, 182, 195, 198, 206, 228, 239; as ancient inhabitants of Palestine, 3, 4, 5; and the Egyptian-Israeli

peace treaty, 199–200, 202–3; and the Lavon affair, 209; and the 1948 war, 11, 13; and the 1973 war, 46, 52, 53, 54, 55, 56; and the 1967 war, 36, 37, 39; on Palestinian refugees, 28; and the Suez crisis, 30, 31, 32; United States aid to, 114; and the War of Attrition, 48–51

Eisenhower, Dwight D.: and the Suez crisis, 30, 31, 32, 33, 34

Eisenhower administration, 175, 198

Eitan, Rafael, 61, 62, 127, 168

el-Edroos, Syed Ali, 14

Ellis A. G., 211

El Salvador, 149, 150

Emerson, Steve, 103

Ennes, James, 41

Epp, Frank, 5

Eretz Yisrael, concept of, 70, 180

Eshkol, Levi, 48, 49, 132, 168–69, 181, 182

Ethiopia, 7, 144, 145

European Community (EC), 82, 180

Evans, Rowland, 41

Export-Import Bank, 230, 231

Eytan, Rafael, 21

Fahd, Prince, 203

Fahd peace plan, 203

Faisal, King, 216, 217

Fatah Revolutionary Council, 58

Federal Bureau of Investigation (FBI), 125

Federenko, Nikolai, 40

Feintuch, Yossi, 174

Fez peace plan, 204

Fisk, Robert, 68

Flag and Emblem Law, 93

Flapan, Simha, 11, 13, 14, 23; on Palestinian refugees, 27

Fonda, Jane, 67

Ford, Gerald, 156, 158, 179, 199

Foreign Military Sales Program, 113

Forrestal, James, 105

Fourth Geneva Convention Relative to the Protection of Civilian Persons in Time of War, 81–82, 84, 85, 178, 179, 185, 221; United Nations Security Council resolutions about, 190, 193, 194

France, 7, 30, 31, 130, 134, 213

Friedman, Robert I., 102

Friedman, Thomas L., 62, 67; on the intifada, 79–80

Galilee, 10, 23. See also Upper Galilee

Garcia, Romeo Lucas, 150

Gaza Strip, 8, 17, 26, 154, 202; Bedouin driven out of, 22; and the Begin autonomy plan, 161; death rate in 1949, 20; and the Fourth Geneva Convention, 180; intifada in, 77, 83, 85, 155; Israeli control of after 1967 war, 17, 37, 153; Jewish settlements in, 71, 72, 122, 178, 182; in United Nations Resolution 242, 43, 44; United Nations Security Council resolutions concerning, 188, 193

General Electric, 210

General Motors, 211

Glubb, Pasha, 14, 20

Golan Heights, 17, 154, 158, 181, 202; annexation of, 71, 220; Jewish settlements in, 71, 72, 122, 123, 159, 160, 178, 181, 182, 207; and the 1967 war, 35, 37, 40, 41, 153; in United Nations Resolution 242, 43, 44; United Nations Security Council resolutions concerning, 190, 193

Goldberg, Arthur, 39–40, 44, 45, 66, 182

Goldmann, Nahum, 8

Gore, Albert, 220

Goren, Shlomo, 37

Goulding, Marrack, 80, 81–82

Gower, William L., 20

Great Britain, 3, 5, 8, 9, 14, 175, 212, 213, 222; and the Suez crisis, 30, 31

Greeks, 4, 5

Guatemala, 149, 150

Guinea-Bissau, 146

Gur, Mordecai, 107

Ha'aretz, 67, 92, 144

Hadashot, 120

Haifa, 224

Haig, Alexander, 235

Haiti, 7, 150

Hansell, Herbert, 180

Harari, Mike, 150

Hare, Raymond, 34

Harkin, Tom, 106

Hauser, Rita, 103

Helms, Jesse, 176

Hersh, Seymour, 126, 132, 137, 139–40, 143
Herzl, Theodor, 23
Herzliya Women's Center, 128
Hickenlooper, Bourke, 131
Histadrut, 232
Hitchens, Christopher, 27
Hitler, Adolf, 6, 70
Hittites, 3
Honduras, 149
Hoover, Herbert Jr., 32
House Committee on Energy and Commerce, 211
House Foreign Affairs Subcommittee on Foreign Operations, 206
Huleh, lake of, 187
Human Rights Watch, 85
Hussein, King, 97; and United Nations Resolution 242, 44, 45
Hyksos, 3

ICRC. *See* International Committee of the Red Cross (ICRC)
IDF. *See* Israel Defense Forces (IDF)
Imwas, Latrun Salient, 22
Institute for Advanced Strategic and Political Studies, 231
International Atomic Energy Agency, 133
International Children's Emergency Fund, 20
International Committee of the Red Cross (ICRC), 84
intifada, 77–88, 154; beginning of, 77; critical reports on, 81– 85; Friedman on, 79–80; permit system under, 80–81; Rabin's suppression of, 154–56; United Nations Security Council resolutions concerning, 194; United States State Department's reports on, 86–88
Iran, 149, 210; and Israel, relations with, 142–45
Iran-Contra affair, 12, 142, 143, 144–45, 211–12
Iraq, 8, 13, 99, 145, 190, 223, 228; Osirak raid, 133–34; Rabin's criticism of American policy on, 145
Irgun, 15, 70

"Israel: Foreign Intelligence and Security Services" (Central Intelligence Agency (CIA)), 125
Israel Aircraft Industries, 12, 214, 224
Israel and Israelis: and African nations, relations with, 145–47; and the American Israel Public Affairs Committee (AIPAC), 95–109; assassinations by, 228; and the Balfour Declaration, 5–6; and the Begin autonomy plan, 161–62; and the Buy America Act, exemption from, 212; and Central America, relations with, 148–49; costs to United States for its support of, 208–17; criticism of the United States by, 234–35; and the demographic problem, 24–26; expansionist policies of, 16–18, 71–73; fraud cases involving, 210–11; and the intifada, 77–88; and the invasion of Lebanon, 57–68; and Iran, relations with, 142–45; and the Iran-Contra affair, 142, 143, 144–45, 211–12; and Jerusalem, claims to, 170–77; and kidnapping, condoning of, 228–29; and the Lavi project, 213–14; *Liberty* attack perpetuated by, 40–41, 209; Likud governments in, 69–73; loan guarantees for, 116–23; looting of civilian property by, 16, 17, 63–64; and the 1948 war, 9–18; and the 1973 war, 52–56; and the 1967 war, 35–41; nuclear weapons in, 130–35, 162–63; and Palestine, claims to, 3– 9; Palestinian citizens in, 89–94; and Palestinian refugees, 19– 29; and the peace process, 195–207; Rabin's regime in, 153–63; racist tendencies of, 168–69; requirements to resolve Arab-Israeli conflict, 236–39; and Romania, relations with, 147–48; settlements in occupied territories, 72–73, 122–23, 159–60, 178–83, 203, 205; socialist economy of, 230–34; and South Africa, relations with, 136–41; Soviet immigration into, 119, 120, 230; spying on the United States by, 124–29; as a strategic ally, 218–24; and the Suez

crisis, 30–34; terrorist activities practiced by, 227–28; and Third World countries, relations with, 142–50; transfer of American technology to, 216; and the United Nations, relations with, 184–94; United Nations General Assembly resolutions concerning, 165–68; and the United Nations Partition Plan, 7–8; and United Nations Resolution 242, 42–47; United States aid to, 110–15, 230, 231, 232, 239; and the War of Attrition, 48–51

Israel Chemicals, 127

Israel Defense Forces (IDF), 37, 41, 62, 133, 210

Israeli Aeronautical Industries, 211

Israeli Commission of Inquiry. *See* Kahan Commission

Israeli Mazlat Ltd., 211

Israeli National Defense College, 65

Israel's Declaration of Independence, 3, 5, 6, 17; on equality, 92, 93

Italy, 134, 209

Jabara, Abdeen, 86

Jabotinsky, Vladimir, 70

Jabotinsky, Zeev, 24

Japan, 222

Jarring, Gunnar, 201

Jerusalem, 8, 12, 23, 45, 154, 185, 188, 221; in the Carter peace plan, 202; future of, 238; Israel's claims to, 170–77; Jewish settlements in, 160; in the Reagan peace plan, 203; United Nations Security Council resolutions concerning, 188, 189, 190, 192; United States policy on, 179–80. *See also* East Jerusalem; Old City of Jerusalem; West Jerusalem

Jerusalem Post, The, 139, 214

Jewish Defense League, 169, 209

Jewish Institute for National Security Affairs (JINSA), 86

Jewish National Fund, 91, 92

Jewish settlements in occupied territories, 72–73, 122–23, 159–60, 178–83; in the Bush peace plan, 205, 206; in the Reagan peace plan, 203; Scranton's speech on, 179–80; United Nations Security

Council resolutions concerning, 190, 193

Jihad, Abu (Khalil Wazir), 228

JINSA. *See* Jewish Institute for National Security Affairs (JINSA)

Jiryis, Sabri, 63–64

Johnson, Lyndon B., 45, 55, 182, 198; on the *Liberty* attack, 40; and the 1967 war, 38, 39

Johnson administration, 38, 40

Joint Distribution Committee, 12

Jordan, 8, 70, 98, 144, 182, 195; and the 1948 war, 11, 14; and the 1967 war, 37; on Palestinian refugees, 28; peace talks with, 206, 207; "security" settlements in, 159; in United Nations Resolution 242, 44, 45; United Nations Security Council resolutions concerning, 188, 189

Jordan River, 8, 181

Jordan Valley, 159

Kahan Commission, 62

Kahane, Rabbi Meir, 169

Kasten, Robert W. Jr., 109, 116

Katz, Harold, 211

Kenen, I.L., 97, 185

Kenen, Sy, 101

Kennedy, John F., 131, 198

Kennedy, Robert, 209

Keren, Moshe, 92

Khissas attack, 10

Khomeini, Ayatollah Ruhollah, 142, 143, 144

Kibbutz Merom Hagolan, 181

Kimche, Jon, 51

King David Hotel, Jerusalem, 15

Kirkpatrick, Jeane, 67, 187

Kissinger, Henry, 33, 53, 107, 156, 198, 199, 216; on the intifada, 79; on the invasion of Lebanon, 66; on the peace process, 196; and Rabin, negotiations with, 157, 158; on the Saunders Document, 167

Klein, Yair, 150

Klerk, F.W. de, 139

Klieman, Aaron S., 8, 149

Knesset, 90, 128, 168, 173, 174, 175

Koenig, Israel, 93, 94

Koenig Report, 93, 94

Kollek, Teddy, 12

Kurds, the, 144

Kuttab, Jonathan, 80–81
Kuwait, 99, 223

Labor party, 69, 70, 71, 89, 94, 128, 168, 196
LAKAM, 127
Lance, Bert, 103
Land Acquisition Law, 92
Latin America, 148, 149
Latrun Salient, 22, 45
Lavi project, 138, 213–14
Lavon Affair, 209
Law and Administration Ordinance, 173
Law for Requisitioning of Property in Time of Emergency, 92
Law of Return, 91
Lawson, Edward, 175
Lawyers Committee for Human Rights, 85
Lebanon, 8, 41, 49, 134, 149, 185, 195; American hostages in, 211, 229; Israel's invasion of, 57–68, 235; and the 1948 war, 13; on Palestinian refugees, 28; peace talks with, 206, 207; Rabin's retaliatory policy in, 156; "security belt" in, 17–18; United Nations Security Council resolutions about, 189, 190, 191, 192, 193, 194; United States Marines in, 98, 209–10
Lerner, Michael, 118
Lesotho, 146
Levin, Carl, 106
Levine, Mel, 106, 109
Lewis, Bernard, 104
Lewis, Michael, 104
Lewis, Samuel, 234
Liberia, 7
Liberty, 40–41, 209
Libya, 163
Likud party, 69–73, 89, 153, 159, 168, 196
Lilienthal, Alfred, 102
Lodge, Henry Cabot, 34
Los Angeles Times, 215
Lustick, Ian, 17
Luxembourg, 7
Lydda, 156

McCloskey, Robert, 38
McConnell, Mitch, 106
McCormick, Anne O'Hare, 16, 29

McDonald, James G., 20
McGovern, George, 104
Majdal, 90
Malawi, 146
Maltz, Yaacov, 214
Marcos, Imelda, 148
Marcus, Yoel, 137
Maronites, the, 144
Marshall, George, 13, 205
Martin Marietta Corporation, 211
Master Defense Development Data Exchange Agreement, 216
Matateh (Broom), 23
Mathias, Charles, 101
"Media Sold Their Conscience to the PLO, The" (Ha'aretz), 67
Meir, Golda, 9, 14, 52, 53, 54, 169; on peace, 197
memorandum of understanding (MOU) with Israel, 157–58
Memorandum of Understanding on Strategic Cooperation, 218, 220
Meshad, Yahya, 134
Middle East, 21, 53, 66, 120, 177, 180, 218, 220, 237, 239; and the American Israel Public Affairs Committee (AIPAC), 101; American policy on, 98, 120, 158; and Israel's nuclear weapons, 130, 132; and Israel's "periphery strategy", 144; missile projects in, 163; and the Palestine Liberation Organization (PLO) peace plan, 205; War of Attrition in, 50
Middle East Watch report, 84
Milhollin, Gary, 163
Moorer, Thomas, 41, 107
Morris, Benny, 14, 21, 22, 23; on Palestinian refugees, 27
Mozambique, 146
Municipal Corporations Ordinance, 173
Murphy, Richard, 98
Myths and Facts (American Israel Public Affairs Committee (AIPAC)), 29, 102

Nakhleh, Issa, 4
Nasser, Gamal Abdel, 30, 39, 49–50, 52, 66, 196
Nation, 103
National Association of Arab Americans, 68

Nationality Law, 91
National Security Council, 39, 53
NBC in Lebanon: A Study of Media Misrepresentation (Americans for a Safe Israel), 67
NBC's War in Lebanon: The Distorting Mirror (Americans for a Safe Israel), 67
Near East Report, 27, 101–2
Neeman, Yuval, 235
Negev Desert, 130, 131
New Republic, 27, 66, 67
New York Times, 16, 67, 93, 129, 155, 169; on the American Israel Public Affairs Committee (AIPAC), 96, 97, 100; on the intifada, 79–80; on the Iran-Contra affair, 143; on the Osirak raid, 133; on Palestinian refugees, 29; on the Phalange militia, 62; on South African-Israeli relations, 137
Nicaragua, 150, 211
Nidal, Abu, 58, 134
1948 war, 9–18, 65; Israeli advantage in, 13–14; Khissas attack in, 10; Palestinian refugees created by, 19–21; Plan Dalet in, 10–11
1973 war, 51, 52–56, 65, 196, 197; and the Arab oil embargo, 216–17; duration of, 52; Israel's intelligence failure in, 54–55
1967 war, 35–41, 42, 54, 65, 153, 156, 172; ceasefire agreement in, 48–49; Johnson administration's support of, 38–40
Nixon, Richard N., 53, 54, 105, 179; and the Arab oil embargo, 216–17; peace efforts by, 198–99; Rabin's endorsement of, 108
Nixon administration, 175
Nordau, Max, 6
Noriega, Manuel, 150
North, Oliver, 149
"North Bank", 18, 59
Novak, Robert, 41

Oakar, Mary Rose, 104
Obeid, Sheikh Abdul Karim, 229
Obey, David R., 106
October Surprise conspiracy, 143
October War. *See* 1973 war
Odeh, Alex, 209
Ofek-1 (Horizon), 132

Old City of Jerusalem, 37, 172, 182. *See also* East Jerusalem; Jerusalem; West Jerusalem
Old Testament, 3
Operation Litani, 17
Operation Peace for Galilee, 57, 60, 66
Operation Sphinx, 134
Osirak nuclear facility, 133
Ostrovsky, Victor, 125, 127, 134, 211
Ottoman Empire, 8
Overseas Private Investment Corporation, 112
Overseas Workload Program, 112
Owens, Wayne, 106

Paisley, Melvyn R., 211
Palestine and Palestinians, 5, 7–8, 57, 146, 229, 236, 237, 238; ancient inhabitants of, 3–4; and the Begin autonomy plan, 161–62; centrality of in Arab-Israeli conflict, 164–65; dehumanizing of, 168–69; and the demographic problem, 24–26; forced from Jerusalem, 172–73; and the intifada, 77–88; and the invasion of Lebanon, 57, 61, 63, 65; as Israeli citizens, 89–94; and Jewish settlements, 72–73, 122–23, 159–60, 178–83; laws discriminating against, 91–92; and the 1948 war, 9–18; and the 1967 war, 35, 37; peace negotiations involving, 195, 202, 203, 207; Rabin's position on, 154–56, 161; society established in, 6; United Nations General Assembly resolutions about, 165–68, 186; and the United Nations Partition Plan, 7–8; United Nations Security Council resolutions about, 187–88, 190, 191, 192, 193, 194. *See also* Palestinian refugees
Palestine Human Rights Information Center of Jerusalem and Chicago, 78
Palestine Liberation Organization (PLO), 154, 158, 167, 191, 196, 204; assassination campaign against, 228; and the Fez peace plan, 204; and Israel's invasion of Lebanon, 58, 59, 60; peace plan offered by, 204–5

Palestine Liberation Organization's Research Center, 63–64
Palestine Red Crescent, 63
Palestinian refugees, 19–29, 67, 153, 156, 195, 197, 201; Arab governments' response to, 28–29; and the demographic problem, 24–26; forced flight of, 26–28; after 1967 war, 21–22; Sabra and Shatila massacre, 61–63; United Nations data about, 186; United Nations Security Council resolutions about, 188. *See also* Palestine and Palestinians
Palmach, 153
Panama, 149–50
Paraguay, 7, 150
Pasha, Glubb, 14, 20, 26
Patriot antimissile missiles, 215, 223
Pault, Steven, 230–31
Peace Now group, 73, 122
Peled, Mattiyahu, 36, 51, 148–49
Pell, Claiborne, 106
Penthouse, 67
Percy, Charles, 100
Peres, Shimon, 124, 142, 143, 169; on the Iran-Contra affair, 149
Peretz, Martin, 66
Perez de Cuellar, Javier, 84
"periphery strategy," 144
Persian Gulf War, 112, 133
Phalange militia, 61, 62
Philippines, 7, 148
Philistines, 3, 4
Physicians for Human Rights, 82
Plan Dalet, 10–11, 23
Plan Gimmel, 10
Podhoretz, Norman, 67
Poindexter, John, 149
"political" settlements, 159–60. *See also* Jewish settlements in occupied territories
Pollard, Anne Henderson, 126, 127, 128
Pollard, Jonathan Jay, 124, 126, 127, 128, 210
Porter, Dwight, 41
Portugal, 146
Posner, Michael, 85
Pratt & Whitney, 210
Prittie, Terrence, 13

Qibya, 188

Quandt, William, 39, 53
Quayle, Dan, 107
Quigley, John, 6
Quneitra, 18, 181

Rabbinical Courts Jurisdiction Law, 226
Rabin, Yitzhak, 20, 36, 45, 56, 94, 109, 144, 199, 234; autonomy plan offered by, 161–62; and the Bush peace plan, 207; government under, 153–63; on the intifada, 78; on Iraq, 144, 145; on Jewish settlements, 179; and Nixon, endorsement of, 108; on nuclear weapons, 162; on peace, 154; position on Palestinians, 154–56; on shared values, 228; on South African-Israeli relations, 137–38; on Zaire, 147
Rabushka, Alvin, 232–33
Rafael, Gideon, 39, 40
Rahall, Nick Joe, 104
Ramadan war. *See* 1973 war
Ramle, 156
Rasnic, Ruth, 128
Reagan, Ronald, 98, 99, 128, 200, 212; on the invasion of Lebanon, 64, 65; on Jewish settlements, 180
Reagan administration, 45, 64, 143, 148, 179, 218; and the American Israel Public Affairs Committee (AIPAC), 97–98; and the Iran-Contra affair, 143, 144–45, 149, 211, 212; on Israel as a strategic ally, 220, 221–22; Lavi project under, 213–14; peace plan offered by, 203–4
Redman, Charles E., 205
Revisionist Zionism, 69, 70
Rhodesia, 146
Richman, Sheldon L., 119
Roche, John, 38
Rogers, William P., 46, 201
Rogers plan, 201–2
Roman Empire and Romans, 4, 5
Romania, 147–48
Rostow, Eugene, 37, 38
Rostow, Walt, 38
Roth, Kenneth, 85
Rothschild, Lord, 5
Roy, Sarah, 85

Rubenberg, Cheryl A., 100, 103, 111, 220
Rubenberg, Martin, 83
Rubinstein, Dani, 92
Rusk, Dean, 41, 44, 45

Sabra and Shatila massacre, 61–63
Sachar, Howard M., 232
Sadat, Anwar, 52, 53, 55, 56, 202
Saddam Hussein, 133, 134
Saguy, Yehoshua, 62
Saudi Arabia, 97, 98, 99, 206, 212; oil embargo imposed by, 216– 17
Saunders, Harold H., 167
Saunders Document, 167
Save the Children Fund, 79
Say, Peggy, 104
Schifter, Richard, 78, 85, 86
Schweitzer, S., 144
Schwimmer, Adolf ("Al") William, 12
Scope, 125
Scranton, William W., 179–80
SDI. See Strategic Defense Initiative (SDI)
"security" settlements, 159, 160. See also Jewish settlements in occupied territories
Segev, Tom, 16
Seko, Mobutu Sese, 146, 147
Sela, Abraham, 11
Sella, Aviem, 127
Semiramis Hotel, Jerusalem, 15
Senate Appropriations Committee, 122
Senate Foreign Relations Committee, 131
Senate Intelligence Committee, 212
Service Airways, 12
Shabak, 80
Shahak, Israel, 16, 229
Shahak-Lipkin, Amnon, 133
Shamir, Yitzhak, 15, 62, 123, 168, 200, 227, 235; and the Bush peace plan, 205, 206, 207; and the Congressional Black Caucus, 138, 139; and the Fahd proposal, 203; and the Fez peace plan, 204; on the intifada, 78–79; on Jewish settlements, 181; Likud government under, 70, 72–73; and loan guarantees for Israel, 116, 118, 119–21; and Pollard, 126; on terrorism, 227–28

Sharett, Moshe, 7, 26
Sharon, Ariel, 8, 54, 132; and the invasion of Lebanon, 58, 59, 60, 61, 62; on Jewish settlements, 122, 183
Shipler, David, 93
Shultz, George, 44, 45, 97–98, 177, 214, 219, 220, 235
Silver, Eric, 71, 72, 234
Simba project, 138
Simon, Paul, 106
Sinai Peninsula, 17, 18, 22, 156, 202; and the 1967 war, 35, 37, 153; and the Suez crisis, 31, 32; in United Nations Resolution 242, 43, 44; War of Attrition in, 48
Sinai II, 156, 157
Sirhan Sirhan, 209
Slabodkin, Gregory D., 103, 104
Smilansky, Moshe, 16
Smith, Hedrick, 99, 102
Smith, Lawrence J., 109
Solar, Edna, 128
Solarz, Stephen J., 96, 109, 134, 137
Sonneborn, Rudolf G., 12
Sonneborn Institute, 12
South Africa, 146, 185, 214; and Israel, relations with, 136–41
South America, 149
Soviet Union, 119, 126, 145, 147, 157, 206, 213, 220, 230; and the 1973 war, 53, 55; and the War of Attrition, 50
Specter, Arlen, 120
Sperry Corporation, 211
Spiegel, Steven L., 223
Star Wars. See Strategic Defense Initiative (SDI)
Steiner, David, 105, 109
Stern Gang, 15
Strategic Defense Initiative (SDI), 114, 221–22
Straus, Richard B., 98
Streisand, Barbra, 103
Stroessner, Alfredo, 150
Sudan, 209
Suez Canal, 48, 49, 50, 51, 55, 158
Suez City, 49
Suez crisis, 30–34
Sulzberger, C.L., 137
Sumerians, 4
Sunday Times, 64, 135
Sununu, John, 104

Swaziland, 146
Sykes, Christopher, 10
Syria, 4, 144, 158, 163, 206; and the invasion of Lebanon, 57; Jewish settlements in, 182, 195; and the 1948 war, 13, 17; and the 1973 war, 46, 52, 54, 56; and the 1967 war, 37; on Palestinian refugees, 28; "security" settlements in, 159; United Nations Security Council resolutions about, 188, 192

Tadiran, 211
Talmon, Jacob, 161–62
Tel Aviv, 10, 23, 45, 174, 175, 176
Tel Nof, 128
Tet offensive, 55
Textron Lycoming, 211
Thalmann, Ernesto, 173–74
Thant, U., 50
Tikkun, 118
Times, The, 68
Tivnan, Edward, 107
Tov, Bar-Siman-, 53
Tower Commission, 149
Traficant, James Jr., 104
Transjordan, 8, 13, 14
Treaty on the Non-Proliferation of Nuclear Weapons, 133, 135, 139
Tricontinental Solidarity Conference, 146
Truman, Harry, 20, 197–98
Truman administration, 7
Tsomet (Junction) party, 168
Tsur, Yaacov, 128
Tuchman, Barbara, 66
Turkey, 8, 29, 144
Turner, Stansfield, 140, 222–23
Tzur, Jacob, 10

Uganda, 146
Ugarte, Augusto Pinochet, 150
United Nations, 64, 115, 146, 221, 238; condemnation of the intifada by, 81; and Israel, relations with, 184–94; and Jerusalem, 171, 172; on Jewish settlements, 178, 179, 181; and the 1967 war, 39; on Palestinian refugees, 21; on South Africa, 138; and the Suez crisis, 31, 34

United Nations Commission on Human Rights, 67
United Nations General Assembly, 3, 7, 28, 184, 185, 220; on the intifada, 83; on Israel's relations with South Africa, 137; on Jerusalem, 171, 173–74; on Palestinian rights, 186; resolutions passed against Israel, 165–68, 185; on the Suez crisis, 31, 32
United Nations Partition Plan, 7–8, 17, 23, 37, 70, 156, 196; designation of Jerusalem in, 170, 171; and the 1948 war, 9, 10, 11, 17
United Nations Relief and Works Agency, 79
United Nations Resolution 338, 47, 158, 204
United Nations Resolution 242, 42–47, 49, 54, 56, 70, 154, 158; in peace negotiations, 200, 201, 202, 203, 204, 205, 207
United Nations Security Council, 7, 31, 115, 184, 185, 202; on the intifada, 84–85; resolutions passed against Israel, 187–94
United States, 24, 108, 153, 184, 196, 226, 227, 233; aid to Israel, 110–15, 230, 231, 232, 233, 239; and the American Israel Public Affairs Committee (AIPAC), 95–109; and the Arab oil embargo, 216–17; costs of support for Israel, 208–17; criticism by Israel of, 234–35; espionage activities against, 124–29; fraud cases involving Israel and, 210–11; on the intifada, 83, 84, 85; and the invasion of Lebanon, 64, 66; and the Iran-Contra affair, 142, 143, 144–45, 211–12; Israel as a strategic ally to, 218–24; and Israel's nuclear weapons, 130–34, 162–63; and Jerusalem, policy on, 174–77; and Jewish settlements, opposition to, 178, 179, 180, 181, 182; and the Lavi project, 213–14; loan guarantees for Israel by, 116–23; and the 1948 war, 12; and the 1973 war, 52, 53, 55, 56, 107; and the 1967 war, 36, 38, 39, 40, 41; and the Palestine Liberation

Organization (PLO), talks with, 205; and Palestinian refugees, indifference to, 20–21; and peace negotiations, 196, 197–201, 202, 203, 205, 206, 207; and the Rabin regime, 156–58; requirements to resolve Arab-Israeli conflict, 236–39; and Romania, relations with, 147; and the Saunders Document, 167; and the socialist economy of Israel, 230, 231, 232, 233; and the Suez crisis, 30, 31, 32, 33, 34; transfer of technology to Israel, 216; and United Nations General Assembly resolutions, 166–68; and United Nations-Israeli relations, 184, 185, 186, 188, 192; and United Nations Resolution 242, 43, 44, 45, 46

United States General Accounting Office, 121, 233

United States State Department, 155, 180, 182, 220; *Country Reports on Human Rights Practices*, 86–88; on Soviet immigrants, 121–22

United States Supreme Court, 128

Upper Galilee, 187. *See also* Galilee

US-Israel Free Trade Area: How Both Sides Gain, A (American Israel Public Affairs Committee (AIPAC)), 101

U.S. King-Crane Commission, 4

Vance, Cyrus, 180

Vanunu, Mordechai, 135

Vargas, Virgilio Barco, 127

Vela, 140

Vietnam, 55

Vorster, John, 137, 138

Wallop, Malcolm, 232

Wall Street Journal, The, 103, 106, 215

War of Attrition, 48–51, 52, 56, 65

Washington Jewish Week, 117

Washington Post, The, 73, 140, 149, 224, 233; on American Middle East policy, 98; on espionage, 124;

on the intifada, 80; on Jewish settlements, 122–23; on the Lavi project, 214; on Rabin, 108

Watergate, 217

Wazir, Khalil. *See* Jihad, Abu (Khalil Wazir)

Webster, William H., 129

Weinberger, Caspar, 104, 127, 209, 220

Weizman, Ezer, 24, 36, 51, 160

Weizmann, Chaim, 13, 23

Welles, Sumner, 7

Wesley Theological Seminary, 5

West Bank, 8, 26, 154, 200, 202; and the Begin autonomy plan, 161; Dayan on, 235; and the Fourth Geneva Convention, 180; intifada in, 77, 83; Jewish settlements in, 71, 72–73, 122, 123, 178, 182; and the 1967 war, 17, 37, 153; "security" settlements in, 160; in United Nations Resolution 242, 43, 44, 45; United Nations Security Council resolutions about, 188, 193

West Beirut, 57, 58, 60, 65, 191. *See also* Beirut

West Germany, 222

West Jerusalem, 12. *See also* East Jerusalem; Jerusalem; Old City of Jerusalem

What Price Israel? (Lilienthal), 102

Whetten, Lawrence, 50

Williams, Angela, 79

Wilson, R.D., 15

World War I, 8

World Zionist Organization-Jewish Agency (Status) Law, 91, 92

Wyden, Ron, 106

Yaacovi, Gad, 235

Yalu, Latrun Salient, 22

Yaron, Amos, 62

Yates, Sidney R., 106

Yom Kippur War. *See* 1973 war

Yost, Charles W., 179

Zaire, 146, 147

Zangwill, Israel, 6

Zionism, 69–70